GALLANTRY IN ACTION

GALLANTRY
IN
ACTION

Airmen Awarded the Distinguished
Flying Cross and Two Bars 1918-1955

NORMAN FRANKS

Foreword by Air Cdre Philip J. Robinson OBE DFC** MA RAF

GRUB STREET • LONDON

Published by
Grub Street
4 Rainham Close
London
SW11 6SS

Copyright © Grub Street 2019
Copyright © Norman Franks 2019

A CIP record for this title is available from the British Library

ISBN-13: 978-1-911621-28-7

Cover and book design by Jorge Sagradas

Printed and bound by Finidr, Czech Republic

CONTENTS

FOREWORD

This is an extraordinary collection of stories of exceptional valour, courage and devotion to duty. The tales of bravery shown by this eclectic mix of airmen from as far afield as Australia, South Africa, Canada, New Zealand, Belgium, Poland, America and Norway makes for compelling reading. They were from all walks of life and yet they had in common a determination consistently to go beyond what was expected of them in the face of a determined enemy and frequently with the odds stacked against them.

This book gives us an insight into the type of men they were and whilst a few moved on to great things and some went on to live relatively normal lives, too many paid the ultimate price. It is fitting that they received national recognition for their efforts and future generations should not forget their sacrifice. I am delighted to be able to contribute to this publication and also humbled to be mentioned in the company of such heroic and brave airmen.

The last 100 years has seen some amazing acts of bravery in the air and I have no doubt that the accounts detailed in this wonderful book will serve as an inspiration to current and future generations. Aircraft have changed beyond recognition since the inception of the Distinguished Flying Cross in 1918, but I recognise the character of the individuals mentioned in this book in the airmen and airwomen of today's Royal Air Force, Royal Navy and Army Air Corps and I have no doubt that at some time in the future we with see the sixty-second award of a second Bar to the Distinguished Flying Cross.

Air Commodore Philip J. Robinson OBE DFC** MA RAF
October 2018

ACKNOWLEDGEMENTS

A number of people helped complete the biographies of the men depicted in this book, and/or provided photographs. In no specific order, they are: Paul Baillie, Larry Milberry, Andy Thomas, Gordon Leith of the RAF Museum, Janet Lacroix of the Canadian Forces Joint Imagery Centre, Julie Robinson of Lewisham Library, Matthew O'Sullivan, Air Force Museum of New Zealand, Mrs Kit Syder, Kenneth Pearce, Peter Wheeler, Harriet Patrick of the King's School, Worcester. Nor must I forget those who have left us: the late Chaz Bowyer, Mike Allen, Bobby Oxspring, Frank Carey, Neville Duke, Colin Gray and Bob Tuck.

INTRODUCTION

Until the Royal Flying Corps and Royal Naval Air Service merged to form the Royal Air Force on 1st April 1918, the RFC was part of the British Army and any awards for gallantry were the same as army decorations, namely the Military Cross (MC), Military Medal etc. Although very little changed initially, the war had still to be fought, but the RAF decided to have its own awards, and the army equivalent to the MC was the Distinguished Flying Cross (DFC). This was established on 3rd June 1918 and by the end of the war, no fewer than 1,100 DFCs had been awarded, plus seventy first Bars, but only seven airmen went on to win second Bars. The first of these went to an Australian, Capt Arthur H. Cobby, promulgated in the *London Gazette* on 21st September 1918. The other WW1 airmen awarded second Bars were those who received second Bars after 1918, either due to late awards for their war service, or for actions in foreign wars prior to WW2.

During World War Two, these seven airmen had been joined by others, the total standing at fifty-seven. Three more followed in the 1950s but to men who had received earlier DFCs during the war. This made a grand total of sixty second Bar awards, mostly gazetted during the war, or immediately afterwards, either late 1945 or in 1946. Although not covered in this book, the sixty-first second Bar has been awarded to a serving RAF air commodore for his gallantry in Iraq and Afghanistan. He has contributed a foreword to this book.

The DFC was instituted in 1918 by King George V, awarded to officers for 'an act or acts of valour, courage or devotion to duty performed whilst flying in active operations against the enemy'. In 1932 this was amended to the simpler 'for exceptional valour, courage or devotion to duty whilst flying in active operations against the enemy'.

For recognition of brave or good service in the air not flying against the enemy, the Air Force Cross was instituted, mostly awarded for saving an aircraft away from front-line fighting, or for continued valuable service in flight instruction and training. Despite this, there was an occasional AFC awarded for other brave acts, notably in rescue operations.

NCO airmen, hitherto being eligible for Distinguished Conduct Medals or Military Medals, could be awarded Conspicuous Gallantry Medals (CGM), Distinguished Flying Medals (DFM) or Air Force Medals (AFM).

The original DFC medal ribbon was produced in the exact same colours, white and deep purple. Whereas the MC ribbon had three vertical stripes, with purple in the middle, the original DFC ribbon was white with a single horizontal purple stripe across the middle. This was obviously not particularly distinguished looking, so the white and purple stripes were made diagonally, which became permanent and stood out. The DFM was the same but the diagonal stripes were smaller. The AFC and AFM ribbons were identical, except the colouring was white with red stripes.

The list below shows the *London Gazette* date for each second Bar. The individual biographies of each airman are then produced in an alphabetical list.

A chronological list of when second Bars to the DFC were promulgated in the *London Gazette,* or announced.

1918-1933

Arthur H. Cobby	21st September 1918	Australian
Ross M. Smith	8th February 1919	Australian
Walter H. Longton	3rd June 1919	British
Robert Halley	12th July 1920	British
John W. B. Grigson	28th October 1921	British
Harold A. Whistler	15th March 1929	British
Stafford B. Harris	8th September 1933	British

1941-1955

Alistair L. Taylor	7th March 1941	British
Robert R. S. Tuck	11th April 1941	British
Brendan E. F. Finucane	26th September 1941	Irish
Desmond A. P. McMullen	12th December 1941	British
Frank R. Carey	24th March 1942	British
Maurice M. Stephens	3rd November 1942	British
Adrian Warburton	3rd November 1942	British
Petrus H. Hugo	16th February 1943	South African
Robert W. Oxspring	16th February 1943	British
Lance C. Wade	27th April 1943	American
John R. D. Braham	15th June 1943	British

Stanislaw Skalski	1st July 1943	Polish
Jacobus J. LeRoux	9th July 1943	South African
James E. Walker	9th July 1943	Canadian
Charles M. Miller	27th July 1943	Irish
James A. F. MacLachlan	30th July 1943	British
Raymond H. Harries	7th September 1943	British
George U. Hill	28th September 1943	Canadian
Frederick D. Hughes	28th September 1943	Irish
Robert W. McNair	26th October 1943	Canadian
Colin F. Gray	12th November 1943	New Zealander
James A. McCairns	14th January 1944	British
Neville F. Duke	23rd June 1944	British
Edward R. Butler	15th September 1944	British
Michael S. Allen	13th October 1944	British
Harold E. White	13th October 1944	British
Harold B. M. Martin	14th November 1944	Australian
Arthur A. O'Leary	14th November 1944	British
Tony Ballauf	8th December 1944	British
Martin Y. Gran	22nd January 1945	Norwegian
Ivor G. Broom	27th February 1945	British
Alfred W. G. Cochrane	27th March 1945	New Zealander
Daniel B. Everett	27th March 1945	British
Keith F. Thiele	8th May 1945	New Zealander
Frederick A. O. Gaze	1st June 1945	Australian
Kenneth R. Triggs	17th June 1945	British
Edward B. Sismore	22nd June 1945	British
Arthur N. Crookes	29th June 1945	British
David C. Fairbanks	20th July 1945	American
Remi Van Lierde	24th July 1945	Belgian
John B. Shepherd	14th September 1945	British
Roy O. Calvert	15th September 1945	New Zealander
John T. Caine	19th October 1945	Canadian
Charles Brameld	26th October 1945	British
Kenneth J. Gordon	26th October 1945	British
Herbert V. Peterson	26th October 1945	Canadian
Thomas J. Broom	26th October 1945	British
Ralph Van den Bok	26th October 1945	British

Joseph Berry	12th February 1946	British
Mack D. Seale	5th March 1946	Australian
Wilfred G. G. D. Smith	29th August 1952	British
Noel T. Quinn	22nd June 1954	Australian
Charles F. St. D. Jeffries	22nd March 1955	British

MICHAEL SEAMER ALLEN

Michael Allen was born in Croydon, Surrey, on 15th March 1923, and attended Hurstpierpoint College in Sussex, while also studying mechanical engineering at night school. Leaving school he was apprenticed to the Fairey Aviation Company. When war came in September 1939, he was living in Ashford, Middlesex, and requested leave to enlist into the Royal Air Force, but the company was not keen to lose him and in saying he was in an important civilian position, thwarted his attempts to do so. However, he finally managed to free himself from Fairey, and joined the RAF in June 1941.

He was selected for navigation and within two months paired with Plt Off H. E. White (q. v.), at No. 54 Operational Training Unit (OTU). Little did they know they were to continue together until November 1945, and remain friends until Harry White's death in 1990.

Both men were to form a night-fighting team, and the RAF soon found that a good team was one that stayed together for long periods of time, during which they worked and trained together, so much so, that each knew almost instinctively what the other was thinking and would do. Other similar successful teams were John Cunningham and Jimmy Rawnsley, Branse Burbridge and Bill Skelton, Des Hughes and Lawrence Dixon, Alan Owen and Mac McAllister, etc.

In the early days of night-fighting, the main difficulty was in finding a hostile aircraft in a dark sky, but this was soon overcome with the introduction of AI – airborne radar. This necessitated a pilot being guided by ground control into the area in which a raider had been discovered by ground radar, and once in the general area, the other person in the aircraft, usually a Beaufighter, should be able to pick it up on his airborne radar. Once these principles had been established, the second crewman's brevet became a single wing with the letters RO – radar operator.

White and Allen's first posting, once training had been completed, was to 29 Squadron but then they went to 534 Flight where they flew Havoc aeroplanes, which were converted Douglas Boston bombers. With AI still in its infancy, all manner of schemes were considered in combating night raiders over Britain. These flights consisted of a few Havocs and a few Hawker Hurricanes. The idea was for the Havoc crew to locate a raider in the night sky, and with a Hurricane close by, the Havoc would light the sky with a powerful searchlight installed in the nose of the machine, that illuminated the raider allowing the Hurricane pilot to go in and shoot it down. There were several of the flights formed, but overall they were not a success. However, all these things helped Mike Allen and his pilot to gain valuable experience during the next fifteen months.

Being given something of a rest period, they spent some time ferrying Beaufighters to the Middle East, but finally they were sent to 141 Squadron, commanded by Wg Cdr J. R. D. Braham DFC (q.v.), flying Beaufighter VIFs. It was now 1943, and RAF Bomber Command were fully committed to attacking German targets, and being hotly engaged by German radar-carrying night-fighters. Fighter Command began flying their night-fighters along with RAF bombers, in order to combat the Luftwaffe's night-fighters.

I had met Mike Allen in a chance meeting at the RAF Club in London in the 1990s and we corresponded for some time afterwards. He explained to me how easy it was on many nights to pick out RAF bombers, not only on their radar but visually, especially when the night sky was not that dark, or over a burning German city. However, their job was to seek out German fighters and either destroy them or at the very least deter them from attacking RAF Lancaster and Halifax bombers.

Their first success was on the night of 3rd/4th July 1943 over Aachen. They found and attacked a Me 110 but could only claim it as damaged. They were more successful two weeks later, destroying another 110, this time near the French town of Reims. In August and September they damaged another 110 but destroyed two Ju 88s. Both these types of enemy night-fighters carried radar and were the main type of opposition to RAF bombers. They were called *zahm sau* (Tame Boar), but they also used single-seat day-fighters in the night role, controlled into the RAF bomber stream by ground control, where it was hoped they would pick up targets. These were called **wilde sau** (Wild Boar). Harry White and Mike homed in on one towards the end of January 1944, a Me 109, and shot it down north of Berlin.

This was also their first kill flying a de Havilland Mosquito II, with which the squadron had been re-equipped during that winter. It was a far better type in which to operate over Germany, and the two crewmen were closer together in the cockpit, rather than separated in the Beau, seated down the back. The other new innovation was in their radar. The boffins had now improved the mark IV AI, and night-fighter crews were now allowed to operate over Germany, because if an AI set was captured, it no longer mattered. These boffins had found they could use the new radar to home in on the German's Lichtenstein airborne radar which enabled the RAF crews to find the enemy night-fighters. It was called 'Serrate' and Mike Allen was among the first to prove its worth. As Mike described:

'We had a switch on the AI which gave us a different picture on our tubes if there was a German night-fighter nearby. It was a herring-bone pattern of lines on both screens, the strength of the signal giving some idea of the range. So although we were alone over Germany with no ground control, we had our AI sets and a means of identification. The Germans, of course, had no rearward-looking radar and we were happy that we were doing something really useful in helping our bomber formations.

'The whole thing was called Serrate because the herring-bone pattern showing the presence of a night-fighter had a serrated edge at the side of the picture. Harry and I got our first success on 15th/16th July 1943 – a 110 near Rheims. We were so elated that for some minutes the Beau flew itself while we congratulated ourselves. The only trouble was that it took us over a searchlight belt at Dreux and we nearly got ourselves shot down!'

Over the next few months, Harry and Mike knocked down six more night-fighters, and damaged another. Both men received decorations for their work. By July they had accounted for twelve enemy aircraft and damaged a further three. Their last two, both Ju 88s, went down on the night of 28th/29th July. These must have been very satisfying for Mike, as, sadly, both his parents were killed when a falling V2 rocket smashed into their house earlier that month.

Rested from operations, they later received a posting to Bomber Support Development Unit (BSDU) at Foulsham, Norfolk, now flying the Mosquito XXX. However, their successful period had ended. They damaged a Ju 88 on the 1st/2nd January 1945 east of Dortmund, their final claim. On their ninety-first operation together a few days later, one of their engines failed as they took off, and the Mosquito dived into the ground, disintegrated and caught fire. Luckily both men survived although Mike became trapped in the wreckage by one leg. In desperation Harry was about to free his companion by using an axe to hack off the offending leg, but fortunately two local farmers got to the crash site and extricated Mike just in time.

Demobbed in 1946, Mike Allen later became personnel manager for Avros, and later still had a similar job with Pye, BTR and Rank Hovis. Mike married Vivian Hallett in 1949 and they had one son and one daughter. In 1966 the family moved to South Africa, returning to Britain in 1982. During this time the marriage came under pressure and was dissolved in 1977. Mike then married Pamela Miller and in the final years of his life, Mike lived in Plymouth, Devon. He was a keen member of the Royal Air Force Association, one job being to answer questions from

Mike Allen and his pilot, Harry White, were lucky to survive this crash in January 1945, being rescued by two farmers from the blazing wreck.

people seeking information of family members lost in the war. He often asked me to help locate records at the Public Archives at Kew. He also wrote his story, where I also helped him; the book *Pursuit Through Darkened Skies* being published in 1999. He died in June 2001, aged seventy-eight.

Distinguished Flying Cross (*London Gazette* 5th November 1943)

As observer, Fg Off Allen has undertaken very many sorties at night and has assisted in the destruction of three enemy aircraft. This officer has displayed exceptional keenness, skill and determination.

Bar to DFC (*London Gazette* 14th April 1944) Joint citation with Fg Off H. E. White DFC

As observer (Allen) and pilot (White) respectively, these officers have completed many sorties since being awarded the Distinguished Flying Cross. They have set a fine example of keenness and devotion to duty throughout and have now destroyed at least five enemy aircraft at night. Their achievements have been worthy of much praise.

Second Bar to DFC (*London Gazette* 13th October 1944)

By his exceptional skill and co-operation, Flt Lt Allen has enabled his captain to destroy three enemy aircraft since the award of the Bar to his Distinguished Flying Cross. This officer has always shown the greatest courage and resourcefulness and has set a high standard of skill and devotion to duty under adverse conditions.

TONY BALLAUF

The son of Harry John Roslyn Ballauf, Tony was born on 18th October 1923. His family originally came from Hanover, Lower Saxony; Tony appears to have resided in the Marylebone area of London prior to joining the RAF. After training to become a pilot, he was posted to 149 Squadron in 1942, flying Short Stirling bombers. He successfully completed a tour of thirty-three operations and received the Distinguished Flying Cross.

'Resting' from operations he was posted to No. 1651 Heavy Conversion Unit (HCU). For his tireless work helping pilots to convert from two- to four-engine bombers, he was awarded the Air Force Cross in the New Year Honours List on 1 January 1944.

Returning to operations he was posted to 139 Squadron, operating de Havilland Mosquitos. The squadron was flying all sorts of bombing missions, especially pathfinding, where the crews would arrive at that night's target, identify it, and once this had been done, mark the target with marker flares, to enable approaching bombers of Main Force squadrons to head in and bomb accurately. In all, he completed sixty-five operations with 139 Squadron, bringing his total night ops to an impressive ninety-eight. For his efforts with 139 he received a Bar to his DFC and then a second Bar before 1944 was out.

Ballauf married Patricia Ainslee Harland and they had a son Christopher, born in March 1948. Sadly, Tony Ballauf died at the age of twenty-five on 8 November 1948.

Distinguished Flying Cross (*London Gazette* 27th October 1942)

Fg Off Ballauf has participated in many attacks on important and heavily defended targets in enemy territory, and has displayed a great determination in the performance of his tasks. Often, in spite of intense opposition, he has remained over the target area for considerable periods of time to ensure the accuracy of his attacks.

Air Force Cross (*London Gazette* 1st January 1944)

This officer has shown tireless devotion to duty as an instructor pilot in a heavy conversion unit. He has averaged over seventy hours flying per month and has done extremely valuable work in instructing on Stirling aircraft both by day and night. He has a very strong influence on his pupils, imparting to them some of his enthusiasm and an appearance of the necessity for attaining a high standard of flying skill.

Bar to DFC (*London Gazette* 15th September 1944)

Flt Lt Ballauf is now on his second tour of operational flying. Since the award of the DFC he has completed a further fifty-four sorties. Seventeen have been on Berlin, and one once occasion his aircraft was hit by anti-aircraft fire, putting his starboard engine out of action. Undeterred, he flew his aircraft safely back to this country on one engine. This officer has at all times shown great keenness and courage. He has set a magnificent example to the rest of the squadron.

Second Bar to DFC (*London Gazette* 8th December 1944)

Since being awarded a Bar to his Distinguished Flying Cross this officer has taken part in further operational sorties and has completed a tour of operational duties. On several occasions his aircraft has been damaged by fire from the enemy defences. Flt Lt Ballauf is an outstanding pilot who can always be relied on to press home his attacks with the utmost courage and determination.

JOSEPH BERRY

Joseph Berry was born in Quarrington, Teeside, County Durham, on 28th February 1920, the son of Arthur Joseph and Mary Rebecca Berry. He was their second of three children, and the first son. His siblings were Ivy and Jack and their home was 55 Ramsey Street, Quarrington. Later the family moved to Hampeth, Felton, Northumberland, where Joe attended Duke's School, Alnwick, between 1931 and 1936. Once free of schooling he became a civil servant with the Inland Revenue, as a tax officer in Nottingham. In August 1940 he joined the RAFVR.

Once pilot training had been completed his first posting was to 256 Squadron, operating Boulton Paul Defiants in the night-fighter role, as a sergeant. On 4th November 1941, he and his gunner were forced to take to their parachutes over the coast near Hambleton, Lancs, in T4053 due to engine failure. Berry landed safely but his gunner, Flt Sgt E. V. Williams, was blown out to sea and drowned.

Berry was commissioned in March 1942 and married Joyce Margaret five days later. His next posting was to 255 (Night Fighter) Squadron, operating over the Mediterranean with Beaufighters. Over Italy he claimed one Ju 88 destroyed on 9th September 1943 and soon afterwards shot down two more. He was awarded the DFC in March 1944. His next posting was to FIU – Fighter Interception Unit – that was forming a special flight of Hawker Tempest fighters in the night role, due to the German V1 rocket campaign. As the invasion of Normandy was in its final stages of preparation, the Germans were firing off scores of these pilotless flying bombs, not only by day but also at night. On 28th June Berry claimed his first two flying bombs, and had scored over six in total by the end of the month. By the first week in August he had shot down an amazing fifty-two and shared another. At least twenty-eight of these were at night.

In mid-August the flight moved to Manston where it became 501 Squadron, with Berry taking command. During August and September, Berry knocked down a further seven 'doodlebugs', making a total of fifty-nine and one shared. He was awarded a Bar to his DFC in August.

With the V1 threat mostly at an end, 501 Squadron began flying ranger sorties over the Continent in support of the Allied armies. On the night of 27th/28th September, he shot up two trains in Holland. On a pre-dawn ranger on 2nd October he led three Tempests to attack German airfields south-west of Aachen

but his Tempest (EJ600 SD-F) was hit by ground fire at fifty feet over Veen-
dam, Groningen, Holland, and crashed in flames near the village of Kibbelgaarn.
His final message was: "I've had it chaps; you go on." He was buried in Scheemda
Protestant Cemetery. In February 1946 came the award of a second Bar to his
DFC, back dated to April 1945.

Distinguished Flying Cross (*London Gazette* 3rd March 1944)

This officer is an exceptionally capable pilot who has destroyed three enemy
aircraft in the course of a long and strenuous tour of duty. During operations at
Salerno in September, 1943, he shot down a Junkers 88 in flames, and on the
following night destroyed a Messerschmitt 210 over the Italian coast. His third
victory took place over Naples in October 1943 when he shot down another
Junkers 88. Fg Off Berry has been forced to abandon his aircraft on two occasions and has operated with coolness and courage in the face of heavy enemy
action.

Bar to DFC (*London Gazette* 1st September 1944)

Flt Lt Berry is a highly skilled and resolute pilot. He has completed a very large
number of sorties and throughout his keenness and devotion to duty have been
exceptional. This officer has, within a short period, destroyed numerous flying
bombs.

Second Bar to DFC (*London Gazette* 12th February 1946)

Since the award of the Bar to his DFC, this officer has flown on many operational
sorties and has destroyed a further forty-one flying bombs bringing his total to
fifty-eight bombs destroyed at night. As squadron commander, Sqn Ldr Berry
has displayed courage and devotion to duty of a high order and under his inspiring leadership the squadron has attained many successes.

JOHN RANDELL DANIEL BRAHAM

'Bob' Braham, as he was universally known, came from Holcombe, Somerset, born in Bath on 6th April 1920 to Ernest Goodall Braham BA, a Church of England vicar and former Royal Flying Corps pilot. He was educated at Belmont Primary School and then at a Taunton public school and finally at Queen Elizabeth's Grammar School, Crediton, Devon. During the late 1930s he lived in London and later in Blackburn, then in Wigan where he worked for the Greater Manchester Police as a clerk. The family had also resided in Hendon from where Braham left in 1933 to attend a boarding school in Taunton. Securing a School Certificate he left in 1936. In December 1937 he applied for a short-service commission with the RAF. By the war years his father was living in Duxford.

Once trained at an FTS at Desford and No. 11 FTS at Shawbury, his first posting was to 29 Squadron at West Malling, firstly with Hawker Demon biplanes and then Bristol Blenheims. Once war came there was an urgent need for airborne radar and 29 Squadron was one of the pioneering units. On 24th August 1940, his radar operator (under training), Sgt A. A. Wilsden, guided Braham to a night raider. Braham's fire damaged a German machine that was later reported to have crashed into the sea near the Humber – a Heinkel He 111. The following month the squadron re-equipped with Beaufighters.

A car accident halted his progress but once back in operation he did much to train squadron crews, having completed a blind-flying course, and for his good work he was awarded the DFC on 17th January 1941. The next major event was when he married Joan Hyde, a VAD nurse, on 15th April 1941, the ceremony conducted by Bob's father.

For the rest of 1941, Braham continued with night interceptions and by the end of that year, his victory score stood at eight and one damaged. His radar operator, Sgt Murray Ross, received the DFM. Soon afterwards, Braham teamed up with a former band drummer, Flt Sgt W. J. 'Sticks' Gregory, flying with him and Ross. A Bar to Braham's DFC was awarded in November. He was then attached to 141 Squadron, helping the crews convert on to Beaufighters before being rested at the start of 1942, going to 51 OTU, but while on a forty-eight-hour pass, he returned to 29 Squadron and taking part in a night patrol, shot down a Dornier.

During 1942, Braham continued his successful night interceptions with five more victories plus three others damaged. He received the DSO in October.

Just before Christmas 1942, he was given command of 141 Squadron, taking 'Sticks' Gregory with him. During the summer of 1943 the squadron began flying ranger operations over France and Holland and also night interceptions of German night-fighters attacking Bomber Command raids into Germany using the new Serrate radar.

On the night of 29th/30th September, they shot down a Me 110 G-4 flown by Hauptmann August Geiger, Staffelkapitän of 7./NJG1, with his crewman Unteroffizier Dietrich Koch. Both men baled out but fell into the Ijsselmeer and drowned. Geiger had by this time downed fifty-three Allied aircraft at night. By October 1943, and flying the Beaufighter Mark VIF, Braham's victory score had increased to twenty.

Rested again in October, he attended Staff College and in February 1944 was appointed wing commander Night Operations at 2 Group HQ, 2nd TAF. Not content with a ground job, he frequently flew operational daylight sorties with various squadrons within his control flying Mosquito VIs, and during the period March to May 1944, he shot down nine more hostile aircraft. After the last of these kills on 12th May, his own aircraft was damaged by flak and then fighters, and he was forced to ditch seventy miles off the Norfolk coast, but was rescued by a minesweeper. He was grounded until D-Day but received a second Bar to his DSO in June.

He carried on flying operations but on 25th June, flying in a 21 Squadron Mosquito, he was shot down over Denmark by Leutnant Robert Spreckels of JG1. He and his navigator, Flt Lt Don Walsh RAAF, were taken prisoner, Bob ending up at Stalag Luft III. Spreckels ended the war with twenty-one kills.

Braham remained in the RAF post-war, joining the Night Fighter Development Wing at the Central Flying Establishment. He was also awarded the Belgian Order of the Crown and the Croix de Guerre with Palm for his wartime work. In the New Year Honours List, 1950, the award of the Air Force Cross was announced.

After two years at Air Ministry he resigned his commission in May 1952 and went to Canada where he joined the RCAF as a wing commander. From October 1957 to July 1960 he commanded 432 Squadron flying North American CF100s, then was sent to Paris, France as senior officer at Supreme HQ Allied Powers Europe (SHAPE), till 1964. He resigned from the RCAF in January 1968 and settled in Nova Scotia with his wife and three sons. In January 1961 he had published his story in the book *Scramble*.

At the age of forty-eight he joined the Department of Indian Affairs and Northern Development, becoming an area superintendent for the next five years. However, his health began to deteriorate and he died from a brain tumour on 7th February 1974, aged fifty-three. Joan died in 2012.

WILLIAM JAMES 'STICKS' GREGORY came from West Hartlepool, born in November 1913, attending the Lister Sealy School and began work as a plasterer for his father's building company. He joined the RAFVR in April 1938 and in May 1940 he was helping to ferry aircraft to France. Posted to 29 Squadron on 25th May he and Plt Off R. A. Rhodes

'Sticks' Gregory and Bob Braham in the cockpit of their Mosquito.

shot down a He 111. In 1941 Gregory retrained as a navigator/radar operator and teamed up with Bob Braham and on 23rd/24th June they claimed a probable He 111, which in fact ditched. By October the team had shot down four more and damaged another, Gregory being awarded the DFM.

Gregory and Braham stayed together for most of the war, Gregory being awarded the DSO, DFC and Bar plus his DFM. He became expert at detecting German night-fighters with the Serrate radar. On 17th/18th August 1943 they shot down three German night-fighters, including a German ace (Ofw Georg Kraft), during the RAF's attack on the rocket establishment at Peenemünde. On 29th September their victim was another high-scoring German ace (Hpt August Geiger). Their last victory came in May 1944, a Fw 190 WSW of Arlborg, although they had to ditch their Mosquito, luckily being picked up by a minesweeper. He retired from the RAF as a wing commander in June 1964 and became an estate agent in Eastbourne, Sussex. 'Sticks' married Jean Atkinson in 1942 and they had a daughter. He died in October 2001.

Distinguished Flying Cross (*London Gazette* 17th January 1941)
Since war began, this officer has been continuously employed on night-fighting duties and during the period has carried out over seventy night operations involving 100 hours flying. He has displayed the greatest zeal and efficiency and performed many courageous flights, often in adverse weather conditions.

On one occasion in August, 1940, by his skilful flying he enabled his rear gunner to destroy a Heinkel 111, at short range.

Recommendation for Bar to DFC

"Flt Lt Braham has been employed on night-fighter duties with this squadron since the outbreak of hostilities. During this time he has destroyed seven enemy aircraft, shared in the destruction of another, probably destroyed one and damaged two. He always shows the utmost zeal and keenness to engage the enemy and has flown with great skill in adverse weather conditions on many occasions.

On the night of 24th October 1941 whilst under control of Foreness C.H.L., he made AI contact with a bandit at 8,000 feet above cloud. Contact was maintained for twenty-two-and-a-half miles as the bandit began to lose height and fly in and out of the cloud. When the bandit was approaching a clear patch Flt Lt Braham instructed his operator to bring him up to minimum range. This resulted in a visual at 300 feet. Flt Lt Braham then closed to fifty yards and gave the bandit a three-second burst which sent it crashing down in flames into the sea just off Yarmouth. In recognition of this pilot's great skill and courage I strongly recommend him for the award of a bar to his DFC."

This recommendation was written by 29 Squadron's CO, Wg Cdr E. L. Colbeck-Welch, endorsed by Biggin Hill's station commander, Gp Capt P. R. Barwell, strongly recommended by the AOC No. 11 Group, AVM T. Leigh-Mallory, and approved by AM W. S. Douglas, AOC in Chief of Fighter Command.

Bar to DFC (*London Gazette* 21st November 1941)

Since January 1941, this officer has carried out many operational sorties at night during which he has destroyed six hostile aircraft bringing his total victories to at least seven destroyed, one probably destroyed and a further two damaged. His most recent success was one night in October 1941, when he intercepted a raiding aircraft and, following a burst from his guns at short range, the raider went down in flames, finally crashing into the sea. This officer has always shown the utmost zeal and keenness and has flown with great skill in adverse weather condition on many occasions.

Distinguished Service Order (*London Gazette* 6th October 1942)
Since being awarded a bar to the Distinguished Flying Cross, Sqn Ldr Braham has destroyed a further four enemy aircraft, bringing his total victories to ten. On one occasion his aircraft sustained much damage and one engine was put out of action when at an altitude of only 150 feet. Nevertheless, displaying great courage and determination he completed the return journey and made a safe landing on a small emergency landing ground. Sqn Ldr Braham has led both his flight and his squadron with courage and resolute determination.

Second Bar to DFC (*London Gazette* 15th June 1943)
This officer is a fearless and determined leader, whose impressive qualities have inspired the squadron he commands. Wg Cdr Braham has destroyed eleven enemy aircraft, whilst his more recent achievements include a damaging attack on a U-boat and another attack on a motor torpedo boat which was set on fire. His fine fighting spirit and keenness have set a praiseworthy example.

Bar to DSO (*London Gazette* 21st September 1943)
Since being awarded a second Bar to the Distinguished Flying Cross, Wg Cdr Braham has undertaken many sorties a night during which he has destroyed a further five enemy aircraft. He is a brilliant leader, whose exceptional skill, gallantry and unswerving devotion to duty have been reflected in the fine fighting qualities of the squadron which has obtained notable successes.

Second Bar to DSO (*London Gazette* 9th June 1944)
Since being awarded a Bar to the Distinguished Service Order, this officer has taken part in many sorties, including numerous successful attacks on rail targets and on mechanical transport. In air fighting he has destroyed many more enemy aircraft, bringing his victories to at least twenty-nine. This officer has displayed the highest qualities of skill and leadership and his achievements are a splendid testimony to his courage and fighting spirit.

Other Honours
Officier in de Kroonorde and the Croix de Guerre (Belgian) awarded on 27th August 1948

Air Force Cross (*London Gazette* 1st January 1950)

CHARLES BRAMELD

Brameld came from South Yorkshire, born in Rawmarsh, Rotherham, Yorkshire in 1921. Going to Mexborough Secondary School, he received his final education at St. John's College, York, from where he volunteered to join the RAF in 1939. In March 1941 he applied for aircrew duties and became an air observer. He was sent to America to go through the Arnold Scheme, obtained his observer brevet and was posted to 142 Squadron in October 1942. In December, part of the squadron departed for North Africa, equipped with tropicalised Vickers Wellington III bombers, following the Allied landings in Tunisia, and based at Blida. Brameld was twenty-one years old and joined the crew of Sgt C. G. Cook. He completed a tour of thirty-two operations and returning to England became an instructor at an operational training unit for the next nine months.

Volunteering for a second tour, he was posted to 109 Squadron, equipped with the de Havilland Mosquito, part of Bomber Command's Pathfinder Force (No. 8 Group), whose job it was to mark targets for Main Force bombers to attack. As a navigator he had to become well versed in Oboe, a radar-controlled bombing device. He served with 109 Squadron, where during 1944-45 he completed further operational trips, bringing his overall total to eighty-six. He was commissioned in July 1944 and became a flying officer on 18th January 1945.

Charles Brameld post-war as a school teacher and headmaster.

Brameld left the RAF on 6th February 1946, became a schoolteacher and later headmaster, for thirty-six years.

Mentioned in Despatches (*London Gazette* 14th January 1944)

Distinguished Flying Cross (*London Gazette* 27th March 1945)

> **Recommendation:** 'Plt Off Brameld has now to his credit eighty-six operational sorties with Bomber Command, fifty-four which were with this squadron, of which thirty-seven are marker trips.
>
> 'His quiet manner and unassuming way serve only as a cloak for his keenness and determination to press on our offensive against the enemy.
>
> 'His duties here have consisted of marking targets or of carrying out highly precise bomber attacks on pinpoint targets; his ability continually to produce excellent results can be attributed to his high degree of navigational skill and accuracy, and to his aggressive spirit.
>
> 'He is much deserving of the award of the Distinguished Flying Cross.'

Bar to DFC (*London Gazette* 17th July 1945)

Since being awarded the Distinguished Flying Cross, this officer has participated in many operational sorties. These have included bombing attacks against heavily defended and important targets in Germany and occupied territory. He has, throughout, displayed a fine fighting spirit, outstanding ability and great devotion to duty.

Second Bar to DFC (*London Gazette* 26th October 1945)

This officer has a long and distinguished record of operational flying. He has completed three tours of operational duty, and since the award of a Bar to his DFC he has participated in attacks against some of the heaviest defended targets in Germany. A navigator of outstanding ability, Fg Off Brameld has never either intense anti-aircraft fire or adverse weather deflect him from accomplishing his allotted attacks in a cool and efficient manner.

IVOR GORDON BROOM

Born in Cardiff, Glamorgan, on 2nd June 1920, the son of a district manager for the Prudential Assurance Company, and a Baptist preacher, Ivor was educated at the West Monmouth Grammar School and the Boys County School in Pontypridd. At the age of seventeen he passed his civil service exam and started his working life as a civil servant, working for the Inland Revenue in Banbury, for whom he played Rugby. In March 1939 he was moved to Ipswich, where he met and later married Jess. With the advent of WW2 he joined the RAF and leant to fly as a sergeant pilot in 1940.

After training at Aberystwyth and Cranfield, he converted to Blenheims at RAF Bicester. With a total of 181 flying hours in his logbook, in 1941 he went to 114 Squadron as a sergeant-pilot, flying Blenheim IVs where he operated on low-level daylight operations against shipping in the English Channel and the North Sea, plus targets along the French and Dutch coasts, as well as into Germany. On an attack on the power station at Knapsack that summer, a spectacular photo was taken of a Blenheim banking away from the target, coded RT-V; its pilot was Ivor Broom.

In the autumn he led six Blenheims out to the island of Malta, via Gibraltar, en route for Singapore. The AOC Malta, Hugh Pughe Lloyd, well known for his 'scrumping' of aircraft and crews stopping off on Malta, retained Broom, while the other five crews left to complete their journey to the Far East. All five were either killed or taken prisoner at Singapore.

On the island was 107 Squadron, but they had lost all their officers so Lloyd told him to move into the officers' mess while he sorted out the paper work for his commission. On his first mission, six Blenheims went to attack barracks at Homs, near Tripoli, Libya, led by Wg Cdr Don Scrivier AFC. Over the target Scrivier and another Blenheim collided and crashed. Heading out to sea, the survivors formed up behind Broom but then his gunner reported another Blenheim was some way behind, struggling to keep up and with an Italian fighter in evidence. Broom turned back to help protect the lagging bomber whose airspeed and altimeter had been knocked out. As they headed for Malta, one of Broom's crew, using an Aldis signalling lamp, flashed the speed and height back to the straggler and both aircraft got back.

Broom attacked on 7th November the port of Argostoli on the Greek island of Cephalonia, which included the sinking of two ships. On 17th November he bombed and set on fire a 4,000-ton ship in the Gulf of Sirte as well as attacking a destroyer. Despite the horrendous operating environment, Broom completed forty-three trips, received the DFC and finally returned to the UK in January

1942 for a rest. In 1942 he married Jess Cooper, a union that produced two sons and one daughter.

In May he was with the Central Flying School, teaching pilots in low-level bombing techniques, and then began to fly Mosquito IIIs in May 1943 with the Light Night Strike Force (LNSF). However, on 5th July he was injured in a crash, his pupil being killed. Four months later he was back, flying with 571 Squadron, awarded a Bar to his DFC, and later he became a flight commander with 128 Squadron of the LNSF, where he received his second Bar to his DFC. Later he was promoted to acting wing commander to lead 163 Squadron in January 1945. During this period Broom flew fifty-eight operational sorties, including twenty-two against Berlin. For his leadership he received the DSO. In May 1944 he had teamed up with Tommy Broom (q.v.) and they became known as the 'Flying Brooms'. Indeed, they had an insignia of crossed brooms painted on their aircraft. Their last trip was flown on 29th January 1945, at which time he was promoted to wing commander and went to form 163 Squadron. By VE Day Broom had flown a total of 103 operations.

Post-war he went to Singapore, then became CO of 28 Squadron, flying Spitfire XIVs. Returning to England, he attended the Staff College as a flight lieutenant, then took a conversion course to fly jets, being promoted to squadron leader. In April 1953 he re-formed 57 Squadron, flying English Electric Canberras. With its new jet-bomber aircraft, the RAF flew several goodwill tours, giving flying displays in the Middle East and Canada. Broom received the Air Force Cross for

Wg Cdr Ivor Broom DSO, DFC★★, AFC (left) with his navigator Sqn Ldr Tommy Broom DFC★★.

pioneering a route from Ottawa to London via the North Pole. In 1955 he was at the RAF Flying College at Manby.

In May 1957 he was responsible for the Bomber Command Development Unit at Wittering, heading trials not only with the Canberra, but also the new Vickers Valiant bomber, in the nuclear-deterrent force role. Between 1959 and 1962 he became station commander of RAF Brüggen, Germany, then spent two years at the Imperial Defence College and at MoD, before taking command of the Central Flying School. Whilst flying one of the Red Arrows' Gnat aircraft to Germany, his machine lost power to its controls, resulting in a crash in which Broom broke both legs and ankles. Once recovered, he was appointed as AOC of the RAF's No. 11 Group, and he flew with both the Lightning and Phantom aircraft. He was made a CB in 1972. He rose to the rank of air marshal in July 1974, and was knighted in 1975 (KCB), retiring from the service in July 1977.

In 1977 he was with the National Air Traffic Service, and in 1993 became president of the Mosquito Aircrew Association, the Blenheim Society and the Bomber Command Association. He also worked for the RAFA (vice president) and its Benevolent Fund. He was also a supporter of the Pathfinder Association, the Aircrew Association and the Bomber Command Association. Other jobs included being a member of the Civil Aviation Board, 1974-77, and chairman of Farnborough Aerospace Development Corporation from 1985 to 1992. He died on 24th January 2003, aged eighty-two.

Distinguished Flying Cross (*London Gazette* 7th April 1942)

This officer has completed forty-five sorties. He has participated in attacks on a wide variety of targets with much success, obtaining hits on a factory at Catanzaro, on military barracks at Buerat, and on mechanical transport and barracks near Tripoli. In November 1941, he bombed and machine-gunned a 4,000-ton ship, setting it on fire. This officer has at all times displayed great leadership, courage and determination.

Bar to DFC (*London Gazette* 3rd October 1944 – a group citation for one award of the DSO, one award of a first Bar to the DFC, one award of the DFC, one award of the DFM)

One night in August 1944, these officers and airmen participated in a sortie involving a mine-laying mission over the Dortmund-Ems Canal. The operation called for the highest standard of resolution as the area is most heavily defended. Nevertheless the mines were laid with great precision. The success achieved reflects the greatest credit on the outstanding skill and great daring of these members of aircraft crew, so ably led by Wg Cdr [J. M.] Birkin [DFC AFC] who also planned the operations.

Second Bar to DFC (*London Gazette* 27th February 1945 – a group citation for two awards of the DSO, one award of a second Bar to the DFC, one award of a first Bar to the DFC, ten awards of the DFC and one award of the DFM)
Three members of aircraft crew have completed very many sorties against enemy targets. In January 1945, they were detailed for an operation which necessitated releasing heavy bombs, from low level, at the openings to various tunnels on the enemy's railway system leading to the Western Front. The mission called for a high degree of skill. The good results obtained reflect the greatest credit on the efforts of the above personnel who, throughout a dangerous and difficult sortie, displayed exceptional ability, great determination and devotion to duty.

Distinguished Service Order (*London Gazette* 26th October 1945)
Since the award of a second Bar to the Distinguished Flying Cross this officer has completed numerous sorties, many of which have been directed against Berlin. Throughout he has displayed the utmost fortitude, courage and determination. At no time has enemy opposition deterred him from completing his allotted tasks. Wg Cdr Broom has at all times set a high standard of devotion to duty.

Other Honours
Air Force Cross, 1955.

Queens Commendation for Valuable Service in the Air.

THOMAS JOHN BROOM

Born in Portishead, Bristol, on 22nd January 1914, Tommy Broom was educated at Slade Road School, leaving at the age of fourteen, to work as a garage hand. When he was eighteen he enlisted into the RAF and trained as an armourer, and saw service in the Middle East and in the Sudan. In 1937 he was serving with 6 Squadron in Palestine.

Requesting aircrew duties, he returned to England in February 1939 and became an observer. When war began he was with 105 Squadron, flying in Fairey Battles in the French Campaign in 1940. Surviving the Battle of France, his squadron continued operations from England with Blenheims, but on 27th/28th November, returning from a trip to Cologne, the crew was forced to abandon their aircraft (T1884) near Stockport due to cloud and flak damage. All three crew landed safely by parachute.

Tommy became an instructor before returning to 105 Squadron in January 1942, now flying in Mosquitos. During an operation on 25th August, his pilot, Flt Lt E. A. Costello-Brown (who had been with him in the bale out back in November 1940), narrowly missed flying into a pylon, although they clipped it, and crashed into some pine trees north-east of Antwerp. Both men survived the crash and were lucky to be picked up by the Resistance people and Broom was sent down the Comet line to Spain, from where he returned to Greenock on the battleship HMS *Malaya* on 5th October. His pilot followed shortly afterwards but was killed in a flying accident in 1943.

In August 1943 he teamed up with Ivor G. Broom DFC (q.v.) at the Mosquito Training Unit where Tommy was chief ground instructor, staying together for the rest of the war. Initially they flew with 571 Squadron, from May 1944, part of the Pathfinder Force. They soon became known as the 'Flying Brooms'. On 9th August 1944 they took part in a spectacular night mission to plant mines along the Dortmund-Ems Canal from 150 feet. Tommy's brilliant navigation helped in making the operations a success. Tom and several others on the mission were decorated. In all the team completed fifty-eight trips, twenty-two of them against Berlin.

Another successful operation came on 1st January 1945, several Mosquito aircraft sent to block railway tunnels at Kaiserslautern, to stop German reinforcements getting into the Battle of the Ardennes. They dropped 4,000-lb bombs, completely demolishing both ends of the tunnel, into which a train had been seen to enter as the attack began. Again several decorations were awarded, Tommy a Bar to his DFC.

When Ivor Broom was given command of 163 Squadron, he took Tommy with him, and continued to operate till the war's end, Tommy receiving a second Bar to his DFC.

After the war Tommy married a German war widow who was working as an interpreter for the Control Commission in July 1948. They set up home back in Portishead, and later had a daughter, Mary-Ann, and later still, a grandson. Tommy worked for the Esso Petroleum Company, within the aircraft fuel department. His wife, Annamarie, died in 1963 and Tommy on 18th May 2010, aged ninety-six. Tom Parry Evans wrote a book about Tommy, published in 2007 called *Squadron Leader Tommy Broom DFC**: The Legendary Pathfinder Mosquito Navigator*.

Distinguished Flying Cross (*London Gazette* 3rd October 1944)
For the joint citation see award for Ivor G. Broom

Bar to DFC (*London Gazette* 27th February 1945)
For the joint citation see award for Ivor G. Broom

Second Bar to DFC (*London Gazette* 26th October 1945)
This officer has a long and distinguished record of operational flying. He first flew against the enemy in September 1939, and since then he has completed a large number of day and night sorties against heavily defended targets in Germany. On one occasion he was forced to leave his aircraft by parachute and another time his aircraft crashed in occupied territory but he evaded capture and returned to this country where he resumed operational flying with undiminished enthusiasm. The sterling qualities of courage, leadership and devotion to duty displayed by Sqn Ld Broom have materially contributed to the operational efficiency of each squadron with which he has served. In addition his fine work as squadron navigation officer has been worthy of the highest praise.

EDWARD ROBERT BUTLER

From Uxbridge, Middlesex, Butler was born on 5th February, 1910, son of Edward Robert and Eleanor Kate Butler, residing at 'Binfield', Basset Road. Mr Butler came from Binfield, Berkshire, hence the name of their house, while his wife came from west Tottenham, north London. Edward Junior, named after his father, had two older sisters, Eleanor Kate (same as her mother) and Dorothy Clare, all three born in Uxbridge. Mr Butler worked for Alfred Button & Sons, in the town, which was a grocery business. His particular job was to tour the local grocery shops collecting their orders, much like a commercial traveller, which would then be delivered later by lorry.

Edward began his education at Cowley Road Boys School, and then the Church of England School at High Wycombe, and later still, the Royal Grammar School, also in High Wycombe. Finally he went to Uxbridge County School in September 1921, leaving in March 1926. Once he had left school his job was as a grocery assistant, no doubt with the same company as his father.

By the time World War Two began he was living in Caversham, near Reading, when he enlisted into the Royal Air Force Volunteer Reserve in 1940. Following training as a navigator he received a commission in 1941.

He was posted to 97 Squadron, flying Avro Manchesters, stationed at Bourn, Cambridgeshire, where he was awarded the Distinguished Flying Cross in late 1942. This was quickly followed by a Bar to this decoration, his citation referring to his part in the daylight Augsburg Raid on 17th April 1942. This was flown in company with 44 Squadron, both units equipped with the new Avro Lancaster, John Nettleton, leading the raid, winning the Victoria Cross for this daring operation against the MAN diesel engine factory there. Seven of the twelve Lancasters involved failed to return. Butler's pilot on this raid was Fg Off E. A. Deverill DFM in Lancaster L7575 (OF-Y), and the others in the crew were Sgts J. S. Cooper, R. P. Irons, K. O. Mackay, J. A. Devine and Flt Sgt W. H. Keene. Ernest Deverill also received the DFC for his part in the operation. Deverill also received the AFC on 1st January 1944 for his instructional work with AFDU, but was killed before it was promulgated.

Their part in this famous daylight raid was far from routine, quite apart from sending a force of these new Lancaster bombers 900 miles into Germany. They took off at 1459 hours. Nearing the target, their Lancaster was hit by ground fire that knocked out the starboard outer engine, and ripped open the starboard side of the fuselage. The hydraulic pipes were severed, putting both rear and upper turrets out of commission, and setting fire to the hydraulic oil. Deverill carried on to bomb, while the fire was contained and put out by Sgt Ronald Irons and

Fg Off Edward Butler DFC★★ (second from right) with his pilot Fg Off E Deverill DFC★, DFM on his right with members of 97 Squadron. In the background, their Lancaster sports thirty-six bomb raid symbols alongside its Popeye insignia. To the extreme left stands Sgt R. P. Irons DFC.

Sgt Kenneth MacKay, both receiving the DFM. They headed for base and managed to get the engine re-started before reaching the French coast. They got home at 2315 hours.

Following a rest from operations, Butler volunteered for a second tour, being sent to 630 Squadron at East Kirby, Lincolnshire, again flying Avro Lancasters. At the end of this tour he received a second Bar to his DFC as an acting squadron leader. During his tours he had flown on the 1,000 bomber raids, and attacks on Le Creusot, Milan and Genoa.

Distinguished Flying Cross (*London Gazette* 6th November 1942)

Plt Off Butler has displayed great skill as a navigator in attacks against some of the most heavily defended areas in Germany. On one occasion, during a low-level daylight attack on Augsburg, despite heavy damage to his aircraft from anti-aircraft fire, this officer, displaying great determination, persisted and successfully achieved his mission. By his keenness and devotion to duty Plt Off Butler sets a fine example to the squadron.

Bar to DFC (*London Gazette* 20th November 1942)

As navigator, Fg Off Butler has taken part in many successful sorties against the most heavily defended areas in Germany, including the daylight attack on Augsburg. Recently he participated in the daylight attacks on Le Creusot and Milan and a night attack on Genoa. His navigational standard has always been exceptional whilst his keenness and courage have materially assisted in the successes achieved by his squadron.

Second Bar to DFC (*London Gazette* 15th September 1944)

Since joining his squadron in December 1943, Sqn Ldr Butler has taken part in attacks on many strongly defended targets in Germany, including Berlin, Brunswick and the Ruhr. He is a navigator of high merit and his technical skill has contributed greatly to the success of operations. This officer has used his knowledge and experience to the full in assisting less experienced navigators. His enthusiasm and unfailing determination makes him an invaluable officer to his squadron.

JOHN TODD CAINE

From Edmonton, Alberta, Canada, born 2nd September 1920, son of Mr and Mrs H L Caine. Educated at Queen Alexandria Public School in Edmonton and then employed by his father who was a fur rancher. In order to increase his education qualifications he studied with the Canadian Legion Educational Services, attaining Grades X and XI in correspondence courses. Johnny Caine enlisted into the RCAF on 1st December 1941, and part of his training was at No. 2 Initial Training School, between April and July 1942, then at 19 and 11 EFTS (Empire Flying Training Schools). In early 1943 he sailed for England, arriving on 13th February where he completed his training and was then posted to 418 Canadian Squadron, flying with this unit from 30th September to May 1944, operating Mosquito VIs on intruder missions.

Fg Off John Caine pictured through the damage to his Mosquito on 2nd May 1944.

Over those months, often flying with Earl W. Boal as his navigator, he gained considerable success in air fighting and ground-attack sorties. This began on 20th/21st December by destroying a twin-engine aircraft on Delune airfield near Metz. As 1944 began, he and another crew shared a Ju W 34 shot down and then Caine disposed of a Ju 88 south-east of Bourges. A third kill was another Ju W 34 at Clermont Ferrand airfield, on the 27th. A month later a ground-attack sortie on a German airfield netted him a Me 110 on the ground and on 12th March a Ju 52 and a Ju 86 were burned on the ground.

Multiple claims were achieved on 12th April with two Ju 52s destroyed and one damaged, followed by a He 111, all on the ground. A bit of a field day occurred on 2nd May, with two Do 18s on the water and four more on the ground – a Ju 52, a Ju 88, a Ju W 34 and a Ju 86, plus two more Dornier flying-boats damaged. On the sortie on 2nd May his Mosquito was hit by ground fire forcing him to nurse his damaged aircraft back to England on one engine. So serious was the problem that he radioed fellow pilot Charlie Scherf that he and Boal were considering a bale out. He received the DFC in April. On 8th/9th May he destroyed as BV 138 and a Do 18 on the water and damaged two others. In June he received a Bar to his DFC and Earl Boal received the DFC, to which he added a Bar in July. Caine eventually received his decorations from King George VI on 13th July 1945. A report mentions the following operations:

> "On 20th March, Fg Off Caine carried out a long daylight penetration of France and destroyed a Junkers 52 and a Junkers 88 at Clermont. Again on 14th April, Fg Off Caine took part in a highly successful day ranger to Copenhagen. During the course of this sortie, Fg Off Caine shot down and destroyed two Junkers 52s over the Pomeranian Sea, destroyed a Heinkel 111 and damaged a Junkers 52 on the ground at Copenhagen Kastrup. On the return journey by skilful manipulation of his aircraft, Fg Off Caine evaded the attacks of two Focke Wulf 190s and returned to base without injury to his crew or damage to his aircraft."

He was posted back to Canada for a rest where he spent some months as an instructor at an operational training unit at Debert, Nova Scotia, before returning to England to join 406 Squadron RCAF, on 30th March 1945. Caine continued his ranger sorties in a Mosquito XXX and on 24th April he destroyed a Ju 88 and damaged two Fw 190s on the ground. On 2nd May, exactly one year following his close call, he made his final claims, two Ju 52s destroyed on the ground. His third DFC was gazetted in October.

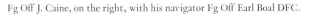

Fg Off J. Caine, on the right, with his navigator Fg Off Earl Boal DFC.

He married LACW Olive Jane Ford (WAAF) on 1st May 1945, with Wg Cdr Ross Gray DFC and Bar, who had been with Johnny in 418 Squadron, now commanding 406 Squadron, as his best man.

Caine was released from the RCAF at the end of 1945, and eventually lived in British Columbia. He re-engaged with the RCAF Auxiliary in Edmonton, made squadron leader in 1950 and retired in January 1952. Post-war he joined his father's fur farm and later opened his own just outside Edmonton. By 1966 the Caine mink farm was one of the largest in Canada. He closed the business in 1973. Edmonton has Caine Memorial Park on 106th Street, named in his honour. He died in Vancouver on 1st June 1995.

EARL WILLIAM BOAL flew as Caine's navigator in the latter part of the war. Born in Weyburn, Saskatchewan on 25th January 1921, to Roy L. and Etta M. Boal (née Taylor). Shattered by the Great Depression Earl and his sisters were raised by his Aunt Rebecca Taylor in Regina, where, leaving school, he enlisted on 11th July 1940 as a wireless operator. The following year he became a wireless electrical mechanic and gradually rose from AC2 to sergeant by September 1942. Sent overseas in October he was commissioned on 31st January 1944 and became aircrew, posted to 418 Squadron RCAF, where he teamed up with Johnnie Caine.

Boal did the navigating on 9th March for two Mosquitos that penetrated 500 miles into enemy territory, and all at low level. By his skill he located their target which resulted in a Ju 52 and a Ju 86P being destroyed.

On 14th April 1944, two Mosquitos, Caine and Boal, Robert Kipp and Peter Huletsky, spotted four Ju 52s with mine-detecting rings, flying over the sea between Denmark and Sweden and shot them all down into the sea. They then strafed a number of aircraft on nearby Kastrup airfield, near Copenhagen. On 2nd May Charles Scherf/William 'Red' Stewart, Caine and Boal, headed into the Baltic and approaching Ribnitz, found several float-planes and flying-boats on the water. While Scherf shot-up two He 115s, Caine and Boal blew up two Do 18s and damaged two more. At Barth they found twelve aircraft on the airfield and attacked. Scherf blew up a He 111 and a Do 217, while Caine destroyed a variety of Junkers. Their port engine was knocked out from flying debris so they quickly headed for home. Over the sea Caine and Boal were certain they were not going to make it, so called Scherf, saying: 'Our airplane is damaged and we shall not be able to get home. We are preparing to bale out.' In the event they did struggle back, Boal navigating the 470 miles back to base. Three days later they were strafing Griefswald air base, destroying a Do 18 on the water, damaged two more, and set a BV 138 on fire. In all Caine and Boal had destroyed more than twenty enemy aircraft in the air and on the ground/water.

Boal received the DFC and Bar for his work with 418 Squadron and upon his final return to Canada he left the service on 9th November 1945. He went to McGill University where he graduated with a bachelor of engineering degree in 1949. At McGill he met Gisella Pearl Anderson and they married in 1948. Boal worked for Northern Telecom in several parts of Canada until he retired. He died in West Park Health Care Centre, Toronto, on 13th June 2010.

Distinguished Flying Cross (*London Gazette* 4th April 1944)

This officer has completed many sorties during which he has shot down four enemy aircraft, two of them at night; he has also destroyed two more on the ground. He has displayed exceptional devotion to duty and his successes are an excellent tribute to his skill and determination.

Bar to DFC (*London Gazette* 2nd June 1944)

This officer continues to display the finest qualities of skill and determination. On a sortie in March, 1944, he shot down two enemy aircraft, whilst in another operation in April 1944, he shot down two Junkers 52s and damaged a Heinkel III on the ground. Since then, Fg Off Caine has destroyed another enemy aircraft. This officer is a fearless and relentless fighter and has been responsible for the destruction of nine enemy aircraft in the air and four damaged on the ground.

Second Bar to DFC (*London Gazette* 19th October 1945)

Flt Lt Caine has completed many operational sorties since the award of a Bar to the DFC. In May 1944 whilst on a patrol in the Barth area, he inflicted much damage on the enemy's lines of communication and destroyed several enemy seaplanes at anchor. In April 1945 whilst over south-east Germany he destroyed one enemy aircraft and damaged a further two. Despite the fact that on this sortie Flt Lt Caine's aircraft was hit by anti-aircraft fire which damaged the flying controls, a successful return to base was made. His indomitable fearlessness and skill have merited the highest praise. Since his previous award he has destroyed a further eleven enemy aircraft, bringing his total victories to at least twenty.

ROY OLDFIELD CALVERT

Calvert came from New Zealand, born on 31st October 1913 at Cambridge, Waikato Region, the son of George Calvert, owner of a department store. After schooling at Cambridge Primary School, Southwell School in Hamilton, and King's College School in Auckland, he became a farmer and wool grader. Keen to fly, he joined the Rukuhia Aero Club, Hamilton, training on a DH60 and later flew at the Waikato Flying Club. Once war was declared he applied for the air force and was finally accepted into the RNZAF on 1st December 1940. In April and May 1941 he trained on Oxfords at Ohakea, and shortly before being sent overseas, married May. She was on the quayside as the ship sailed, waving her scarf till the boat was out of sight. He later wrote to her asking that she send that scarf to him, which she did. He wore it throughout all his operations.

His first stop was Canada and after further training sailed for Liverpool, England, going to No. 25 Operational Training Unit at Cranage, where he flew Avro Ansons.

In April 1942 he was posted to 50 Squadron at Skellingthorpe, the first RAF squadron to received Avro Manchester bombers and his first operation was to Lille on the 16th. He continued with his tour and was awarded the DFC in October. Meantime, the squadron had re-equipped with Lancasters. On the night of 9th/10th November, a trip to Hamburg resulted in the award of a Bar to his DFC. His Lancaster (R5702), with its bomb doors open, was hit by flak over the city and sustained severe damage. One AA shell exploded near the port wing, spraying the fuselage with shrapnel and blowing out most of the Perspex. A second shell hit the aircraft squarely, killing the wireless operator, Sgt L. H. Austin RAAF and wounding both Calvert and the navigator, Flt Sgt John Medani RNZAF. Much of the aircraft's equipment was damaged and the bomber became very difficult to handle. Nevertheless, although wounded in one arm, Calvert succeeded in getting his crippled aircraft clear and flew it back to England to land at Bradwell Bay, despite the undercarriage collapsing leaving the bomber to belly land along the runway.

Medani was awarded an immediate DFM, having continued with his navigational duties despite losing a good deal of blood. Back in England he had to have two blood transfusions to save his life.

Calvert left the squadron on 14th February 1943, joining No. 1660 HCU two days later. In January 1944 he volunteered for another tour, being sent to 630 Squadron, at East Kirby, on Lancasters. Between 17th January and 24th August 1944, he brought his total number of operations to fifty-nine, and received a second Bar to his DFC.

Top: Roy Calvert's 50 Squadron Lancaster (R5702) at RAF Skellingthorpe in 1942. Bottom: Calvert crash landed his shot-up Lancaster at Bradwell Bay on 9th November 1942, his thirty-first operation. The word 'Taipo' can be seen in the insignia and it means 'evil spirit' or 'goblin' in New Zealand.

Roy returned to New Zealand in late 1944 and was finally discharged on 15th March 1945, to return to farming. He died on 26th March 2002 aged eighty-eight, of emphysema and cancer and is buried at the RSA Cemetery at Hautapu. Cambridge, NZ.

Distinguished Flying Cross (*London Gazette* 20th October 1942 – joint citation with Plt Off J. A. Sears RAAF)

Fg Off Calvert and Plt Off Sears as pilot and navigator of aircraft respectively have flown together on many sorties. Whatever the weather or the opposition they have always endeavoured to press home their attacks and, on numerous occasions, have obtained excellent photographs. Throughout their tour of duty, these officers have displayed a high standard of skill, together with great devotion to duty.

Bar to DFC (*London Gazette* 18th December 1942 – joint citation with Flt Sgt J. Medani [DFM])

As pilot and navigator of aircraft respectively, Fg Off Calvert and Flt Sgt Medani have participated in numerous sorties, including attacks on heavily defended areas in western Germany and daylight raids on Le Creusot and Milan. During a recent sortie, Fg Off Calvert's aircraft was subjected to heavy anti-aircraft fire, sustaining much damage. The wireless operator was killed and both the pilot and navigator were wounded. The aircraft became difficult to control but Fg Off Calvert, although he had a piece of shell splinter embedded in his left arm, set course for home. Flt Sgt Medani, despite the severity of his wound and subsequent loss of blood, continued his duties until he collapsed. Even so, he succeeded in giving his pilot a final course which enabled him to reach an airfield in this country where he make a skilful crash landing in bad visibility. Both these members of aircraft crew displayed great courage and tenacity in the face of harassing circumstances.

Second Bar to DFC (*London Gazette* 15th September 1944)

Since joining this squadron in January 1944, Sqn Ldr Calvert has taken part in attacks against many strongly defended targets in Germany, including Berlin and Leipzig. He has consistently showed skill, determination and reliability, and, as captain of aircraft, he has set a high example to the other members of his squadron. His operational experience and enthusiasm have been invaluable in the training of new crews.

FRANK REGINALD CAREY

The son of Alfred John and Elsie Mabel Carey, Frank was born on 7th May 1912 in Brixton, south London. He had two younger brothers, Hugh and Roy. The family moved to Blackheath, south of Greenwich and later to Shepherd's Bush. However, his mother suffered from TB that led to another move into the country, going to Lindfield, in Sussex, his father opening an ironmonger's shop there. Frank went to Belvedere School, in Haywards Heath. Sadly his mother's health did not improve and she died in 1924.

From an early age, young Frank became interested in aviation but with limited education his only way of joining the RAF was as an apprentice and with some extra tuition from his old headmaster at Lindfield School, just managed to scrape through the entrance exam to join the Halton Apprentice Scheme in September 1927, aged fifteen.

By 1930 Frank had become a full-blown mechanic and as such was sent to 43 Squadron at RAF Tangmere, equipped with Siskin fighters. It was not long before Frank was applying for permission to become a pilot, but it was a rocky road. However, his persistence paid off and in 1936 he was selected for pilot training, going to No. 6 FTS at Netheravon. Frank appeared to be a natural pilot and soon gained his 'wings'. Amazingly his first posting was to his old squadron (43) as a sergeant pilot.

During this time he had met Kathleen Ivy Steele, known to everyone as Kate, who lived on a farm near Winchester. She was twenty-two years of age, he twenty-four and they were married at Winchester Registry Office on 1st July 1936, Kate setting up home in Arundel. For the next three years Frank honed his flying skills so that by the time war came, he was an established senior NCO pilot, flying Hawker Hurricanes. The squadron's war station was Tangmere but in November 1939 they were sent to Acklington, north of Newcastle.

Although what air fighting was going on was in France, German raiders did occasionally make forays to England and Scotland. Frank's first success in air combat came on 30th January 1940 against a Heinkel III bomber that he and his flight commander, Caesar Hull, shot down. On 3rd February, he and Sgt P. G. Ottewill shared another HeIII, while on 28th March Frank, Hull and Sgt T. A. H. Gough shared another. This led to Frank being awarded an immediate Distinguished Flying Medal. This in turn led to him being commissioned and posted to 3 Squadron in April 1940.

The Germans began their offensive into the Low Countries and France on the morning of 10th May, an event that sent 3 Squadron to Merville to support the few Hurricane squadrons already in France against the enemy onslaught. That evening Frank Carey, amazingly, destroyed three Heinkels and damaged two more in a single action between Merville and Lille, and before the day was over, he shared in another destroyed, along with Flt Lt M. M. Carter and Fg Off A. R. Ball. The next day he shot down another Heinkel, followed by another plus a damaged on the 12th. What was a wonderful achievement on the 10th was overshadowed on the morning of the 13th, Frank destroying two Ju 87 dive-bombers, with two more probably destroyed, one He 111, a Dornier 17 and a Henschel 123 also destroyed, a total of seven destroyed and three probables. During a second patrol before noon, Frank shared yet another He 111, with his CO, Sqn Ldr W. M. Churchill and Sgt D. A. Allen.

On the 14th he shot down a Dornier 17 on a dawn patrol near Wavre, but the rear gunner got in a telling burst that set Frank's Hurricane on fire, another bullet hitting one leg below the knee. Having problems baling out of his stricken fighter he eventually crash landed. He was picked up by two Belgian soldiers who handed him over to British sappers, preparing to blow a bridge. Later he got a lift in a truck and later still, by ambulance, he wound up in Dieppe. A few days later he and some other RAF bods, stole a Bristol Bombay aircraft they found abandoned on an airfield, with Frank manning a rear gun. Far from being inconspicuous, the Bombay transport 'plane was painted bright yellow, but they made it to England.

For his actions over France, Frank received not only the DFC, but a Bar too. In those few days he had shot down a dozen German aircraft, with others damaged. Back in England his wound was treated and by mid-June he was back, posted to 43 Squadron again. In July he was made A Flight commander.

Frank was heavily embroiled in the Battle of Britain, until he was wounded again on 18th August and again crash landed. He had, however, destroyed a further six German aircraft, probably four more and damaged another six. No doubt 'higher authority' decided he had been rewarded enough in recent months, for he received no recognition of these victories.

He returned to 43 Squadron on 23rd September, but the squadron had been moved north for a rest, and took no further part in the battles over southern England. In February 1941, Frank was posted as an instructor to No. 52 Operational Training Unit where he remained until given command of A Flight in 245 Squadron, in Northern Ireland. However, his next posting, in August, was to command 135 Squadron, at Kirton in Lindsey, a new Hurricane squadron just forming.

Frank Carey by a Vampire V at RAF Gütersloh, Germany in 1949.

Before the summer was out the squadron became operational but it was then announced that it was to leave England for the Middle East. By the time the convoy taking them reached Sierra Leone, the Japanese had attacked Pearl Harbor, and so 135 Squadron were re-routed to India and finally Rangoon. This meant flying their Hurricanes across Africa to Egypt, then on to Burma. It arrived piecemeal, but a few of the early arrivals managed to get some action against Japanese aircraft before Rangoon fell, followed by the retreat north. On 29th January 1942, Frank shot down a Japanese fighter and damaged another over Mingaladon.

In February, with the retreat almost over, Frank was asked to command 267 Fighter Wing. During that month he shot down six more Japanese aircraft, plus another two destroyed on the ground. His final victory came on 25th October, another Japanese fighter near Chittagong. In all, Frank was credited with twenty-eight enemy aircraft destroyed in the air, two on the ground, eight more probably destroyed and ten damaged. When I wrote Frank's biography, some of the men he had flown with thought he deserved a DSO for his actions over Burma. However, 'higher authority' was at it again, so he was only awarded a second Bar to his DFC. After all, he was an ex-NCO, and Burma was a retreat, not a victory.

Once the retreat had been halted, 267 Wing returned to India and Frank had some sick leave before commanding 165 Wing at Dum Dum, taking this wing back to the Arakan in December. However, his air fighting days were over, and in February 1943 he took command of the air fighting training unit at Amarda Road, Orissa. Here he passed his knowledge to many of the existing and new fighter pilots in theatre, and many a number of these men remember Frank's skill, and especially his numerous aerobatic displays. Frank left India in June, went back to England for a gunnery course, although he no doubt passed on more information that he learnt, and went back to India and AFDU in September.

Promoted to group captain in November he commanded No. 73 Operational Training Unit at Fayid, Egypt, and for his good work there, received the Air Force Cross in the 1945 New Year Honours List. In June 1945 he went to the Central Fighter Establishment, Tangmere as OC Tactics, and flew as part of the famous Battle of Britain flypast that September, led by Douglas Bader.

In May 1946, as a wing commander, he attended the Army Staff College and that November was OC Training 84 Group at Celle, Germany, while in January 1948 he was OC 135 Wing at Gütersloh. His career continued with various command posts, promotion back to group captain and he retired from the service on 1st June 1960, having been made CBE on 1st January.

One of his last appointments was with the United Kingdom Joint Services Liaison Staff at Canberra, Australia, and following retirement from the RAF,

Frank Carey with the author in Majorca, May 1992.

he returned to Australia to a position with Rolls-Royce aero engine division, as sales representative for them in Australia, New Zealand and Fiji. By this time, his marriage to Kate had produced two daughters.

Frank retired from Rolls-Royce in 1972 when he reached the age of sixty. However, his wife died in 1991, which was sad, and a pity for me, for she was trying to persuade Frank to let me write his life story. However, he met Marigold Crew-Read in 1992 and they married in April 1993, setting up home in Bognor Regis.

Frank died on 6th December 2004, having spent three years in a rest home in Chichester. Shortly afterwards, I contacted Marigold about a biography, and she was all for it. Going through his papers we discovered many handwritten accounts of his time in France and in the Battle of Britain, all of which added to a wonderful life story. *Frank 'Chota' Carey* was published by Grub Street in 2006.

Distinguished Flying Medal (*London Gazette* 1st March 1940)
On 30th January 1940, with his section leader, he successfully engaged an enemy aircraft over the North Sea whilst it was attacking shipping. Again on 3rd February 1940, Sgt Carey, this time acting as section leader of a section of two aircraft, engaged an enemy aircraft over the North Sea and shot it down. The weather conditions during these engagements were such that low cloud

provided almost immediate cover for the enemy and it was mainly due to Sgt Carey's initiative, determination and skill that this cover was denied the enemy and the engagement brought to a successful conclusion. It is recommended that he be decorated by the award of the Distinguished Flying Medal.

Distinguished Flying Cross (*London Gazette* 31st May 1940)

This officer has destroyed five enemy aircraft early in the operations in May 1940, and by his dash and courage set the highest example of gallantry to the squadron.

Bar to DFC (*London Gazette* 31st May 1940 – both awards promulgated on the same date)

This officer has shot down four more enemy aircraft bringing his total to nine. Throughout the operations he was continuously on the search for enemy aircraft and was an inspiration to all who flew with him. His morale was always of the highest order.

Second Bar to DFC (*London Gazette* 24th March 1942)

When leading the squadron or wing, this officer has displayed high qualities of leadership and has set a high example by his courage and devotion to duty. Wg Cdr Carey has destroyed at least five enemy aircraft.

Other Honours

Air Force Cross (*London Gazette* 1st January 1945)

Czechoslovakian Flying Badge – 20th January 1941

American Silver Star – June 1945

Ordinary Commander to the Military Division of the Most Excellent Order of the British Empire (*London Gazette* 3rd June 1960)

ARTHUR HENRY COBBY

Harry Cobby was the first World War One airman to receive a second Bar to the DFC and actually be awarded it prior to the war's end. Born in the Melbourne suburb of Praham on 26th August 1894 (the second of four sons), his parents were Arthur E. S. Cobby, a tram conductor, and Alice Cobby. He completed his studies at the University College, Armadale, and joining the militia was commissioned into the 46th Infantry Regiment (Brighton Rifles) in 1912, later transferring to the 47th Infantry Regiment.

His civilian occupation was as a clerk with the Commonwealth Bank of Australia, Melbourne office, and when war came his manager refused to allow Harry to enlist, saying his job was an essential occupation. Eventually, however, he did manage to join the Australian Imperial Force on 23rd December 1916, despite having no real interest in flying, and after training at the Central Flying School, sailed for England arriving on 17th January 1917 to become a founder member of 71 Squadron RFC which later became 4 Squadron AFC, equipped with Sopwith Camels.

Once in France he became a gifted fighter pilot claiming his first two victories on 21st March 1918. In May he became a flight commander and was awarded the DFC, followed by a Bar in June. By the end of that month his score stood at eighteen. Following his twenty-fourth victory he received a second Bar. Shortly before the end of the war he was awarded the DSO for his leadership in attacking the German airfields at Haubourdin and Lomme.

With a final tally of twenty-nine victories (including five kite balloons), he was the highest-scoring Australian ace, and he returned to England in September to become an instructor. In December he was mentioned in despatches, and then chosen to lead the AFC's Anzac Day flypast over London before the Prince of Wales on 25th April 1919.

Cobby returned to Australia in May 1919, and married Hilda Maude Urban in Caulfield, Victoria, on 24th April 1920, resulting in one son and one daughter. Harry remained in the RAAF and was the CO of 1 Squadron between 1925-26, and as a squadron leader returned to England in 1928 to attend the RAF Staff College. Back in Australia in 1930 he became CO of 3 Squadron while also commanding RAAF Station Richmond. Made wing commander in May 1933, and later appointed RAAF director of intelligence.

During WW2 he became a group captain in July 1940, as director of recruiting, and in August 1942 was AOC North-East Area, Queensland. On 7th September 1943, as an air commodore, he was a passenger in a Catalina that crashed at Townsville, Queensland. Although injured he helped to rescue two survivors and was recommended for the George Medal, which was gazetted on 10th March 1944.

He became commandant of the RAAF Staff College and in June 1944 was made CBE for his conduct of air operations over New Guinea. In August 1944 Cobby became AOC of 10 Group, later called 1 Tactical Air Force in the South-West Pacific. He left the service in August 1946 and was awarded the American Medal of Freedom in April 1948. He then served with the

Gp Capt 'Harry' Cobby photographed during WW2.

Department of Civil Aviation and then as regional director in New South Wales in 1947-1954. In 1955 he became director of flying operations.

On Armistice Day, 11th November 1955, he collapsed in his office and passed away later than day in Heidelberg Repatriation General Hospital Victoria, and four days later he was given a military funeral at St Mary's Church in Caulfield, and cremated at Springvale Crematorium. Cobby Street, in the Canberra suburb of Campbell, is named in his honour.

Distinguished Flying Cross (*London Gazette* 2nd July 1918)
He has proved himself a very gallant and successful fighter and patrol leader, setting a fine example to the squadron. Within the last few months he has destroyed a number of enemy balloons and aeroplanes.

Bar to DFC (*London Gazette* 21st September 1918)
An officer whose success as a leader is due not only to high courage and brilliant flying, but also to the clear judgement and presence of mind he invariably displays. His example is of great value to other pilots in his squadron. During recent operations he shot down five machines in eleven days, accounting for two in one day.

Second Bar to DFC (*London Gazette* 21st September 1918)
One evening this officer, in company with another machine, attacked five Pfalz Scouts, destroying two; one fell in flames, and one broke up in the air.

The officer who accompanied him brought down a third machine out of control. While engaged in this combat they were attacked from above by five triplanes. Displaying cool judgement and brilliant flying, Captain Cobby evaded this attack and returned to our lines in safety, both machines being undamaged. A determined and most skilful leader, who has destroyed twenty-one hostile machines or balloons, accounting for three machines and two balloons in four days.

Distinguished Service Cross (*London Gazette* 2nd November 1918)
On 16th August this officer led an organised raid on an enemy aerodrome. At 200 feet altitude he obtained direct hits with his bombs and set on fire two hangars; he then opened fire on a machine which was standing out on the aerodrome. The machine caught fire. Afterwards he attacked with machine-gun fire parties of troops and mechanics, inflicting a number of casualties. On the following day he led another important raid on an aerodrome, setting fire to two hangars and effectively bombing gun detachments, anti-aircraft. The success of these two raids was largely due to the determined and skilful leadership of this officer.

George Medal (*London Gazette* 10th March 1944)
On 7th September 1943, Air Cdre Cobby was returning from Dutch New Guinea and upon arrival at Townsville the Catalina in which he was travelling crashed on alighting, exploding one of the two depth charges with which the aircraft was armed. The aircraft was badly shattered and thirteen of the nineteen occupants were either killed or drowned. Air Cdre Cobby managed to extricate himself from the wreck and although injured, he re-entered the submerged hull on three occasions in order to rescue members of his staff. As a result of his strenuous efforts against the great pressure in the cabin, he was able to assist Wg Cdr W. L. B. Stephens, who had a badly broken arm, and brought him to the surface. The second time he extricated Wg Cdr B. P. Macfarlan and brought him to a position on top of the blister. He re-entered the cabin a third time but was unable to effect any further rescues. Owing to the fact that at least one other depth charge was unexploded, and that any moment the wrecked aircraft might slip under the water, Air Cdre Cobby displayed outstanding courage in risking his life while effecting rescues of these members of his staff. His devotion to duty on this occasion is worthy of the highest praise.

Commander of the Order of the British Empire (June 1944)
[For his conduct of air operations over New Guinea] "… and good leadership, personal example, keen understanding and continued encouragement."

American Medal of Freedom

For meritorious service which has aided the United States in the prosecution of the war against Japan, from 26th September 1944 to 31st January 1945. While under the operational control of the Thirteenth Air Force, Air Cdre Cobby directed his planes in continuous action against enemy installations in the Celebes and Halmahera Islands, and inflicted heavy damage on enemy shipping, supply areas and radar positions. His services were distinguished by exceptionally sound judgement and far-sighted planning, and his forces were so well co-ordinated with those of the Thirteenth Air Force that all available aircraft were employed with maximum effect. He greatly assisted in denying the enemy water or land movement in the northern Celebes and the Halmaheras, and materially assisted in the support of the operations in the Philippines Liberation Campaign. Air Cdre Cobby rendered a material contribution to the success of the United States Army Forces in the South-West Pacific Area.

ALFRED WILLIAM GORDON COCHRANE

From Rawene, New Zealand, born 10th October 1916, son of W. M. Cochrane. Upon leaving school, Gordon as he preferred to be known, got a job as a shop assistant in his uncle's general store but with the coming of WW2 he enlisted into the RNZAF in September 1940. Once trained as a pilot, that he began at No. 6C Course at No. 3 Service Flying Training School, at Ohakea, he was retained as an instructor before finally able to get onto an operational squadron, joining 156 Squadron, flying Vickers Wellingtons. In the summer of 1942 he was awarded his first DFC, an immediate award. He completed thirty-three operations, including all three of the thousand-bomber raids.

Left: Alfred Cochrane photographed during his time on No. 6C course at No. 3 Service Flying Training School in Ohakea on 20th December 1940.

After attending an instructor's school, he spent the next eighteen months as an instructor before returning to 156 Squadron in June 1944. He flew two tours with 156, later flying Avro Lancasters, onto which he had converted in early 1943. 156 became part of the Pathfinder Force, marking targets for Main Force bombers. In all Cochrane flew fifty-five operational trips, fourteen of these while acting as master bomber, directing bombers onto the targets, while remaining over them for a longer period to ensure the right markers were being bombed.

His next decoration was the award of the Distinguished Service Order, his citation referring to an attack on Eindhoven airfield. Early in 1945 he received a Bar to his DFC for his part in a daylight raid upon an airfield at Düsseldorf. His third DFC was a reward for his efforts on the night of 7th/8th February 1945, the target being troop concentrations at Goch, Germany. Over the target his Lancaster was in collision with another Lancaster, part of Cochrane's aircraft port wing being torn away. However, he regained control and managed to get his crippled bomber on an even keel, and continued to direct the attack. Afterwards he headed for home – and made it. Among his crew, two were decorated: Flight engineer John B. Elder and rear gunner Tom E. Drew, both received DFMs, having completed fifty-four and sixty trips respectively.

In all Cochrane flew eighty-eight operational trips during three tours of bomber operations and was an acclaimed Pathfinder captain. After the war he remained in the RNZAF until April 1947, then joined the British Overseas Aircraft Corporation (BOAC) and flew a succession of air liners for that company, including Avro Yorks, Handley Page Hermes, Boeing 377 Stratocruisers, de Havilland Comets and Boeing 707s. He retired at the end of 1971 as a senior captain after twenty-five years of service.

He had married Josephine Hughes, from Bristol, England, and remained in the UK afterwards. Cochrane died in Wimborne Minster, Dorset, England, in 1994 aged seventy-eight.

Distinguished Flying Cross (*London Gazette* 11th August 1942)

This officer is employed as captain of aircraft. Throughout he has completed his attacks with skill, courage and determination. On one occasion in March 1942, his aircraft would not climb above 1,000 feet. Despite strong enemy opposition and the presence of balloons, Plt Off Cochrane, with great resolution, flew on and successfully bombed his objective at Essen. His aircraft was damaged by anti-aircraft fire. His high devotion to duty is shown by the completion of six successful night sorties between 30th March and 7th June, 1942. His fearlessness in the face of danger has inspired a high standard of morale in his crew. Plt Off Cochrane has attacked many important enemy targets, including Brest, Cologne, Bremen and Hamburg.

Distinguished Service Order (*London Gazette* 2nd January 1945)

This officer has displayed the highest standard of skill and courage against the enemy. He has completed a very large number of sorties, involving attacks on a wide range of enemy targets and throughout has displayed outstanding determination and devotion to duty. On a recent occasion, Sqn Ldr Cochrane participated in an attack on the airfield at Eindhoven. His accurate and determined bombing in the face of concentrated anti-aircraft fire set a very fine example. His achievements have won great praise.

Bar to DFC (*London Gazette* 16th February 1945)

Sqn Ldr Cochrane is a cool and courageous captain and pilot, whose qualities of leadership and determination have been well illustrated in many operations against the enemy. In December 1944, Sqn Ldr Cochrane participated in an attack on the airfield at Düsseldorf. In spite of intense and accurate fire from the ground defences, Sqn Ldr Cochrane pressed home his attack with his usual skill. His aircraft was hit but he flew back to base. His devotion to duty has been unfailing.

Second Bar to DFC (*London Gazette* 27th March 1945)

On one night in February 1945, Squadron Leader Cochrane, as captain of aircraft, was detailed to attack enemy troop concentrations at Goch. Soon after reaching the target the port wing of his aircraft sustained severe damage and part of it fell off. Undeterred, Sqn Ldr Cochrane, with superb airmanship and courage, continued with his task. This officer has set a magnificent example of fearlessness. His tenacity of purpose and cheerfulness have been an inspiration to his squadron.

Other Honours

Other than these decorations, Cochrane also received the **French Croix de Guerre and from Belgium,** he was made **Commandeur in de Order van Oranje Nassau.**

ARTHUR NORMAN CROOKES

Norman Crookes was born in New Tupton, Chesterfield, Derbyshire on 23rd December 1920, the son of Frederic Norman and Hyacinth Marie Crookes. He was educated at Clay Cross, Tupton Hall County School (Head Boy 1938/9) before studying at King's College, London University, where he achieved a BA degree in history. Joined the RAFVR in July 1941 and trained as a navigator and radar operator. His first squadron was 125 that after a period with Defiants, was re-equipped with Bristol Beaufighter IIF night-fighters. Here he teamed up with a New Zealand pilot, G. E. Jameson, known as Jamie.

Fg Off Arthur Crookes DFC★★ with his pilot Flt Lt 'Jamie' Jameson DSO, DFC of 488 Squadron RNZAF standing by their Mosquito.

Most successful night-fighter crew stayed together as a team, and so it was with Jameson and Crookes. By mid-February 1943 they had achieved three victories and damaged a fourth. There followed a period for both of them as instructors. They were put together again in 1944 and sent to 488 New Zealand Squadron, equipped with Mosquito XIIIs. In May, with the invasion of Normandy approaching, the squadron was based at Zeals, Wiltshire, and following the landings in France, the pair had a successful run of night victories over France. By 6th August, they had shot down eight enemy aircraft and damaged one more. Their best night was on 29th/30th July, achieving four kills, three Ju 88s and one Do217 over Caen and Lisieux.

However, their time together now came to an end. Jamie's mother asked for her son to return home following the deaths of his father, and his two brothers, who had both lost their lives in the war.

With Jameson gone, Norman teamed up with Fg Off Ray Jeffs, another New Zealander, and they shot down a German aircraft on their first patrol on 18th/19th August. Over the Ardennes in December, they damaged a Ju 88, later confirmed in the 1990s by an air historian. This action was over Malmédy in the American sector and in consequence, Norman received an award of the American DFC. On 16th April, 1945, taking off for an air test, their Mosquito XXX suffered an engine failure that caused them to run into a partially filled bomb crater. Both men were slightly injured. However, Crookes' final mission was over Berlin on 24th April.

Leaving 488, Norman spent the next year as commanding officer of No. 11 Ground Control Unit with the rank of squadron leader, helping to guide Allied aircraft to a safe landing in poor weather. After the war he was declared unfit for post-war service with the Royal Air Force due to colour blindness! Norman left the RAF in October 1946. Returning to King's College, he studied for a teaching diploma and became history master at Brockley County Grammar School in Lewisham, south-east London.

He and his wife, Kathleen Elvin, whom he had married in 1944, had moved to Chesterfield, remaining there for the rest of his life, teaching at Clay Cross Boys' School from 1957 to 1961. He had formed an Air Training Corps squadron while in south London, and another in Chesterfield, and became training officer for the Derbyshire ATC Wing, and later chairman of the East Midlands ATC Wing. Crookes became headmaster at the William Rhodes Secondary School in Chesterfield until his retirement in 1981 after twenty years in post. He was made an MBE in 1974 for his work with the Air Training Corps. Crookes also formed a school brass band, which on four occasions in the later 1970s, won the National Festival of Music for Youth.

He and his wife had one son, Richard and a daughter Linda. Kathleen died in 1987 and he remarried Sheila in 1988. Norman died in Chesterfield Royal Hospital on 17th April 2012 after suffering a heart attack. He was ninety-one years old.

GEORGE ESMOND JAMESON, from Rotherham, North Canterbury, New Zealand, was born on 29th November 1921 in Canterbury, NZ, so was a year younger than Crookes. Joining the RNZAF in February 1941 from his farming background, he teamed up with Norman Crookes in 125 Squadron. He received the DSO, DFC and Bar for his eleven night kills, to become the top New Zealand night-fighter pilot of WW2. He and Crookes had their most successful night on 29th/30th July 1944, downing three Ju 88s and a Do217. When his father died at home, and having news that one brother had been killed in Tunisia, and the second died in a flight training accident, he was pulled out of combat and sent home in August 1944, where he took over the running of the family farm. He and Crookes remained friends post-war until George's death on 21st May 1988.

Distinguished Flying Cross (*London Gazette* 15th August 1944)

As observer, Fg Off Crookes has taken part in a large number of sorties and has displayed commendable courage and resource. He has assisted in the destruction of five enemy aircraft, success which is an excellent tribute to his high skill and excellent co-operation.

Bar to DFC (*London Gazette* 22nd September 1944 – Joint citation with Flt Lt G. E. Jameson)

These officers have completed many sorties as pilot (Jameson) and observer (Crookes) respectively. They have displayed great skill and co-operation, qualities which were well displayed on one occasion in July 1944, when they destroyed four aircraft in one sortie. Their devotion to duty has been unfailing.

Second Bar to DFC (*London Gazette* 29th June 1945)

Since the award of a Bar to the Distinguished Flying Cross, Flt Lt Crookes has been instrumental in attacking a further four enemy aircraft at night, of which his pilot destroyed two and damaged the other two. An outstanding navigator, he has repeatedly shown exceptional ability and has now been responsible for the destruction of twelve enemy aircraft by night. At all times this officer's courage and determination have been worthy of high praise.

Other Honours
American Distinguished Flying Cross (1944)

NEVILLE FREDERICK DUKE

Born in Tunbridge, Kent on 11th January 1922, to a Kentish father and a mother from Northumberland; they also had a daughter Peggy. Nev went to Judd School in Tunbridge, and spent all his pocket money on pleasure flights and making flying model aircraft. Leaving school in early 1939 he took a job as an auctioneer and estate  agent while awaiting his eighteenth birthday. Once of age he tried to join the Fleet Air Arm, and was turned down, but was accepted by the RAF and joined in June 1940.

Learning to fly, his first operational squadron was No. 92 at Biggin Hill in February 1941 and he was engaged in fighter sweeps and circus operations over Northern France. In the spring and summer he damaged two Me 109s before gaining his first confirmed successes over 109s on 25th June and 9th August. On occasions he flew as number two to the wing leader, Wg Cdr A. G. 'Sailor' Malan DSO DFC.

In October he was posted overseas, ending up in North Africa, where he joined 112 Squadron, flying P-40s. His first positive action over the desert came on 21st November, a share in an Italian CR42 biplane fighter. The next day he shot down a Me 109F of JG27, its pilot baling out to become a prisoner. For the next two or three weeks he was in constant action over and around Tobruk and by the end of the year he had shot down four enemy machines, damaged three and damaged others on the ground. This did not come without damage to his pride, for he was shot down twice in December, but managed to crash land on both occasions.

On 14th February 1942 he shot down two more Italian fighters and in March received the DFC. Resting after his first tour he went to the Fighter School at El Ballal in the Canal Zone as an instructor, a post he held until November. By this time his old squadron (92) were in North Africa and he returned to it and in the new year was made a flight commander. No. 92 were still equipped with Spitfires of course.

In the first four months of 1943 Neville really got into his stride. He was a superb pilot and his prowess as an air fighter was fast becoming well established. By mid-April he had added twelve more victories to his tally and a damaged, and was awarded the DSO. With North Africa in the hands of the Allies, Sicily and Italy were soon to be on the cards. He was promoted to squadron leader and once more became an instructor, at No. 73 Operational Training Unit at Abu Sueir.

In March 1944 he started his third tour, commanding 145 Squadron in Italy, adding a further five victories by 7th September and receiving two more bars to his DFC. On 7th June he was brought down by ground fire, baling out only to splash down into a lake. He was helped by Italian partisans, staying with them until overrun by advancing American troops.

His final confirmed victory score came to twenty-six and two shared destroyed, one probable, six damaged with others damaged on the ground. He was the RAF's top-scoring fighter pilot in the Mediterranean Theatre. He had flown 486 sorties during his three tours.

Returning to England he became a production test pilot for Hawkers and a year later took a course at the Empire Test Pilot's School at Cranfield, before joining the RAF's High Speed Flight in June 1946. After a period at A&AEE at Boscombe Down, and being awarded the Czech War Cross in 1947, he received the Air Force Cross in 1948. In 1947 he married Gwen Fellows.

Resigning from the RAF in June 1948 he went back to Hawkers as a test pilot, becoming chief test pilot in 1951, and also joining the Royal Auxiliary Air Force, commanding 615 Squadron. His work on the Hawker Hunter fighter was recognised by becoming an Officer of the Order of the British Empire in January 1953.

The Farnborough Air Show on 6th September 1952 became famous for the spectacular crash of a de Havilland 110, flown by Nev's friend John Derry, a former Typhoon pilot. As the aircraft flew across the airfield at high speed it suddenly disintegrated, killing both Derry and his observer. Debris was strewn across the watching crowd killing twenty-eight spectators. Shortly afterwards, Neville Duke took off in his Hawker Hunter and made his usual spectacular display, even ending it with a sonic boom. He was later congratulated for his performance despite the carnage below. Winston Churchill wrote to him the next day: 'My dear Duke, it was characteristic of you to go up yesterday after the shocking incident. Accept my salute. Yours in grief, WS.' As Neville said to me, I was next on the flight schedule, so I merely got into the Hunter and took off.

On 7th September 1953, in an all-red Hunter (WB188) he took the World Air Speed Record. However, in August 1955 he crash landed a Hunter near Thorney Island, injuring his back. The following year he damaged his back again in a hard landing in a P1099, but received the Queen's Commendation for Valuable Service in the Air.

He took up freelance flying, and formed Duke Aviation, while also becoming the personal pilot of Sir George Dowty, of the Dowty Group who specialised in landing gear. However, in order to concentrate on his freelance work he shut down Duke Aviation and became involved with Brooklands Aerospace Group in 1987. His main occupation was with the Optica aircraft used by the police,

Neville Duke, now a test pilot, with an all-red Hunter at Tangmere.

and the Fieldmaster and Firemaster machines. In 1953 he had written his biography, *Test Pilot*, which is still in print.

I was in correspondence with Neville in the mid-1990s, at the time Grub Street were republishing his famous book. Neville was then persuaded to hand over to me his wartime diaries, which I edited, and Grub Street published these in 1995 under the title of *The War Diaries of Neville Duke, 1941-44*.

By this time Neville was having serious hearing problems following years of aero-engine noise, but he was still wonderfully fit and more than capable of carrying on flying. He had a special 'bone dome' made which enabled him to hear clearly any instructions from ground controllers, and after so many years of flying, what he could not hear he knew by experience what was being said – or so he told me!

He was still flying in 2007, at the age of eighty-five, but on 7th April of that year he was flying with Gwen on a trip to Popham airfield. After a safe landing he became unwell and was taken to hospital where he died that evening. He was a very gentle man, an excellent pilot, and we shall not see his like again.

On 11th October, 2007, I attended a service of thanksgiving at St. Clement Danes Church in the Strand. After the service a Spitfire flew over the church in salute.

Distinguished Flying Cross (*London Gazette* 17th March 1942)

One day in February 1942, Plt Off Duke was the leader of a section of a wing when he sighted thirty-five enemy aircraft. He informed the wing leader and led his section to attack. In the ensuing combat eleven enemy fighters were destroyed by the squadron, two being destroyed by Plt Off Duke. This officer's leadership contributed materially to the success achieved. He has destroyed eight enemy aircraft and probably destroyed and damaged a further six.

Bar to DFC (*London Gazette* 19th February 1943)

One day in January 1943, this officer led his flight in an engagement against a large force of enemy fighters over Beurat. During the combat, Fg Off Duke fought with great resolution, destroying two enemy aircraft before all his ammunition was expended. Since being awarded the Distinguished Flying Cross he has destroyed three hostile aircraft, bringing his victories to eleven. Fg Off Duke has led his section and the flight with distinction.

Distinguished Service Order (*London Gazette* 9th April 1943)

In recent intensive air fighting this officer has led his flight and often the squadron on most of the sorties which have been undertaken. He has displayed exceptional skill and dash, achieving great success. During the first week of March 1943, he destroyed seven enemy aircraft, bringing his total victories to nineteen. His courageous leadership and fine fighting qualities are worthy of the highest praise.

Second Bar to DFC (*London Gazette* 23rd June 1944)
This officer has displayed the highest standard of skill, gallantry and determination, qualities that have been well reflected in his squadron which has destroyed twenty-three hostile aircraft within a period of several weeks. Recently, over Anzio, he led the squadron in a sortie during which eight enemy aircraft were shot down. Four of them were destroyed by Sqn Ldr Duke himself. He had destroyed twenty-six and damaged several other enemy aircraft.

Other Honours
Air Force Cross (*London Gazette* 10th June 1948)

Czech War Cross – 1946

Officer of the Order of the British Empire (OBE) – 1st January 1953.

Queen's Commendation for Valuable Service in the Air – 1955.

WILFRED GEORGE GERALD DUNCAN SMITH

Born 28th May 1914, in Madras, India, the son of Lieutenant-Colonel Wilfred Arthur and Anna Cecilia Smith (née Duncan), where his father was serving. Sent to England for schooling aged seven, he was educated at Nairn and Morrison's Academy, in Crieff, Scotland, where he also joined the school's officer training corps. Returning to India in 1933 he became a coffee and tea planter. His early skill at shooting was clearly shown on the occasion he had to shoot two tigers that had been attacking cattle. In 1936 he returned again to the UK having become a mechanical engineer, to join the sales staff for Great Western Motors in Reading. Joining the RAFVR as a sergeant as the war started, he was commissioned in September 1940.

After completing his training he went to No. 7 Operational Training Unit before being posted to 611 Squadron at the end of October 1940, just missing being officially a Battle of Britain pilot. However, a few days before the end of that year he shared the probable destruction of a Dornier bomber. The following year, as RAF Fighter Command began to fly operations over northern France, he was ready, and in February he was credited with another probable off the French coast. He continued to fly during the summer of 1941, and by August he had achieved six victories, with others damaged.

Before August ended he had been awarded the DFC and posted to 603 Squadron as a flight commander. However, he went down with pneumonia and spent much of the rest of the year in hospital, but did receive a Bar to his DFC. Once over his illness he was given command of 64 Squadron, part of the Hornchurch Wing, the first squadron to be equipped with the new Spitfire IXs. He led 64 for most of 1942, gaining more victories over France, and during the Dieppe show on 19 August, was credited with two Dornier 217s destroyed and another shared. In this action his Spitfire was hit by return fire and he was forced to bale out over the Channel, losing his dinghy in the process. Although in the sea just four miles off the Somme Estuary, he was rescued by ASR launch. A couple of days later, Smith was promoted to wing leader at North Weald.

Rested from operations in November, he held a post at Fighter Command HQ in the Tactics Branch and at the School of Tactics at Charmy Down. In 1943 he was posted out to Malta in readiness for the assault upon Sicily, and then became

Wg Cdr Wilfred G. G. Duncan Smith DSO, DFC**, AFC.

wing leader of No. 224 Wing of the Desert Air Force. The day before the invasion, he took off on a lone-reconnaissance sortie but an engine defect caused him to run out of fuel and once again he found himself hanging from a parachute and then in the sea. Once in the 'drink' he discovered yet again there was no dinghy. Six hours later, and near the end of his endurance, he was rescued by an ASR Walrus amphibian aircraft. As its crew hauled him aboard they were attacked by a Me 109, and one bullet from its guns, actually tore through the collar of his Mae West. Taking off the Walrus brought him back to safety.

At the end of 1943 Smith was given command of No. 324 Wing, as a group captain, and led it across Italy via Anzio, through Rome and finally across to southern France. His victories in air combat rose steadily and by mid-June he was credited with seventeen and two shared destroyed, six and two shared probables, and eight damaged. He had been awarded the DSO in 1942 and in March 1945 came a Bar to this decoration.

He decided to leave the RAF at the end of the war, but rejoined in 1948, serving initially with No. 61 Group. In July 1950 he took command of 60 Squadron, flying Spitfire F Mk 18s against communist guerrillas in Malaya. In September he returned to England to attend a course at the Central Fighter Establishment, before returning to Malaya and his squadron. In December he flew an operation that saw the Spitfire fire its guns in anger for the last time in its long history. Smith received a second Bar to his DFC for these operations.

His squadron re-equipped with de Havilland Vampire jets and in April 1952 he was posted to HQ Fighter Command as personal staff officer to the commander-in-chief, Air Chief Marshal Sir Basil Embry. In February 1952 he took command of RAF Turnhouse, near Edinburgh, and led the Scottish Auxiliary Air Force, with Vampires. On an exchange posting in 1955 he went to the USA serving with the US 9th Air Force in South Carolina. His final posting was to HQ RAF Germany in 1958. He retired from the service in 1960, joining the Triplex Safety Glass Company, as aviation sales and commercial manager, and in this role travelled extensively until his retirement.

He retired to Rome in 1973 spending seven years there before heading for Scotland but in 1980 moved to Honiton, Devon. He wrote his biography *Spitfire into Battle* (John Murray Publishing, 1981) I was privileged to meet Gp Capt Smith at the RAF Club in London on one occasion. Now universally known as Duncan Smith (with or without a hyphen) he died on 11th December 1996, aged eighty-two. He had married Pamela Mary Summers in 1946, whom he met while she was appearing as a ballerina at the Opera House in Naples. They had three sons, one of whom is known today as the Conservative MP, Iain Duncan Smith, and two daughters. As was noted on the rear flap of his book:

'A keen big-game hunter and sportsman he has lived a colourful and exciting life, which many young people today might well envy.' He was also a scratch amateur golfer, winning the Malayan Open in 1950.

Distinguished Flying Cross (*London Gazette* 22nd July 1941)
This officer has participated in many operational flights over enemy territory and has always displayed the utmost keenness to engage the enemy. Plt Off Smith has destroyed at least three hostile aircraft.

Bar to DFC (*London Gazette* 26th December 1941)
During 1941, this officer has carried out 190 operational patrols, ninety-eight of which have been over enemy territory. By his skill, coolness and strong sense of duty, Flt Lt Smith has set a splendid example to all. He has always devoted himself unselfishly to the success of his squadron, thereby contributing materially to its achievements. Flt Lt Smith has destroyed at least five enemy aircraft.

Distinguished Service Order (*London Gazette* 11th September 1941)
Since being awarded a Bar to the Distinguished Flying Cross, this officer has completed a great number of sorties. He is a brilliant pilot and a fine leader whose skill has proved a source of inspiration to all. Sqn Ldr Smith has destroyed ten and probably destroyed several other enemy aircraft.

Bar to DSO (*London Gazette* 20th March 1945)
Group Captain Smith has led a fighter wing in the invasion of Sicily and in operations over southern Italy. The high measure of success achieved by the squadrons under his command has been largely attributable to the boldness and soundness of his leadership. Since he took command of his wing, eighty-five enemy aircraft have been destroyed in combat and many others damaged.

Group Captain Smith has taken an important part in the successes thus achieved. He has destroyed in all fourteen enemy aircraft and a large number of transport vehicles and locomotives. As an operational commander, Gp Capt Smith has rendered extremely valuable and devoted service.

Second Bar to DFC (*London Gazette* 29th August 1952)
Sqn Ldr Smith has been in command of 60 Squadron since July, 1949. During this time, his squadron has been engaged in operations against the insurgents in Malaya and he has personally led a very large number of strikes. In addition to the exceptionally fine example of leadership displayed by Sqn Ldr Smith, he has also set an exceptionally high standard of flying to his squadron. It is quite

a usual occurrence for these operations to be carried out in conditions of bad weather and visibility and over difficult mountainous, jungle-covered country, but, regardless of conditions, he and his pilots have been able to identify their targets on all occasions and have pressed home their attacks with determination, skill and accuracy.

The squadron recently discarded their Spitfire aircraft and were re-equipped with Vampires. Their task, and that of bringing the squadron up to its previous high level of operational efficiency, was completed in record time. Sqn Ldr Smith is a born fighter-pilot and leader of men and, by his inspiration to others, he has set a fine example, fully maintaining his reputation as a squadron commander, as demonstrated by his leadership of 60 Squadron. His personal example and ability have created an efficient and spirited squadron, which has proved its worth in the current operations in this theatre.

DANIEL TREVOR BULMER EVERETT

Born on 15th October 1920, the son of Harold B. and Ellen Ada Everett of 30 Woodcote Road, Epsom, Surrey. The youngest of nine children he was educated at Kingswood House Preparatory School, and the City of London Freeman's School, Ashtead Park, Surrey. He became an all-round sportsman and took employment with his uncle, Tom McNab.

Sgt (later Sqn Ldr) 'Danny' Everett DFC★★ (centre) with two crew members.

Daniel joined the RAFVR in May 1940, learning to fly before going to No.13 Operational Training Unit, equipped with Bristol Blenheims. A conversion course at No. 1652 HCU led to a posting to 158 Squadron, flying Handley Page Halifax bombers, on 28th February 1943, initially as a second pilot. He was commissioned on 29th May 1943 and after flying eight missions he was sent to 35 Squadron, part of Bomber Command's Pathfinder Force. Completing a tour of operations, 'Danny' as he had become known, received the DFC following a raid on Kassel in October. After a rest period he returned to 35 Squadron, now flying Avro Lancasters, for another tour on 22nd August 1944.

On the night of 14th/15th January 1945, on a raid against the oil plant at Mersberg-Leuna, his bomber was hit by a falling bomb from another aircraft, ripping off the whole of the rear turret and with it Everett's rear gunner, Fg Off R. T. Salvoni DFC, who had won his DFC with 640 Squadron in mid-1944. Danny Everett was promoted to squadron leader on 25 February.

Despite virtually completing this tour of operations, Everett gathered together a scratch crew for a raid on the Deutsche Erdoel oil refinery at Hemmingstedt late on 7th/8th March, Lancaster ME361 taking off at 1853 hours. In this crew were four DFC winners, and Everett acted as master bomber. It was his eighty-ninth operation, although this number may have been higher. At around 2200 hours Everett's Lancaster was shot down, apparently by the Luftwaffe 3, Flak Division. All eight men aboard were killed and were all buried in Hamburg Cemetery.

Distinguished Flying Cross (*London Gazette* 21st January 1944)
Plt Off Everett was captain of an aircraft detailed to attack Kassel on the night of 22nd/23rd October 1943. En-route to the target the weather was particularly

bad and some of his blind-flying instruments became inoperative owing to icing conditions. This officer carried on despite this handicap as he fully realised the importance of this special task and at the target he made a most successful attack, this being proved by an excellent photograph. Throughout the thirty-three night-bombing attacks in which he has taken part, Plt Off Everett has consistently maintained an extremely high standard of tenacity and reliability, and it is considered that the fine results he achieved in this attack fully merits the immediate [but amended to non-immediate by the AOC] award of the DFC.

Bar to DFC (*London Gazette* 16th January 1945)

On 14th January 1945 he had piloted an Avro Lancaster serial number 'PB684', squadron code TL-B from RAF Gravely to Merseberg-Leuna. Over the target area his aircraft was hit by a bomb dropped from a friendly aircraft, the rear turret was smashed and later broke away, taking with it the body of the rear gunner, Raymond Salvoni DFC, who was believed to have been killed by the impact of the bomb. Everett brought the aircraft home safely.

Second Bar to DFC (*London Gazette* 27th March 1945)

One night in February 1945, Sqn Ldr Everett was pilot and captain of aircraft detailed to attack Goch. Whilst making his first run over the target his aircraft was badly hit. The starboard mainplane was extensively damaged and the starboard inner engine caught fire. Momentarily the aircraft went out of control. Sqn Ldr Everett quickly levelled out though and feathered the propeller of the burning engine. The flames were then extinguished. Although unable to assess the full extent of the damage sustained, Sqn Ldr Everett went on to make several further runs over the target, which he left after he was satisfied as to the success of the operation. He afterwards flew the badly damaged aircraft safely to base. This officer displayed a high degree of skill, courage and resolution throughout.

The recommendation was originally for the award of the Distinguished Service Order but 'higher authority' changed it to second Bar to DFC.

DAVID CHARLES FAIRBANKS

Born in Ithaca, New York, USA, on 22nd August 1922, David was the son of a Cornell University professor and his wife Helen. There was also a sister Caroline. In early 1941 he ran away from home to join the Royal Canadian Air Force. Accepted, he began flight training at No. 21 EFTS on Fleet Finch II aircraft, and received his wings on 21st November. With further training at Prince Edward Island, Trenton, Ontario and then at St. Hubert, Quebec, he became stuck as an instructor for the next two years. Finally posted overseas he sailed for England in February 1943.

Known as 'Foob', David's first posting was to 501 Squadron on 12th January 1944, which was equipped with Spitfire Vb and IX fighters, based at RAF Hawkinge. He gained his first combat victories over the Normandy beachhead, on 8th June, two days after the initial landings – a Me 109 destroyed and another damaged. In August David moved to 274 Squadron, equipped with the Hawker Tempest V fighter and some of its work was against the V1 flying bombs. Fairbanks shot down one of these rocket bombs on 29th August. By September the squadron had moved to the Continent, operating from Antwerp and by the end of the year, David added two more confirmed victories to his tally, by shooting down two Me 109s on 17th December and damaging a third.

Foob Fairbanks moved to 3 Squadron and continued to destroy enemy aircraft in the air and on the ground during January 1945. At the beginning of February he returned to 274 Squadron as CO. During that month he really got into his stride, attacking aircraft both in the air and on the ground. He claimed a Me 262 jet on 11th February but in reality it was an Arado Ar 234B jet of 1(F)/123. His luck ran out on 28th February during a patrol of the Hamm area. His six Tempests ran into a reported forty Fw 190s and although Fairbanks later claimed to have shot down one, he and one of his pilots were also downed, both becoming prisoners.

After the war he returned to the US to attend Cornell University, receiving a BA degree in mechanical engineering in 1950. He then returned to Montreal where he joined the Dominion Bridge Company as a design engineer for the next year. He also joined the RCAF flying with 401 Squadron RCAF Reserve on Harvards and Vampires, and then became associated with the Sperry Gyroscope Company until 1955. He then spent two years in the UK flying Meteor 8s and Sabres.

David Fairbanks standing by his 274 Squadron Tempest V (EJ762) that was badly damaged by flak on 19th November 1944. Burning petrol took off much of the paint and fabric before it went out.

Meantime he became a Canadian citizen, and joined the de Havilland Company of Canada, gaining his commercial pilot's licence. In 1958 he was co-pilot on the first flight of the de Havilland Caribou, then captained a round-the-world demonstration tour in 1964. Over the next few years he tested and delivered aircraft to many parts of the globe, showing at both Paris and Farnborough air shows and also tested STOL aircraft and settled in New York. He died on 20 February 1975, in Toronto's North York General Hospital, two weeks after suffering a heart attack, aged fifty-three. In 1976 he was awarded the McKee Trans-Canada Trophy posthumously for service to Canadian aviation. The citation read: 'In recognition of the valuable service that he contributed to the development of Canada's STOL aircraft in his capacity as a test pilot for over twenty years.'

Distinguished Flying Cross (*London Gazette* 23rd January 1945)
Flt Lt Fairbanks has completed a large number of sorties and has set a fine example of determination and devotion to duty throughout. On one occasion in November, 1944, whilst attacking an enemy locomotive, his aircraft was badly hit and turned completely over whilst at a low altitude. One of the (wing) petrol tanks was pierced and a fire commenced in one of the wings. Displaying admirable coolness and great skill, Flt Lt Fairbanks succeeded in righting the aircraft and set a course for home. The fire in the wing died down but not before it had done much damage. Nevertheless, Flt Lt Fairbanks succeeded in reaching base. This officer has invariably displayed a high degree of courage.

Bar to DFC (*London Gazette* 6th March 1945)

This officer continues to display a high standard of skill and gallantry. Within recent weeks he has destroyed five enemy aircraft, bringing his victories to eight. Flt Lt Fairbanks has also effectively attacked many enemy targets on the ground. His keenness and determination have set a high example to all.

Second Bar to DFC (*London Gazette* 20th July 1945)

Sqn Ldr Fairbanks has destroyed fifteen enemy aircraft. On two separate occasions since his last award he has shot down two aircraft in one sortie and in less than a fortnight he has destroyed six, including a jet-propelled aircraft. As a flight and then a squadron commander he has led many daring and highly successful attacks on enemy communications, principally locomotives and road transport. In three weeks seventy-two enemy locomotives and vehicles were successfully attacked. By the excellent example he has set, his initiative and fine leadership, this officer has inspired the other members of his squadron and all pilots with whom he has come into contact.

BRENDAN EAMONN FERGUS FINUCANE

Universally known as 'Paddy', he was born in Rathmines, County Dublin, Ireland, on 16th October 1920, the son of Thomas 'Andy' A.F. and Florence Louise Finucane, born in Leicester, England. His father was a bank cashier and Paddy had two sisters, Clare and Monica, and a brother Raymond.

Educated at O'Connell's Irish Christian Brothers School, despite being a devout Catholic, where he became a keen sportsman; his first job was in an office at a printing and stationery firm in Sandymount, Dublin. Later he went to Synge Street and Marlborough Street Schools. In 1936 the family moved to England, living in Richmond, Surrey. Andy, having risen to become a company director, ran a company office in the West End of London. Brendan worked in London's Regent Street, but bored with office work decided to apply for a RAF short-service commission in April 1938. Being accepted, he began pilot training at Sywell, Northants. During his training he crashed twice but by July was posted to 65 Squadron, flying Spitfires.

Finucane learnt to fly at No. 6 RFTS, Sywell. In this photograph, he is in the centre of the middle row with his arms folded.

Paddy was in action during the Battle of Britain and his first victories were scored on 12th August, three Me 109s, one of which was confirmed. The next day he claimed another, plus a probable. In 1941, with Fighter Command taking the war to the skies over northern France, by July he had added four more enemy aircraft to his tally, plus a share in a Ju 88 bomber. In April he became a flight commander and posted to 452 Squadron, manned by Australians. After becoming operational, 452 began operations over France and by October his score had risen to over twenty plus three shared. He was rewarded with two Bars to his DFC, and the DSO.

In January 1942 he was commanding 602 Squadron but was wounded in the right leg on 20th February, although in the first six months of the year he had added a further four victories, three more shared, plus numerous probables and damaged.

'Paddy' Finucane, on the right, with two Australian pilots of 452 Squadron, Sgts Keith Chisholm and Ian Milne. This picture was taken on 20th September 1941. On this day Milne was shot down and taken prisoner. Chisholm became a prisoner on 12th October 1941.

In all his claims totalled twenty-six and six shared. On 27th June he was made wing leader of the Hornchurch Wing, but on 15th July, leading a mission to attack an enemy troop camp just inland from the French coast at Etaples, his Spitfire suffered a hit from ground fire. Heading out across the Channel, the Spitfire finally came down on the water but sank almost instantly, taking its pilot with it. He was twenty-one years of age

His brother Ray was also in the RAF, flying as aircrew on bombers with 101 Squadron. Paddy has no known grave.

Distinguished Flying Cross (*London Gazette* 13th May 1941)
This officer has shown great keenness in his efforts to engage the enemy and he has destroyed at least five of their aircraft. His courage and enthusiasm have been a source of encouragement to other pilots of the squadron.

Bar to DFC (*London Gazette* 9th September 1941)
This officer has led his flight with great dash, determination and courage in the face of the enemy. Since July 1941, he has destroyed three enemy aircraft and assisted in the destruction of a further two. Flt Lt Finucane has been largely responsible for the fine fighting spirit of the unit.

Second Bar to DFC (*London Gazette* 26th September 1941)
This officer has fought with marked success during recent operations over northern France and has destroyed a further six enemy aircraft. Of these, three were destroyed in one day and two in a single sortie on another occasion. His ability and courage have been reflected in the high standard of morale and fighting spirit of his unit. Flt Lt Finucane has personally destroyed fifteen enemy aircraft.

Distinguished Service Order (*London Gazette* 21st October 1941)
Recently during two sorties on consecutive days, Flt Lt Finucane destroyed five Messerschmitt 109s bringing his total victories to at least twenty. He has flown with this squadron since June 1942, during which time the squadron destroyed forty-two enemy aircraft of which Flt Lt Finucane has personally destroyed fifteen. The successes achieved are undoubtedly due to this officer's brilliant leadership and example.

Mentioned in Despatches (1st January 1942)

FREDERICK ANTHONY OWEN GAZE

Known as Tony, Gaze was born in Prahan, Melbourne, Victoria, Australia, on 3rd February 1920. His father, Irvine Gaze was a member of the Ross Sea Party, who were preparing for Ernest Shackleton's expedition. Tony was educated at Geelong Grammar School and when war came he had become a student at Queen's College, Cambridge. His father had been a pilot in WW1 and then a flying instructor with the RAAF. Irvine had met his wife Freda, who had been a driver in the RFC.

Deciding to join the RAF in 1940, he trained to be a pilot and was successful in his quest to fly fighters. His first posting was to 610 Squadron in March 1941 where his brother Scott (Plt Off I. S. O. Gaze) was serving but on the 23rd of that month Scott was killed in a flying accident, aged nineteen.

Being part of the Tangmere Wing, Tony's squadron took part in the offensive operations over northern France that summer and on 26th June claimed his first combat victories, a Me 109E destroyed and another as probably destroyed. In July he destroyed another two 109s with two more damaged, rewarded by a DFC. His next posting was to No. 57 Operational Training Unit as an instructor.

His second tour began in June 1942 as a flight commander with 616 Squadron, claiming a couple more victories before taking part in the famous Dieppe Raid on 19th August. During this operation he shot down a Dornier 217 bomber of KG2. Following Dieppe, he received a Bar to his DFC and was given command of 64 Squadron, flying Spitfire IXs. However, on 26th September he led the fighter cover to a force of American B17s to a target at Morlaix. Due to exceptionally high winds, the force was blown well off course resulting in a whole squadron of Spitfires of 131 Eagle Squadron failing to return, just one pilot surviving. Gaze was made the scapegoat for this disaster, stripped of his command, and returned to 616 as a flight commander.

Following a rest period, during which he made factory tours, helped train Mustang pilots on reconnaissance missions, and being attached to two Spitfire squadrons as a supernumerary, he returned to operations, going to 66 Squadron but on 4th September he was shot down by Feldwebel Gerhard Vogt of 6/JG26, the German's fourteenth victory. Losing glycol Gaze had to force land twenty miles inland from Dieppe but managed to evade capture. Fortunately he was

picked up by members of the French Resistance organisation who eventually got him across the Pyrenees into Spain. He was back in England by 28th October.

Gaze did not return to operations for some while, spending his time with the Air Fighting Development Unit, then at 5 Group Bomber Command on liaison duties. Eventually the opportunity arose to return to fighters, so in July 1944, following the invasion of France, he became a flight commander with his old 610 Squadron, on Spitfire XIVs. Fighter Command were in the throes of combating the German V1 rockets at this time, and Tony managed to shoot one down on 5th August.

Late in 1944 his squadron moved to Holland as part of Second Tactical Air Force. When the Germans made their surprise dawn attack on Allied airfields on 1st January 1945, Gaze shot down a long-nose Fw 190D over Y.32 airfield at Ophoven, despite having to chase the German through intense American ground fire.

On 14th February Gaze became one of the few air fighters to down a German jet, this being a Me 262 that he shot down in the Munster area of Germany. Gaze now moved again, this time to 41 Squadron where he claimed his last combat victories, including the sharing of another jet, an Arado 234 bomber. For these actions he received a second Bar to his DFC.

Posted yet again, this time back to 616 Squadron which was flying the RAF's first jet-fighter, the Gloster Meteor. In those last days of WW2 the squadron flew a number of ground-attack sorties.

Gaze remained with 616 immediately after the war, flying demonstration flights to show off the Meteor, and when 616 was disbanded, he helped to form the nucleus of a new 263 Squadron in England, taking command. In December 1945 he was sent to Rolls-Royce at Derby and became OC its engine school. While there he went to 56 Squadron to co-ordinate Meteors that were to fly in the Victory Parade over London. He left the service in July 1947, returning to Australia where, in January 1949 he joined 21 Squadron of the Citizen Air Force. In July the following year he returned to Europe, becoming involved in motor racing, but managed to fly with 600 Squadron RAux AF.

Returning to Australia again he took with him a pre-war Alta sports car in which he successfully campaigned for better racing car circuits. This led him into the world of motorcar racing. In 1946 he had suggested to the Duke of Richmond and Gordon, that the roads around Westhampnett would be perfect for a motor racing track. The Goodwood Circuit was opened two years later.

In 1949 he married widow Kay Wakefield, and back in Britain they settled at Kay's family estate at Ross-on-Wye. He soon turned his attention full time to motor racing taking part in numerous events including the Monte Carlo Rally. He also took up gliding and in 1960 he represented Australia in the World Gliding Championships at Cologne, West Germany.

His wife Kay died in 1976 and the following year he married another widow, Diana Davison. Together they ran Paragon Shoes, the Davison's family business. In 2006 Gaze was awarded the Medal of the Order of Australia (OAM). Tony and Diana returned to Goodwood for the 2010 Revival which marked the seventieth anniversary of the Battle of Britain. Diana died in 2012 and all three of Tony's stepsons became racing drivers.

Tony Gaze died on 29th July 2013.

Distinguished Flying Cross (*London Gazette* 5th August 1941)

This officer has shown persistent desire to engage the enemy on all occasions. In a recent combat he undoubtedly saved his squadron commander from being shot down over enemy territory by destroying his two attackers. He has now destroyed at least three enemy aircraft.

Bar to DFC (*London Gazette* 19th January 1943)

Since June, 1942, this officer has completed a large number of sorties and has destroyed at least two enemy aircraft. By his great skill and fine fighting spirit, Flt Lt Gaze has set an admirable example.

Second Bar to DFC (*London Gazette* 1st June 1945)

Since the award of a Bar to his DFC, this officer has flown a further 140 sorties comprising armed reconnaissances, escorts, sweeps and defensive patrols, and has destroyed a further four enemy aircraft, probably destroyed one, and damaged another. His flying is outstanding and his shooting brilliant, and he has never missed a single opportunity of inflicting losses on the enemy. His keenness and the results he has produced have been an inspiration to his entire squadron.

KENNETH JAMES GORDON

Ken Gordon came from Hall Green, Birmingham where he was born in 1915. Educated at Stanley House School, Edgbaston he enlisted into the RAF in April 1941 and went to Canada to be trained. He flew as a navigator commencing with 38 Squadron, with Wellingtons, which he joined in September 1940 following his air observer's navigation course. After a number of operations his squadron went out to Egypt, operating against such targets as Tripoli and Benghazi. With rest period after thirty-six sorties, WO Gordon returned to the UK. Commencing another tour with 105 Squadron, on Mosquitos, Gordon completed a second tour of operational duty, including many at low level. No. 105 Squadron had been the first to equip with de Havilland Mosquito BIVs in 1942, often flying long-distance daylight-bombing sorties, even as far as Berlin and Copenhagen. In mid-1943 their Mossies began to carry Oboe equipment, and worked with the Pathfinder Force helping to mark targets at night. He often flew with Wg Cdr John Wooldridge DSO DFC DFM, the unit's CO. He then became navigator to Sqn Ldr Peter Channer DFC, awarded the DFC in August, and by the end of his tour he had brought his total ops to seventy-three to receive a Bar to his DFC. He had been commissioned in September 1943.

On the night of D-Day, 6th June 1944, the squadron helped to mark ten coastal gun batteries, in support of the landings in Normandy. On 22nd December 1944, flying with Wg Cdr T. G. Jefferson AFC in ML911, they were returning from a raid on Koblenz only to find foggy conditions over base. During a SBA approach the Mosquito hit an inner marker beacon and crashed in a nearby field but both men scrambled clear unhurt.

Returning from a raid on Nuremberg on another occasion, the Mosquito developed an electrical fault in RV298. The cockpit filled with smoke but Gordon's pilot, Flt Lt J. A. Rusk on this night, got the Mosquito down safely.

Following another period as an instructor, Gordon returned to 105 in December 1944 to begin a third tour of duty. He completed a further twenty-six trips including Berlin and Munich, and eventually made his total operations up to the 100 mark. He received a second Bar to his DFC in the autumn of 1945. He was posted to 162 Squadron in July 1945, before leaving the RAF in mid-1946. He later received the Air Efficiency Award.

Ken Gordon with his pilot Sqn Ldr Peter J. Channer DSO DFC, 105 Squadron.

Distinguished Flying Cross (*London Gazette* 17th August 1943)

WO Gordon, after long experience of night bombing, has recently been leading formations in low-level daylight attacks. He is now a navigator of very considerable experience and continues to maintain a very high standard of skill and courage.

Bar to DFC (*London Gazette* 15th August 1944)

Fg Off Gordon has completed in all seventy-three sorties, including thirty sorties with the Pathfinder Force, eight of these being marker sorties. As a navigator his work has been of the highest standard and he has displayed outstanding courage and endurance under the most arduous conditions.

Second Bar to DFC (*London Gazette* 26th October 1945)

Flt Lt Gordon has now completed a grand total of 100 sorties and he started operating in Bomber Command in September 1940. His first tour of thirty-six sorties was carried out in Wellington aircraft. In April 1943 he joined the Pathfinder Force and he completed a further thirty-eight sorties before going on instructional duties. Then in December 1944 he commenced a third tour and has since then completed another twenty-six sorties with no less than twenty-three of them in the capacity of marker for following forces.

Flt Lt Gordon's great skill and efficiency as a navigator, together with high qualities of courage, have been proved time and time again throughout his long and successful operational career. He has shown himself able to concentrate on his work under the most adverse and arduous conditions and has been determined that nothing shall stand in his way to make each and every sortie as successful as possible. Flt Lt Gordon's operational record is a fine and outstanding example to his fellow pilots in the squadron.

MARTIN YNGVAR GRAN

Born 13th September 1917, in En- ebakk, Norway. Keen to become a pilot, when the war began he, like many of his countrymen following the invasion by German forces, es- caped to England. He sailed from Tromsø aboard HMS *Devonshire*, a British cruiser that also evacuated King Haakon VII and the Norwe- gian government. He was soon on his way to Canada, where he and other Norwegians trained at a base near Toronto, which became known as Little Norway.

Martin Gran (left) with Svein Heglund DSO, DFC* both with 331 Norwegian Spitfire Squad- ron, 1943.

Once he had achieved his aim, he returned to England and posted to one of the two Norwe- gian-manned fighter squadrons, 331 (the other being 332), in ear- ly 1942. He would remain with this squadron till the war's end except for brief rest periods, one being as an instructor at No. 57 Operational Training Unit, becoming firstly a flight commander in 1943 and then in June 1944, taking over command.

Although he managed to claim a few enemy aircraft as damaged, it was not until 17th May 1943 that he was credited with his first combat victory, an Fw 190 north of Guernsey, flying a Spitfire IX. By the end of the summer of 1943 he had managed to increase his score to five with several others damaged on fighter sweeps and escort missions. Awarded the DFC and the Norwegian War Cross, he was again in action during 1944 and into 1945, bringing his score to ten, in- cluding a couple of shared victories, with two more probably destroyed and six others damaged – all fighters. In June 1944 he took command of 331 Squadron, holding this position until March 1945. He received a Bar and then a second Bar to his DFC. He completed his final tour on 3rd March 1945, having flown a total of 345 operational sorties.

Gran attended the RAF Staff College during 1945-46 and from 1947 to 1949 he was a pilot at Braathens but went back to the military, where he commanded

332 Squadron and then 337 Squadron. He was promoted to Oberstløytnant (Lieutenant-Colonel) in 1953 and full colonel in 1963. In 1963 he attended Military High School and also took charge of the operational staff at the Air Defence HQ. The last year of his service he took command of the air base at Mågerø.

Once retired he lived in Tjøme, and between 1964 and 1969, he was chairman of the Norwegian Aviation Club. He died on 16th May 2004.

Distinguished Flying Cross (Approved 4th November 1943)

Captain Gran has been engaged on operational flying since October 1941, and has completed 198 sorties during which he has destroyed at least four enemy aircraft and damaged others. As flight commander he has displayed outstanding keenness, skill and determination.

Bar to DFC (Approved 20th December 1944)

Over a long period of operational flying Major Gran has rendered very valuable service. On 15th June, 1944, he was appointed to command his present squadron and since that date the squadron has destroyed at least thirteen enemy aircraft and inflicted much other severe damage to the enemy. Throughout, Major Gran has displayed courage and tenacity of purpose and qualities which have contributed materially to the high standard of efficiency maintained by the squadron.

Second Bar to DFC (Approved 22nd January 1945)

Since being awarded the first Bar to the Distinguished Flying Cross, Major Gran has completed a further thirteen sorties during which he has continued to display outstanding initiative and leadership. On the afternoon of 29th December 1944, Major Gran led a formation of ten aircraft against twenty-five Messerschmitt 109s. On this occasion Major Gran's superb airmanship and skilful tactics resulted in the destruction of twelve of the enemy aircraft. Major Gran personally destroyed two of them bringing his total victories to at least eight destroyed and many damaged.

On 9th March 1945 the Norwegian government presented Gran with the War Cross with Sword for his service as CO of 331 (N) Squadron, at a time when 331 had flown 134 operational missions and shot down thirty-three German aircraft. He was also awarded the St Olavs Medal with Oak Leaf War Medal, the Norwegian War Medal with Rosette, and the Haakon VII Medal in 1955. The French awarded him the Croix de Guerre with Palm.

COLIN FALKLAND GRAY

The man who would become New Zealand's highest scoring ace in WW2, was born on 9th November 1914, in Papanui, Christchurch. In fact he was an identical twin, with his brother Ken. His father Robert Leonard was an electrical engineer, married to Margaret (née Langford), from Gisborne. From an early age Colin became fascinated with aeroplanes and he would watch the machines flying over nearby Wigram airfield. He was educated at Huntley School in Marton, Wellesley College, Wellington, Christ's College, Christchurch, and the Napier Boys' High School. By the time he was a schoolboy he was determined to become an RAF pilot.

Once he had left school, aged eighteen, his enquiries as to how to achieve his ambition, was by way of commission via a cadetship at RAF Cranwell. However, world events were starting to alarm politicians in England at this time which enabled the flood gates to open for young men who desired to fly. Both he and Ken applied together, passed the interview, and while Ken succeeded in his medical exam, Colin did not. Ken sailed off to England, while Colin was promised a revue in a year's time provided he put himself in the hands of his doctor, not that this doctor was much help.

While waiting Colin got himself a job on a sheep farm on the shores of Palliser Bay. In 1938 he finally passed the medical and in December 1938 sailed to England aboard the RMS *Rangitata* via the Panama Canal. Arriving on 18th January 1939 he found Ken waiting for him on the London dockside. Ken was progressing well, had been commissioned and posted to a bomber squadron. Colin began his pilot training, and soloed in nine hours and forty minutes under civilian instruction in order to acquire an 'A' flying licence. This achieved he was off to No. 11 FTS at Shawbury.

Progressing well through 1939 he had all but finished training by the time war was declared, and was sent off to No. 11 Group's Pilot Pool at St. Athan. In November Colin was posted to 54 Squadron at RAF Hornchurch, which was equipped with Spitfires. During the period known as the Phoney War, because not much military activity happened, Colin was able to hone his skills with the Spitfire, and among his comrades was another New Zealander he was to become friends with, Al Deere. Meantime, brother Ken was bombing the enemy with 102 Squadron, flying Whitleys. In late November he flew a reconnaissance sortie to Cuxhaven and Heligoland. Struggling through flak and a severe snow storm, the aircraft was struck by lightning over the target area and a large portion of fabric was torn away from the port wing and another large area from under the starboard wing. One flap became jammed in the down position and the radio began to cause problems. Nevertheless Ken and his co-pilot managed to fly the 342 miles back to Bircham Newton and land safely. Ken was awarded the DFC. Sadly, Ken was killed in a flying accident in May 1940.

Colin saw his first action during the Dunkirk evacuation that began on 26th May 1940. Fighter Command was stretched to try and defend the soldiers on the French beaches awaiting rescue, and of course, the Spitfire and the Hurricane fighters were designed for defence, not for operating far over the English Channel, with a limited radius of action. No. 54 Squadron, however, had already seen combat two days earlier, on the 24th. Colin in fact claimed two Me 109s as probably destroyed over Calais. The next day he shot down a 109, this time being confirmed.

No. 54 Squadron saw considerable action over and around Dunkirk, and at the end of this operation, all waited for the next phase, the Battle for Britain. As this warmed up, Colin and his squadron had numerous encounters with German aircraft as the latter began testing Britain's ability to defend. By the end of July, he had added two more confirmed kills to his tally, plus a couple of probables. As the battle began, Colin bagged a brace of 109s on 12th August, and was then notified that he had been awarded the DFC.

Colin Gray became a prolific scorer during the summer battles, and by the first anniversary of the war, 3rd September, he had some sixteen victories, plus several probables and damaged. 54 Squadron were pulled out of the battle for a rest and in December Colin was posted to 43 Squadron as a flight commander, but soon returned to 54 doing the same job. In June 1941 he moved to 1 Squadron – flying Hurricanes. In the summer he made another claim, this time while attaching himself to 41 Squadron, where he shot down a 109F on 22nd August. The following month he received a Bar to his DFC.

His next move was to command 403 RCAF Squadron, but two days later was sent off to command 616 Squadron. After this he was rested, spending time at 9 Group HQ, before receiving a posting overseas. He had had two brief stints with 485 NZ and 64 Squadrons to gain present-day combat experience, and was then sent off to Algiers. In late January 1943 he was given command of 81 Squadron with Spitfire IXs, operating over Tunisia. Colin continued his successful fighting career, downing six German and Italian fighters, before commanding No. 322 Fighter Wing, which was moved to Malta to take part in the invasion of Sicily. Here, in June and July, he added four more victories to his score, including

Colin Gray pictured while serving in North Africa in 1943. Note the squadron leader pennant painted by the cockpit although he was about to become a wing leader. He ended the war as the top New Zealand ace.

two transport Ju 52s over Cap Milazzo. Gray had led the Wing to occupy the airfield at Lentini and on 25th July intercepted a large force of transport aircraft that were bringing supplies. The Wing shot down twenty-one of them. These victories raised his overall score to twenty-seven and two shared destroyed, six and four shared probables, with twelve more damaged. His own count noted twenty-seven-and-a-half, thirteen-and-a-half and twelve. He received the DSO and a second Bar to his DFC.

Back in the UK, he commanded a Spitfire Wing at the Fighter Leaders' School at Millfield and then led the Detling Wing. He continued with various postings till the war's end and in July 1945 returned to New Zealand. He came back to the UK in March 1946, and to Air Ministry then attended the RAF Staff College. He remained in the RAF, attaining the rank of group captain in 1955. He was with HQ Far East Air Force in Singapore for the next three years, as group captain operations, responsible for all fighter, bomber, transport, reconnaissance, maritime and helicopter operations, then back to Air Ministry 1959-61. Here he worked in the department of the assistant chief of Air Staff, Air Defence, and later ACAS Operations, responsible for operational aspects of all manned fighters and also the control and reporting systems. He opted to retire in April 1961.

Returning to his native country, he took an appointment with Unilever till 1979, retiring as personnel director. In October 1945 he had married Betty Louis Dinne (née Cook), who had a young daughter, Diane. Colin and Betty had four children, two boys and two girls.

I met Betty and Colin in March 1990, at their home in Waikanae, while visiting New Zealand as guest of both No. 75 NZ Squadron Association and the RNZAF, whilst I was writing 75's history. I had been staying with Fray Ormorod DFC, Colin's cousin, who had been with 75 Squadron in WW2. Fray asked if I would like to meet his cousin. Would I?! Colin had just about finished his biography, *Spitfire Patrol*, which was published later that same year.

Colin died on 1st August 1995, in Kenepura Hospital, Porirva, aged eighty. During the war he had flown 511 operational sorties, covering over 613 operational flying hours. Betty died in July 2013.

Distinguished Flying Cross (*London Gazette* 27th August 1940)
Since May 1940, Plt Off Gray has flown continuously with his squadron on offensive patrols. He took part in numerous engagements against the enemy throughout the Dunkirk operations, and subsequently throughout the intensive air operations over the Kentish coast and in protection of shipping in the Channel. He has shot down four Messerschmitt 109s and, it is believed, destroyed a further four. He also assisted in destroying one Messerschmitt 109 and one

Dornier 215. His example, courage and determination in action have contributed materially in maintaining the high morale of his squadron.

Bar to DFC (*London Gazette* 30th September 1941)
This officer has destroyed a further eight enemy aircraft bringing his total victories to seventeen. In addition he has probably destroyed a further nine enemy
aircraft. Flt Lt Gray has always shown the greatest keenness and enthusiasm and
has been of great assistance to his squadron commander.

Distinguished Service Order (*London Gazette* 15th May 1943)
Sqn Ldr Gray is a first-class fighter whose personal example has fostered a fine
fighting spirit in the squadron. He has taken part in many sorties in operations
in North Africa and has destroyed five enemy aircraft, bringing his total victories
to at least twenty-one. His gallant leadership has been inspiring.

Second Bar to DFC (*London Gazette* 12th November 1943)
Since the award of the Distinguished Service Order, this officer has destroyed
a further five enemy aircraft thus bringing his victories to twenty-seven aircraft
destroyed. He is an exceptionally able pilot and leader who has completed a
long and arduous tour of operations and has discharged his duties as wing commander, in the air and on the ground, in an exemplary and highly praiseworthy
manner.

Other Honours
The Order of the Patriotic War, First Degree (Russian).
During his first tour of operations, whilst serving in February to October 1943,
he commanded a squadron in North Africa and in Sicily. During the latter period, Wg Cdr Gray destroyed another ten hostile aircraft bringing his victories to
twenty-seven. His fine leadership, great skill and courage have inspired all.

JOHN WILLIAM BOLDERO GRIGSON

(P. H. T. Green collection)

From Pelynt, Cornwall, 'Jack' Grigson was born on 26th January 1893, the son of the Reverend Canon William Shuckforth Grigson and his wife Mary Beatrice (née Boldero). In 1913 he joined the Royal Navy.

During WW1 he went to sea and on 8th August 1915 was aboard the armed merchant cruiser HMS *India*, in the 10th Cruiser Squadron. Investigating a suspected blockade runner, *India* was torpedoed by the German submarine *U-22*. Of the crew of 160, twenty-two officers and 119 men were saved. Transferring to the Royal Naval Air Service, he was posted to HMS *Ark Royal* in August 1917, Britain's first aircraft carrier.

On 21st September 1918, along with observer Lieutenant Oswald Gayford, both men won the DFC for their long service and good work. (Oswald Gayford later became an air commodore.) Confirmed as a seaplane pilot in December 1918, Grigson went with 224 Squadron to Russia to support White Forces opposed to the Bolsheviks. He remained based at Petrovsk till 1st September 1919, but then moved to 47 Squadron in South Russia, and where he received a Bar to his DFC.

On 18th February 1920 he and Capt C. F. Gordon shot down an enemy Sopwith 1½ Strutter. For his work here he received a mention in despatches on 31st March 1920. He then became the CO of a flight of DH9 bombers of 55 Squadron in Egypt. Later he saw action in Turkey and in the Eastern Mediterranean, Caspian Sea, and Iraq. For these actions he received a DSO and a second Bar to his DFC.

In August 1922 he became a flight commander with 205 Squadron, then served at the Seaplane Training School, before being given command of 420 (Fleet Spotter) Flight. In 1924 he attended the Staff College. Four years later, Grigson was promoted to squadron leader and took command of 55 Squadron in March 1929. The following year he attended the Imperial Defence College, then commanded No. 2 (Indian Wing) stationed at Risalpur in 1935.

Promoted to group captain in 1939 in WW2 he became AOC with the rank of air commodore, in Palestine and Trans-Jordan. Grigson was part of the Air Staff in Greece and AOC HQ Eastern Wing during the withdrawal from Crete in 1941. He received another mention in despatches, 24th September of that year.

War memorial in Pelynt, Cornwall with the names of 'Jack' Grigson and his brother Aubrey enscribed. (via Andrew Thomas)

His other awards included the Royal Order of George I with Swords from Greece in March 1943.

Later he became SASO to the Rhodesian Air Training Group, then AOC. However, flying in a Harvard IIA (EX163) of the 20th Service Flying Training School on 3rd July 1943, he crashed at Antelope Mine, Bulawayo, and was killed. He was fifty years of age. He left a widow, Mary Isobel, who came from Ottershaw, Chertsey.

The Grigson family had quite a history. Canon Grigson had married three times, the first, Charlotte for twelve years, but she died. Secondly to Mary, and they had a daughter but she and her mother did not survive. They had been married for three years. At age forty-five, Canon Grigson married Mary Boldero and between 1892 and 1905 they had seven sons, all born at the Pelynt parsonage, near Looe.

John was the eldest. Second son Kenneth enlisted into the 7th Cyclist Battalion of the Devonshire Regiment and was commissioned in March 1915. Moving to the 5th Battalion of the Yorkshire Regiment, he went to France. He was awarded the Military Cross on 1st January 1918 but was killed in action on 20th July. Lionel Grigson went to Oxford where he too joined the Devonshires, going to the 3rd Battalion, and later the 1st. He was killed in action on 9th May 1917 during an attack on Fresnoy and has no known grave.

Claude Grigson became an RAF cadet at eighteen, but died in the influenza pandemic in October 1918. Wilfred studied at Oxford and was commissioned into the 30th Battalion of the Machine Gun Corps, seeing action in France,

Mesopotamia, Belgium and Palestine. Post-war he served with the Indian civil service, was knighted in the New Year Honours list on 1 January 1948, only to die in an air crash flying with Pakistan Airlines from Karachi to Lahore on 26th November 1948. Aubrey also attended Oxford. Too young to see service in WW1 he went to Burma and in WW2 became a captain in the Burma Reserve. He was killed at Schwebo by a bomb in April 1942. Seventh son Geoffrey survived becoming an editor, writer and poet.

Distinguished Flying Cross (*London Gazette* 21st September 1918, joint with Lt O. R. Gayford)

These two officers have flown together for a period of twelve months, during which time they participated in a number of bombing raids, carried out a large number of valuable reconnaissance patrols and escort flights in all weathers, by day and night, during the performance of which duties they have brought down hostile aircraft on several occasions. No task is too difficult for these officers.

Bar to DFC (*London Gazette* 22nd December 1919)

In recognition of distinguished services rendered during the war since the close of hostilities in South Russia.

Mention in Despatches (31st March 1920)

Distinguished Service Order (*London Gazette* 12th July 1920)

For gallant conduct and distinguished service in Southern Russia.

Second Bar to DFC (*London Gazette* 28th October 1921)

For gallant conduct and devotion to duty. This officer has always set a fine example to his flight by his courage and devotion to duty and by constant keenness and hard work.

ROBERT HALLEY

From Perth, Scotland, 'Jock' Halley was born on 8th November 1895, the son of Bailie Robert Halley. Educated at Perth Academy, and when war came he enlisted into the Cyclist Battalion of the Royal Highlanders in February 1915. After service with this unit, he decided to join the RNAS in February 1917, and trained at Vendôme. Once a pilot he was posted to 'A' Squadron, which became 16 Naval Squadron, flying Handley Page 0/100 bombers.

These huge bombers were employed in attacks upon targets in Germany at night. On these operations he often flew with the American millionaire, Robert Henry 'Bobby' Reece as his observer. On the night of 24th/25th October, the target was the Burbach Works at Saarbrucken. Flight Sub-Lieutenant Jock Halley's bomber was hit by French AA gunners as he returned and he had to crash land at 2140 hours at St. Dizier.

During 1918 Halley flew over twenty such night raids, including one against Thionville on 17th May. More raids came during the summer and on the night of 24th/25th August 1918 Halley went to Frankfurt. They pressed on in terrible weather, reaching the target despite the difficulties, and landed back at Lunéville after eight-and-a-half hours. Reece was with him on this trip, and their gunner was a new pilot who volunteered to go as their gunner, 2/Lt C. W. Treleaven.

By the end of the war, Jock Halley had received the DFC, quickly followed by a second, while Bobby Reece also received the DFC, the latter for at least the twenty-nine raids noted in his citation. Reece had been the head of the Reece Buttonhole Manufacturing Company, and had volunteered to fly with the RNAS before the Americans joined in the war. In 1919 his book *Night Bombing with the Bedouins* was published.

Halley remained in the service post-war and on 13th December 1918 he was co-pilot to Maj A. S. C. MacLaren, when they took Brig Gen N. D. K. MacEwen to his new appointment as AOC India. They took off in a Handley Page V/1500 (J1936) from Martlesham Heath, named HMA 'Old Carthusian', with a crew of Flt Sgt A. E. Smith, Sgt W. A. Crockett and Sgt T. Brown. The route took them to Paris – Rome – Catania (where the bomber sank up to its axels in a muddy field) – Malta – Cairo – Baghdad and finally Karachi, arriving on 15th January 1919. Later they flew to Delhi, where their arrival was met not only by the Viceroy but also by a crowd of 30,000 people. Halley later received the AFC for this epic flight, that had been flown despite several setbacks, including having to leave Brig Gen MacEwen, who was suffering from sunstroke, at Omara.

The Third Afghan War was being fought, and on 24th May 1919 Halley and his crew were ordered to fly their V/1500 through the Khyber Pass in the pre-dawn darkness to bomb the Royal Palace of Amanullah Khan in Kabul. As well as Messrs Crockett, Smith and Brown, the co-pilot was Lt Ted Villiers. The bomber was loaded up with four 112-lb bombs and sixteen 20-lb bombs but they struggled up to 8,000 feet, an altitude never previously attained by J1936. They arrived safely over the target, making a bomb run from 700 feet. Little actual damage was done, but a wall of the Khan's harem was blown in, and the resulting panic caused the Khan to surrender, thus ending the war. The NCOs all received Air Force Medals, and Halley his second Bar to his DFC.

During the mid-war period, Halley had a number of postings, including stints with the Fleet Air Arm, aboard the carriers *Eagle* and *Glorious*. On 1st July 1938 he was promoted to group captain. As WW2 began he became the assistant commandant at RAF Cranwell, and later CO of No. 200 Group of Coastal Command based at Gibraltar.

He retired from the service on 6th May 1945 and died on 13th December 1979, the sixty-first anniversary of his epic flight to India.

Distinguished Flying Cross (*London Gazette* 3rd August 1918)
A gallant and determined leader in long-distance night-bombing raiding. He has been most successful in many of these raids, generally under adverse weather conditions and intense anti-aircraft fire from the enemy, and having had to fly by compass course owing to density of mist. In his last raid the flight outward and homeward lasted eight hours.

Bar to DFC (*London Gazette* 1st January 1919)

Second Bar to DFC (*London Gazette* 12th July 1920)

Air Force Cross (*London Gazette* 22nd December 1919)
For pioneering flight to India.

RAYMOND HILEY HARRIES

Ray Harries came from Llandilo-fawr, South Wales, born in 1916. He studied as a dental student at Guys Hospital in London, but left to become a district agent for the Prudential Assurance Company in Canterbury. He joined the RAFVR in September 1939 and on completion of his pilot training, was posted to 43 Squadron which was in Scotland on rest. Following a period with 43, during which time he had an inconclusive night action against a German raider, he went to No. 52 Operational Training Unit at Debden as an instructor on 8th July 1941. He returned to operations in February 1942, posted to 131 Squadron flying Spitfire Vb fighters, and as a flight commander. He saw considerable action during that year and by December had achieved several victories, for which he received the DFC, at which time he was living in London, SW1.

Left: LAC Raymond H. Harries at ITW, Trinity Hall, Cambridge.

His next posting was to command 91 Squadron, known as a 'Jim Crow' outfit, as its job was one of coastal reconnaissance from RAF Hawkinge, keeping an eye on enemy activity and shipping in the Channel. In April the squadron re-equipped with Griffin-engine Spitfire XII, one of only two squadrons so equipped. By this time Ray had increased his score, destroying two and sharing two destroyed, plus some others damaged. With the Mark XII he brought his score to fourteen by October, and was now wing leader of the Westhampnett Wing and Tangmere Wings. He received a Bar to his DFC and then a second Bar, followed by the DSO in November.

Two of his victories, on 25th May 1943, were against German hit-and-run Fw 190s near Folkestone. He had only just landed from a coastal patrol when

Ray Harries on the right with Gp Capt J. E. Johnson DSO★★ and DFC★ (centre), post-war. They are talking to Charles Lindbergh.

the scramble signal was given. He and his number two immediately roared back into the air and off Folkestone saw a German fighter heading for France. He attacked and the 190 crashed into the sea. He then spotted another 190 in the failing light and after a four-second burst, the enemy fighter caught fire, hit the sea and sank. Both fighters came from 6./SKG 10.

At the end of the year he went on a lecture tour to the USA and upon his return in early 1944 became wing leader of 135 Wing within 2nd TAF, claiming a V1 flying-bomb on 25th June. In the latter part of the year he added one more confirmed victory and on 26 December managed to inflict damage on a Me262 jet. In January 1945 he converted on to Typhoons and Tempests and for a while commanded the Predannack Wing.

His next posting was as wing training officer at 84 Group, 2nd TAF, a position he retained till the end of the war. He received a Bar to his DSO in 1945, and the Croix de Guerre from both the French and the Belgians. He remained in the RAF after the war, taking command of 92 Squadron in November 1949.

On 14th May 1950 Ray was flying a Meteor F4 (VW267) but strangely he ran out of fuel when at 6,000 feet. He baled out but his parachute became entangled in the tailplane and he was killed in the subsequent crash. The aircraft fell near Sheffield, about six miles west of Worksop.

Distinguished Flying Cross (*London Gazette* 11th September 1942)

This officer, who has completed numerous sorties, is an excellent flight commander. He has spared no effort in the training of his pilots, amongst whom he has fostered a fine team spirit. He had destroyed one and assisted in the destruction of two more enemy aircraft.

Bar to DFC (*London Gazette* 25th May 1943)

This officer is a highly efficient squadron commander whose great keenness and energetic leadership have set a worthy example. In recent operations he has destroyed three enemy aircraft, shared in the destruction of another and damaged three more.

Second Bar to DFC (*London Gazette* 7th September 1943)

Since being awarded a bar to the Distinguished Flying Cross, Sqn Ldr Harries has destroyed a further four enemy aircraft. In May 1943, he led the squadron in an engagement against twelve enemy fighters. In the combat five enemy aircraft were shot down, two of them by Sqn Ldr Harries. During an engagement in July 1943, he destroyed two and damaged another enemy aircraft. This officer is a fine leader and a skilful and tenacious fighter.

Other Honours
Distinguished Service Order (*London Gazette* 9th November 1943)

Recommendation dated 16th October 1943:

> 'This officer has a long and distinguished operational record. His personal score to date is fifteen enemy aircraft destroyed, two probably destroyed and five and a half damaged. On relinquishing command of 91 (Nigeria) Squadron he became a wing commander flying, Tangmere's Spitfire XII Wing on the 19th August 1943, shortly after that Wing was formed. Under his leadership the Wing has destroyed twenty-seven enemy aircraft, probably destroyed four and damaged ten others. Twenty-three of these enemy aircraft were destroyed during the month of September 1943, three being accounted for by Wg Cdr Harries. The losses of the Wing have been light for such intensive operations; ten pilots being lost during the period. Of these, only six are attributable to enemy action. Many of the engagements have been against numerically superior enemy forces which were attempting to attack our bomber formations. In no instance were these attacks successful.'

On 20th October, AVM Saunders supported this recommendation with:

> 'Wg Cdr Harries has shown himself to be a courageous and aggressive wing leader. Under his command, the Tangmere Wing has been doing exceptionally fine work. Only this morning, under Wg Cdr Harries' able leadership the Wing destroyed nine enemy aircraft without loss to themselves. Wg Cdr Harries himself destroyed two, bringing his total for the last seven weeks up to five destroyed.'

Bar to DSO
Recommendation dated 6th May 1945:

> 'This officer has been flying operationally since 1940. He has just concluded his third tour of operations and his record before joining 2nd TAF was quite outstanding.
>
> 'In May 1944, he returned to operations as wing commander flying, North Weald, transferring later to No. 134 Wing. During this time he led the Wing during the strenuous flying which followed D Day. At the end of July 1944 he joined No. 135 Wing as wing commander ops. And continued to fly consistently with the Wing. During this time he flew some fifty sorties. These consisted of long escorts, including the first ninety-gallon-tank missions to the Ruhr, bombing and close support.
>
> 'Personally he has destroyed one e/a, damaged another, and destroyed and damaged MT, and under his leadership the Wing has claimed over 1,000 transport targets. The enthusiasm shown by all squadrons for close support and ground attack under all conditions of weather and in the face of very strong flak has been due to his leadership and great enthusiasm for creating the maximum destruction among these targets.
>
> 'On the ground, under field conditions and very often of discomfort, his personality has been a very fine example to the pilots which has kept the latter in great heart. His total score of enemy aircraft destroyed is twenty-and-a-half.'

Citation for this award (*London Gazette* 24th July 1945)

> 'This officer has been engaged in operational flying since 1940 and has destroyed at least twenty enemy aircraft. He has been operations

wing commander of his wing throughout the strenuous period which followed the invasion of Normandy. During this time Wg Cdr Harries took part in numerous long-escort sorties and in bombing and close support missions. Since the award of the DSO, he has destroyed one enemy aircraft and damaged others. Under all circumstances, in the face of adverse weather and heavy enemy opposition, he has displayed outstanding leadership and gallantry.'

Other Honours
Belgian Croix de Guerre (approved by the Inspectorate-General of the Belgian Air Force, 4th September 1944, awarded on 15th June 1945.)

'Brilliant officier, commandant les operations du 'Wing' dont fait part-ie l'escadrille 349. A effectué trois tours d'operations et remporte dix-neuf victories confirmées. Ses brilliants qualitiés de pilote et de chef lui ont gagné l'admiration et la confiance de son personnel.'

French Croix de Guerre

'After having shared his first success with a French pilot, has now to his credit seventeen enemy aircraft destroyed, two probably destroyed and four damaged. His squadron, containing several French pilots, has destroyed sixteen enemy aircraft, and on 24th May, 1943, destroyed five enemy aircraft without loss.'

STAFFORD BERKELEY HARRIS

Known as 'Bunny', Harris was born in Shepherds Bush, London at 31 St. Stephens Avenue, son to George G. H. (a master mariner) and Bertha J. Harris, on 16th February 1896. Following in his father's footsteps, he entered the Royal Naval Reserve as a probationary midshipman in August 1912 and in WW1 served aboard HMS *Otway*. In February 1916 he was acting sub-lieutenant on HMS *Princess Royal* but then decided to transfer to the RNAS.

By January 1918 he was serving at Luce Bay Airship Station, where he remained for the rest of the year, flying anti-submarine patrols in airships over the Irish Channel and the North Sea. With the formation of the RAF in April 1918 he became a lieutenant dirigibles and then a flying officer, airships, from August. He was awarded the Air Force Cross at the end of 1918, having also been mentioned in despatches on 1st May 1918.

Post-war he remained in the service and qualified as an aeroplane pilot at the RAF Airship Base at Howden, then went to No. 1 FTS at Netheravon for further flight instruction. In November 1921 he was posted to 27 Squadron in India, based at Risalpur, flying DH9A bombers and was engaged in operations during the Waziristan campaign the following year, and in the Razmak campaign in 1923. In 1924 he was flying at Arawali, and was awarded the DFC.

No. 27 Squadron became part of the first long-distance formation flight from Risalpur to Calcutta and back. This was the idea of Wg Cdr R. C. M. Pink (OC 2 Indian Wing), in order to train his crews. On 14th January 1925, the six flight commanders of 27 and 60 Squadrons, with Bunny Harris taking Pink as passenger, made the flight. The other two 27 Squadron flight commanders were Flt Lts J. L. M. Hughes-Chamberlain and S. Graham MC. The flight took a toll on the formation and only four Ninaks arrived at Calcutta on the 18th. They had covered 1,330 miles, although time in the air had only been fourteen-and-a-half hours. Those able, took off on the return on the 23rd – five in number. Two dropped out on the journey, and only Harris and J. W. Baker DFC of 60 Squadron got back to Risalpur.

Harris was sent off to the Staff College at Quetta in February 1925 and two years later he returned to England to be employed on the staff of HQ Air Defence Great Britain. It was back to India in 1929, working at the RAF HQ India in New Delhi, where he became personal assistant to AVM Sir Geoffrey Salmond, AOC India, for the next twenty months. In early 1930 he took command of 39 Squadron, equipped with Westland Wapiti aircraft, and fought against the Mohmands from May to September. Over the 5th and 6th September, the squadron dropped supplies to the Chitral Relief Column at Khar and Chakdora respectively.

Flt Lt Stafford 'Bunny' Harris DFC**, AFC (right). Left is Flt Lt J. L. M. deC Hughes-Chamberlain. They were both flight commanders with 27 Squadron in 1922.

During these campaigns, Harris flew on sixty-six operations, fifty-five of which were bombing, for which he received a Bar to his DFC.

Over the winter of 1931-32 his squadron re-equipped with Hawker Harts and then there was more trouble in the Dir State and the Mohmand territory. He flew a further sixteen operations during February and March, receiving a second Bar to his DFC.

He left 39 Squadron in March 1933, returned to England and took a post at HQ Central Area, Abingdon, where he became a wing commander, for Directing Staff at the Staff College at Andover in August 1935. He was briefly the CO of RAF Hucknall before being sent to Air Ministry to work with the Directorate of Organisation in August 1938. During WW2 he held a number of important posts, one being SASO for Technical Training in 1940, SASO at Air HQ British Forces in Habbaniya, Iraq from February to October 1941, then SASO No. 217 Group in Cairo, 1943-44, then on the staff at HQ Middle East Command, Cairo, in April 1944 to June 1945.

He finally retired from the RAF in April 1946. Harris died at Rossken, Heath Road, Woolmer, Welwyn Hertfordshire, in June 1952.

Mentioned in Despatches (1st May 1918)

Air Force Cross (*London Gazette* 2nd November 1918)
In recognition of valuable services performed in the Royal Air Force.

Distinguished Flying Cross (*London Gazette* 30th May 1924)
In recognition of distinguished services rendered with the Waziristan Force between January 1922 and April 1923.

Bar to DFC (*London Gazette* 26th June 1931)
In recognition of gallant and distinguished service rendered in connection with the operations on the North-West Frontier of India between 23rd April and 12th September 1930.

Second Bar to DFC (*London Gazette* 8th September 1933)
In recognition of gallant and distinguished services in connection with the operations on the North-West Frontier of India during the periods 28th January 1932 to 6th February 1932, and 6th March 1932 to 18th March 1932.

GEORGE URQUHART HILL

A Canadian from Nova Scotia, George Hill was born in Antigonish, on 29th November 1918 and educated at Mount Allison University where he became a BA and began to study medicine. While preparing for medical school he lived in Picton, working as a steeplejack. This came to an end with the declaration of war, and he joined the RCAF on 9th September 1939. Once trained as a pilot at an aero club in Halifax his skills were recognised because he was retained as a flight instructor at Trenton Station from 6th November and then at Camp Borden till April 1940.

He continued with various training units, attaining the rank of flight lieutenant on 1st July 1941, and finally sailed for England in early 1942, where he ended up at No. 52 OTU in early February. In April, he was posted to 421 Squadron, RCAF, then to 453 Squadron in June and then to 403 Squadron in August. Saw action during the Dieppe operation on the 19th of that month, sharing a Fw 190 destroyed and scoring hits on two more.

Posted overseas in December, he arrived in North Africa and was sent to 111 Squadron in February 1943, damaging two Me 109s on the 4th. From then on he scored regularly over the next few months during the Tunisian campaign, and by the end of April he had been given command of the squadron. He received the DFC in May and a Bar less than two weeks later. By the time he was due for a rest his score had risen to ten destroyed, seven shared destroyed and ten damaged. On 4th March, during a heated battle with Ju 87s of II/StG3, he shot down two and damaged another but then his own aircraft suffered hits and he just managed to reach the front lines before having to crash land.

Another eventful day was on 1st May, on his second day in command of 403 Squadron. On his first mission he shared in the destruction of a He 111 bomber over the Mediterranean, between Tunis and the island of Pantelleria. In the afternoon he and his pilots were able to bounce some fifteen Me 110s and ten Me 109s. His score in that fight was one 110 destroyed, and two others shared destroyed. He also saw action during the landings on Sicily. On 11th July he shot down an Italian MC.200. Two days later, over Sicily, he shot down a Ju 88 at dawn, but its rear gunner hit his Spitfire and he had to make a forced landing at Pachino. On a later sortie he got a 190, his last kill in the Middle East.

Leaving 403 he went to HQ Middle East before going home to Canada. At this time came the award of a second Bar to his DFC.

He returned to England in January 1944 and in March was given command of 441 Squadron RCAF. However, on one of the unit's first sorties, on 25th April, he shared in the destruction of a Fw 190 but was himself shot down, having to make a forced landing near Épernay. Managing to evade capture, he eventually reached the French-Spanish border but was then captured by the Gestapo, and spent the next six months in prison camps at Fresnes, Mainz and Wiesbaden, mainly in solitary confinement and living on one bowl of soup and a piece of bread per day. He was finally transferred to Stalag Luft I at Barth in Pomerania (POW number 5858) in October 1944. George Hill made out the following report of his last wartime flight:

> 'I took off in a Spitfire on 26 April 1944 and owing to one of my [fuel] tanks being blown off I crash landed fifteen kilometres north-west of Épernay. I made contact with a man who gave me some civilian clothes and then continued walking for a few days at the end of which time I met some people who put me on a train to Toulouse. I was then put on another train but had only just got out of the station when the Gestapo made an identity check and I was captured.
>
> 'I was sent to a civilian prison in Biarritz and from there to Bayonne for a week after which I was sent to Fresnes Prison where I remained for two-and-a-half months. At the end of this time I was sent to a civilian prison in Mainz. There were two other British and eleven Americans in this camp. When we refused to answer questions our rations were cut and our interrogators told us that they were not in a hurry but that we would eventually talk. We were in solitary confinement for over nine weeks. At the end of this time we were sent to a civil prison in Wiesbaden where we were crowded seventeen to a room and interrogated again. Some of the men talked and got double rations. We were finally sent to Stalag Luft I.'

With the war over, Hill, back in England, attended an investiture and also a garden party at Buckingham Palace, along with fellow Canadian pilots, recently released from captivity, including Sqn Ldr T. A. Brannagan DFC and Sqn Ldr H. C. Trainor DSO DFC. He then returned to Canada and once released from the RCAF, attended Dalhousie University in September 1945 to continue his medical studies. He qualified as a doctor in 1950. He became a general practitioner in Orangeville, Ontario, while also serving on the public school board and the local medical society. He also stood in the federal and provincial elections, and was active in New Democratic Party politics.

He was killed in a motor accident on 12th November 1969, when driving home following a night call, although another source says he was driving home prior to a curling match. He had stated that in the event of his death he wanted to be buried in Picton. During the interment in Haliburton Cemetery, an RCAF Neptune aircraft from CFB Greenwood made a low pass in salute.

Distinguished Flying Cross (*London Gazette* 21st May 1943)

Flt Lt Hill is a skilful leader whose ability has been well in evidence during recent operations. He has participated in many sorties and has destroyed four enemy aircraft.

Bar to DFC (*London Gazette* 1st June 1943)

This officer has led the squadron with great success and, since early April 1943, has destroyed five enemy aircraft. Early in May, 1943, he led his formation in an operation off the Tunisian coast. During the flight a superior force of enemy fighters were engaged. In the ensuring combats, seven enemy aircraft were destroyed without loss, two of them by Sqn Ldr Hill. This officer is a courageous and skilful fighter.

Second Bar to DFC (*London Gazette* 28th September 1943)

Sqn Ldr Hill, as a fighter pilot, has displayed exceptional courage and determination. He has destroyed at least fourteen enemy aircraft including one by night and damaged many others. During recent operations from Malta, he led his squadron with skill and resolution, personally destroying four enemy aircraft within a few days. On one occasion he remained alone despite repeated and persistent attacks from six Messerschmitt 109s to obtain assistance for a comrade who had been forced to leave his aircraft by parachute.

FREDERICK DESMOND HUGHES

From Donaghadee, County Down, Des Hughes was born in Belfast on 6th June 1919, the son of a linen manufacturer. He went to Campbell College and completed his education at Pembroke College, Cambridge, reading law, and where he was also a member of the university air squadron. Deciding to join the RAF, he began training on the first war course at Cranwell in September 1939 and joined the RAFVR on 3rd October. He had also played rugby for the London Irish team.

His first squadron was No. 26, an air co-operation unit, which he joined in 1940. After a period at No. 5 Operational Training Unit, he was posted to 264 Squadron, which had Boulton Paul Defiants. Although badly outclassed as a two-seat fighter, he and his turret gunner did manage to shoot down two Do 17s on 26th August, operating from RAF Manston. 264 Squadron then went over to night-fighting and before the year was out he had been credited with a He 111 destroyed and another damaged. He continued with the night role into 1941, shooting down a further two He 111s, with another as probably destroyed. He received the DFC in April. His gunner on all these occasions was Sgt Fred Gash, who received the DFM.

Following a rest, Hughes was posted to 125 Squadron, which had Bristol Beaufighters, a twin-engine night-fighter that had the advantage of airborne radar. His radar man was Plt Off Lawrence Dixon. However, his next two victories came in daylight, a Ju 88 in June and another of this type shared in November. Following a year of duty, the pair were posted to 600 Squadron in North Africa, Hughes having received a Bar to his DFC.

Operating for most of 1943 with this squadron, the pair achieved considerable success, and between January to mid-August 1943, they claimed nine German and Italian aircraft shot down, three on the night of 11th/12th August, all Ju 88s. By this time, of course, the squadron were flying operations over Sicily. A second Bar to his DFC came in September and Dixon also received the DFC and Bar.

Returning to England at the end of this tour, Hughes was promoted to wing commander, and sent to take a staff role at HQ Fighter Command and then served with 85 Squadron. In July 1944 he was given command of 604 Squadron, flying de Havilland Mosquito XIII night-fighters, taking it to France, the first night-fighter unit to be based in France following the invasion. On the night of 6th/7th August, over France, he shot down a Ju 88. He continued to lead 604

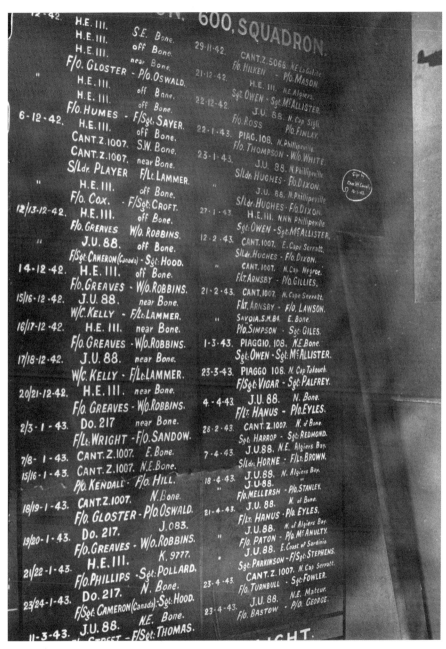

600 Squadron's scoreboard which was the tail fin of an enemy aircraft. The names of Hughes and Dixon can be seen in early 1943.

into 1945, downing his last victory, a Ju 188, on the night of 13th/14th January, over Rotterdam. In March he received the DSO.

After the war he remained in the service, being appointed to a permanent commission and again began working at HQ Fighter Command until 1953 and received the Air Force Cross in June 1954. On the staff of the RAF Staff College 1954-56, he then became personal staff officer to the chief of the Air Staff, until 1958. As a group captain he went to Germany to command RAF Gelsenkirchen from 1959 to 1961, for which he became a CBE. He continued to progress over the next few years holding a number of senior positions and in 1963, as an air commodore, was ADC to HM Queen Elizabeth II. Promoted to air vice-marshal in July 1967 and in 1970 he became commandant of the RAF College, Cranwell, and in 1972 became SASO, Near East Air Force until his retirement in June 1974. He was made CB in 1972 and settled in the Sleaford area of Lincolnshire. In 1983 he became deputy lieutenant of Lincolnshire.

In January 1992 he went down with pneumonia, and died on the 11th. He had married Pamela Harrison in 1941, daughter of Julius Harrison, composer and conductor. They had three sons. Hughes' father-in-law had been a technical officer with the RFC in WW1, and post-war was with the Royal Academy of Music, director of music at Malvern College, and the BBC Northern Orchestra.

LAWRENCE 'LAURIE' DIXON and Des Hughes got together in January 1943 and became one of the best night-fighter crews in the Middle East theatre. They remained together for the rest of the war. Flying with 125 Wing, with Beaufighter VIs, they began with destroying two Ju 88s on 23rd/24th January and on the 12th/13th February, an Italian Cant 1007b, which fell into Allied territory. Soldiers rummaged through the wreckage and sent several documents back for inspection. From these it was clear that the Italian pilot had been Maggiore Pietro Padorani, commanding officer of 262ª Squadriglia, of No. 104° Gruppo. Dixon's contribution for assisting in night victories with Hughes was twelve destroyed, for which he received the DFC and Bar. His DFC citation was a joint one with his pilot, and the Bar mentioned his part in ten victories. Dixon had started out as a LAC in June 1940, then volunteered for aircrew. He joined 600 Squadron as a radar operator in July 1940, and was commissioned in November 1941. Initially with 125 Squadron he teamed up with Hughes in October. Their first success was a Ju 88 which they shared with another crew on a day ranger.

Posted overseas in January 1943, Dixon found himself back with 600 Squadron, where he and Hughes began scoring heavily. In July 1944 Hughes took Dixon with him when he returned to England to take command of 604 Squadron, scoring two more victories.

Dixon left the RAF as a squadron leader in 1947, and died in October 1998.

Distinguished Flying Cross (*London Gazette* 18th April 1941). Joint citation with Sgt F. Gash, awarded DFM.

Fg Off Hughes and Sgt Gash as pilot and air gunner respectively have participated in numerous engagements against the enemy, both by day and night. During these flights four enemy aircraft have been destroyed, of which two were shot down at night.

Bar to DFC (*London Gazette* 13th April 1943). Joint citation with Fg Off L. Dixon.

As pilot and observer respectively, Sqn Ldr Hughes and Fg Off Dixon have flown together on many night sorties in operation in North Africa. During the flights they have destroyed three enemy aircraft. Sqn Ldr Hughes and Fg Off Dixon have displayed great skill and keenness, setting a praiseworthy example.

Second Bar to DFC (*London Gazette* 28th September 1943)

Sqn Ldr Hughes is a brilliant night-fighter whose determined efforts have met with further successes. Since being awarded the DFC he has destroyed seven enemy aircraft. His total victories number at least sixteen, of which thirteen have been destroyed at night. Sqn Ldr Hughes is a highly efficient flight commander and his meritorious work has been reflected in the efforts of his flight which has earned notable successes.

Other Honours
Distinguished Service Order (*London Gazette* 23rd March 1945)

Wg Cdr Hughes has displayed the highest standard of devotion to duty throughout a long period of operational flying. His outstanding keenness, great skill and unsurpassed determination have been well reflected in the success of the squadron which, under his brilliant leadership, has been responsible for the destruction of a good many enemy aircraft. Among his own personal successes, Wg Cdr Hughes has destroyed eighteen enemy aircraft.

Air Force Cross, 1st January 1954.

Commander of the Order of the British Empire, 1st January 1962.

Companion of the Order of the Bath, 3rd June 1972.

PETRUS HENDRICK HUGO

A South African from Cape Provence, Hugo was born on 20th December 1917 at farm Boonste, Pampoenpoort, Victoria West. His parents were Pieter Francois and Susanna Catherine Hugo. He had brothers and sisters. He finished his education at Witwatersrand College of Aeronautical Engineering and in 1938, with the idea of joining the RAF in England, sailed to Britain. He attended the civil flying school at Sywell and applied and received a short-service commission into the RAF in April 1939.

He began training at No. 13 FTS and his assessment after six months was noted at 'exceptional'. Completing his training and a period at an operational training unit, he was posted to 615 Squadron in December 1939, which were in France operating during the Phoney War. His first operational aeroplane was the Gloster Gladiator biplane and then the Hawker Hurricane. He was known as either 'Piet' or 'Dutch'. With the latter aircraft he claimed one victory in France, a He 111 on 20th May.

Once back in England, the squadron took its share of action during the Battle of Britain and by mid-August he had scored at least three more victories. On 16th August he was slightly wounded in the legs and then shot down again two days later, ending up in hospital. He was notified of the award of the DFC a few days later.

Returning to 615 upon recovery, in 1941 the squadron began a very active part in denying the English Channel to the Germans, and becoming a flight commander, Hugo took part in numerous anti-shipping strikes with their 20-mm cannon-armed Hurricane IIs. In fact he took part in sinking over twenty ships of various shapes and sizes. In addition he and the squadron, under Squadron Leader Denys Gillam, also attacked targets in France, destroying oil storage tanks, railway locomotives and distilleries. For these actions he received a Bar to his DFC in November.

Promoted to squadron leader he was given command of 41 Squadron, adding a couple of more victories to his tally, including at least one during the Channel Dash operation on 12th February 1942. In April he was posted to command the Tangmere Fighter Wing. However, on the 27th he was shot down by a Fw 190 over the Channel, wounded and baled out. He was successfully rescued and awarded the DSO.

Flt Lt Petrus Hugo DFC, while flying with 615 Squadron in 1940-41.

Posted to HQ Fighter Command he later resumed operations as wing leader of the Hornchurch Wing in July leading it during the Dieppe operation in August. One of his squadrons was the French 340 Squadron, which led to him being awarded the Croix de Guerre, but shortly after this event, he was posted to the Middle East. Given command of No. 322 Wing for the forthcoming invasion of French north-west Africa, by the end of 1942 his score had risen to over a dozen, plus some shared kills and several probables and damaged. His latter claims were made during the Tunisian campaign and he continued to lead the wing during the invasion of Sicily in 1943, during which time he added at least two more victories to his score. This score now totalled seventeen and three shared destroyed, with several more unconfirmed, damaged or probably destroyed. He was shot down by a Fw 190 near Mount Etna on 2nd September 1943 and his last kill was an Arado 196 floatplane over the Adriatic coast on 18th November.

There followed a second Bar to his DFC, promotions to group captain with further commands with his wing over Corsica and Italy. Combat in the air became less and less as the air war moved north over Italy but he was often leading ground-attack sorties. When the wing was disbanded in November 1944, he was sent to HQ Mediterranean Allied Air Force, and seconded to Marshal Fyodor Tolbunkin's 2nd Ukrainian Army in Romania and Austria.

Posted back to the UK towards the end of the war, he went to the Central Flying School. He remained in the RAF for a time, an American DFC. He left the service in February 1950, returned to Africa, and bought a farm (Ol Kiret) on the slopes of Mount Kilimanjaro in Tanganyika (later Tanzania), which he worked until 1971, when his land was expropriated by the new leaders of the country and he was expelled. He had married a lady from Rhyl, Wales, named Angela Margaret (née Seeds), and they had a daughter Angela Elisabeth Petrus Hugo. Sadly his wife died in 1971 aged fifty.

Returning to his native South Africa he died on 6th June 1986, at Victoria West, and in fact is buried on the farm where he was born.

Distinguished Flying Cross (*London Gazette* 23th August 1940)

Plt Off Hugo has displayed great keenness to engage the enemy on every possible occasion. During June and July, 1940, he destroyed five enemy aircraft.

Bar to DFC (*London Gazette* 25th November 1941)

Since early September 1941, this officer has participated in numerous attacks on enemy shipping during which some thirty-five vessels have been either sunk, set on fire or damaged; also several E-boats were damaged in two further attacks. Other losses sustained by the enemy were a petrol storage tank which was set on fire, and one of their aircraft destroyed. In the execution of operation tasks necessitating the greatest skill and determination, Flt Lt Hugo has displayed high qualities of leadership and courage. Although he has been continuously engaged on operational flying since the war began his enthusiasm remains unabated.

Distinguished Service Order (*London Gazette* 29th May 1943)

This officer has completed over 500 hours of operational flying, a large proportion of which has been on patrols over enemy territory. During the autumn of 1941, he performed outstanding work in attacks on enemy shipping. He is a fine leader, and during a period of five months from November 1941, his unit destroyed at least twelve and damaged several more enemy aircraft. Both as a squadron leader and wing leader, this officer has displayed exceptional skill, sound judgement and fighting qualities that have won the entire confidence of all pilots in his command. He has destroyed thirteen enemy aircraft and damaged a further seven.

Second Bar to DFC (*London Gazette* 16th February 1943)

In operations in North Africa, Wg Cdr Hugo has taken part in many sorties on which he has destroyed at least four enemy aircraft. He has displayed gallant leadership and great skill during an outstanding record of operational flying.

Other Honours

French Croix de Guerre with Bronze Palm, 15th February 1943

Petrus Hugo brilliantly participated in the campaign over France conducted in the autumn of 1941, carrying out many offensive missions against enemy navigation. In 1942, he personally led the Groupe 'Île-de-France' on nineteen offensive missions of which five were carried out in a single day on 19th August 1942, during the course of the combined operations over Dieppe.

American DFC (*London Gazette* 14th November 1944)

For extraordinary achievement while participating in aerial flights from Corsica under American Command from 23rd April to 23rd June 1944. During this period, his command was in tactical support of the Allied Ground Forces in Italy, and [it] flew more than 536 missions, destroying twenty enemy aircraft, 234 motor transport and miscellaneous shipping. Gp Capt Hugo was personally responsible for great destruction and damage to material and communications so vital to the enemy. His inspiring aerial leadership, steadfast devotion to duty and personal example reflect great credit to himself and the Allied air forces.

CHARLES GORDON ST.DAVID JEFFRIES

Born in Llanarth, on 1st March 1920, a small village and community in Cere-digion, Cardiganshire (now Dyfed), located on the A487 between Aberystwyth and Cardigan. He received his education at the Shaftesbury Grammar School, and Cardiff Technical College. The family later moved to Fawley, Hampshire.

With a war obviously on its way, Jeffries joined the RAF on a short-service commission in February 1939 and did his ab initio training course at No. 11 E&RFTS, Perth and in June progressed to No. 2 FTS at Brize Norton. Once he had completed his training and been to an operational training unit, he was sent to 3 Squadron, flying Hurricanes, as part of a group of nine pilots from various squadrons, sent to France as reinforcements.

With the British army in retreat and the RAF on the defensive, Jeffries was in action four days after the blitzkrieg began on the 10th, shooting down a Me 110 over Sedan. At 1625 hours he was in action against a formation of Ju 87s but his fighter was hit by an attacking Me 109 and he was forced to bale out. He landed uninjured and returned to his base. His squadron soon had to pull out of France and set up base at Wick, Scotland, Jeffries returning to his original squadron.

On 17th July he went to Sumburgh, when B Flight was re-numbered 232 Squadron, and on 23rd August he shared in the destruction of a He 111 over Fair Isle, the squadron's first victory. Little further action followed and so by April 1941 he, now a flight lieutenant, had volunteered for overseas duty, and that month he found himself aboard HMS *Ark Royal* bound for the island of Malta. Flying off the aircraft carrier on 30th April he, and around twenty other pilots, landed at the airfield of Hal Far. Jeffries, who had by this time acquired the nickname of 'Porky' due to his rotund appearance, was sent off to join 261 Squadron based at nearby Takali. It wasn't long before he was in action, shooting up a Ju 88 of 9/KG30, on 5th May. This bomber crashed upon its return to home base with the crew lost.

At this stage, C Flight of 261 became the nucleus of 185 Squadron at Hal Far on 12th May, with Jeffries being appointed as A Flight commander. On 4th July he destroyed an Italian MC200 fighter and damaged another. On the 9th Jeffries was part of a strafing mission against Syracuse seaplane base in which a number of enemy aircraft were destroyed or damaged. Jeffries reported seeing several strikes on one seaplane on the water before attacking five others on the slipway. Shooting at these he saw one floatplane burst into flames and after strafing the others, fired a long burst into the nearby hangar, scattering several men working there. Two days later he was in a fight with some Macchi fighters, claiming one and damaging a second. On 4th September and on the 30th he claimed Macchi fighters as probably destroyed. The Macchi on the 4th, it was noted in the squadron diary, received some fifty-two cannon shells from twenty-five yards range which: '.. rather leads one to believe that one little Macchi did *not* get home.'

Jeffries was awarded the DFC on 26th September. The squadron diary records:

> 'If ever a man earned the DFC, Jeff has; he has been leading "A" Flight practically since the formation of the squadron, and leading it most successfully. In England he was a flight commander of 232 Squadron for some considerable time, before that he operated from and over France, and on one occasion had to walk back to base. He now has six confirmed victories to his credit, as well as many other probables and damaged. In the early days of the squadron when things were not going so well for us, Jeff more than anybody else kept us going by his constant cheerfulness and almost continual wisecracking. Good luck Jeff and here's to the next one.'

By now 185 Squadron were taking the war to the Italians. On 30th September Jefferies led a section of Hurricanes to bomb Comiso airfield on Sicily. The squadron lost one pilot so later Jefferies escorted a FAA Fulmar, along with four other Hurricanes, to see if he had come down in the sea. They ran into Macchi 202 fighters but Jeff found he was far more manoeuvrable than one 202 and

Flt Lt Charles 'Porky' Jeffries DFC** in front row, second from left, with members of 185 Squadron in Malta, August 1941.

when he finally had to break off, the Italian was last seen down at 800 feet trailing smoke and leaving bits of aeroplane behind him.

The following month Jeffries was posted to HQ Middle East, and then came a posting to a Wellington bomber squadron, training to drop paratroops, but he managed to get himself back on to fighters. Given command of 155 Squadron, flying Curtiss Mohawks, the unit began operating in India and Burma from November 1942. On 28th January 1943 he probably destroyed a Japanese Ki43 Oscar fighter. A Bar to his DFC had come three days earlier. He continued to command 155 Squadron for a whole year, until November 1943, during which time he led numerous low-level ground-attack missions and also had several aerial encounters.

Little has been recorded about Porky Jeffries' service after 1943 but he remained in the RAF and received a second Bar to his DFC whilst operating with No. 1340 Flight over Kenya during the Mau Mau Rebellion. Initially the flight flew North American Harvard II aeroplanes, strafing and bombing Mau Mau hideouts in the dense jungles. He continued to serve on his return to England, commanded 543 Squadron in 1959 flying Valiants, having become a wing commander in 1955. He retired back to Wales in October 1967, and died on 28 January 1985 being buried in his home village of Llanarth.

Distinguished Flying Cross (*London Gazette* 26th September 1941)

This fighter pilot has been continuously engaged on operational flying for the past year. He has destroyed at least five hostile aircraft and damaged several more. He has led his flight, and on occasion the squadron, with commendable skill and efficiency, while his unfailing cheerfulness and keenness to engage the enemy has been an inspiration to all.

These final citations are often reduced in size from the original recommendations. This one is a case in point, so I show the original as an example:

'The following recommendation for the non-immediate award of the Distinguished Flying Cross to A Flight Lt Charles Gordon St.Davies [sic] Jeffries No.41929 of No. 185 Squadron, is forwarded. This officer has now carried out one year of continuous operational flying as a fighter pilot. In France he shot down two aircraft and damaged two more. In England he shot down one enemy aircraft and in Malta he has shot down a further two enemy aircraft and damaged two more. He has led his flight and at times the squadron with commendable skill and efficiency and has been an inspiration to all pilots under him with his unfailing cheerfulness and keenness to engage the enemy even when

up against heavy odds. This officer has shown a magnificent and determined spirit which has proved most inspiring to the squadron.'

Bar to DFC (*London Gazette* 25th January 1944)

This officer has taken part in numerous and varied operational sorties. Since
March 1943, as squadron commander, he has led his squadron on many bombing and escort duties over enemy targets in Burma. He has at all times set a magnificent example of courage, skill and determination and his inspiring leadership
and has contributed greatly to the high standard of operational efficiency and
morale maintained by his squadron throughout the monsoon period.

Second Bar to DFC (*London Gazette* 22nd March 1955)

In recognition of gallant and distinguished service in Kenya.

JOHANNES JACOBUS LE ROUX

'Chris' Le Roux was a South African, born in Heidelberg, Transvaal, on 12th April 1920. He received his education at Springs, in the Transvaal and Durban High School, and worked as an apprentice in the Springs Mines. Saving his money, he planned a trip to Britain to join the RAF, having been turned down when he and a friend tried to join the SAAF, due to lack of money available within the SAAF.

Both made their way to England and joined the RAF in February 1939, and once trained as a pilot at 6 OTU, the war had started and Le Roux found himself posted to France to fly Fairey Battle light bombers, although it seems he was actually with 85 Squadron. He was wounded in May 1940 and spent the next six weeks in hospital. On his release he became a flight instructor but in February 1941 he was posted to 91 Squadron. No. 91 was known as a 'Jim Crow' squadron, and although a day-fighter unit, spent much of its time patrolling the Channel in search of enemy shipping. Quite expectedly their small patrols often met enemy fighter aircraft and by the end of the year, Le Roux had shot down six Me 109s, damaged two more and damaged a Ju 88. All these combats had taken place around the Folkestone-Calais-Boulogne-Cap Griz Nez areas. He became a flight commander in September and received the DFC. When he shot down two Me 109s on 4th September, he received personal congratulations from the AOC of 11 Group.

Tour expired in December he was posted to No. 55 Operational Training Unit as an instructor until March 1942 and then posted to Rolls-Royce for testing duties. In September he managed to become a supernumerary with his old squadron (91), damaging two Fw 190s on 30th September, and he destroyed two more on 31st October east of Dover, following a German hit-and-run raid on Canterbury. He received another letter of congratulations from the AOC of 11 Group, as well as a 'well done' from Sir Archibald Sinclair, the Secretary of State for Air. The following month he received a Bar to his DFC.

Posted overseas in January 1943, he found himself in North Africa, joining 111 Squadron for Operation Torch, then becoming CO on the 26th. He led Treble One throughout the Tunisian campaign until 30th April, adding four more combat victories to his tally. He was awarded a second Bar to his DFC. He then became a fighter controller. In Tunisia, Le Roux was credited with one of the best 'line-shoots' of the campaign, after he landed in bad weather: "You know, I didn't realise I was down until I heard the ground crew clapping."

In 1944 he began a third tour of operations, taking command of 602 Squadron in France, following the invasion. During July he shot down six German fighters and damaged two more and attacked several ground targets, such as motor transports. After one successful combat on 16th July, he went down and strafed a German staff car at Sainte Foy de Montgomerie, in which it was thought Feldmarschall Erwin Rommel was travelling. The car crashed, Rommell receiving a fractured skull that effectively took him from his post as army commander on the Western Front.

On 29th August, 1944, Le Roux took off from B-19 landing ground to fly to England. The weather was bad and he died crashing into the sea off Selsey Bill. He had married an English woman named Betty, from Shropshire and they had two children.

Distinguished Flying Cross (*London Gazette* 17th October 1941)
This officer has carried out over 200 operational sorties which have included shipping reconnaissances, during which much valuable information has been obtained, and numerous attacks on shipping and enemy aerodromes in the face of heavy enemy fire. Flt Lt Le Roux has destroyed three hostile aircraft in combat and at least one on the ground.

Bar to DFC (*London Gazette* 11th December 1942)
Since being awarded the Distinguished Flying Cross this officer has destroyed a further five enemy aircraft. In addition to his air victories he has attacked shipping and targets on the ground with considerable success. At all times Flt Lt Le Roux has displayed a fine fighting spirit.

Second Bar to DFC (*London Gazette* 9th July 1943)
Sqn Ldr Le Roux's magnificent leadership has played a large part in the many successes attained by his squadron. He has personally destroyed fourteen enemy aircraft and damaged many others, and has also inflicted much damage on enemy shipping.

WALTER HUNT LONGTON

From Whiston, Lincolnshire, 'Scruffy' Longton as he became known, was born on 10th September 1892, eldest born to Walter Henry and Mary Anne Longton, the latter the daughter of a doctor. He had a sister Hilda Mary and three brothers, Eric, Norman and Thomas, all three of whom became doctors, graduating from the University of Liverpool. On leaving school he entered the new world of the motorcar, and eventually became a motorcar test driver with the Sunbeam Motor Company, while also becoming interested in motorcycle racing. At this time he was living in Prescot in order to work for Alldays & Onion Ltd, a motor company in Birmingham, where he also acted as a factory racer, competing in the Isle of Man motorbike TT races.

Some time after the start of WW1 he joined the Queen's Own Worcestershire Hussars, and saw service in Egypt and Gallipolli. However, he then decided that flying was to be his choice of fighting in the war, and learnt to fly in a Hall Biplane at the Hall School at Hendon, gaining Aero Certificate No. 2647 on 31 March 1916. The following month he received a commission in the Royal Flying Corps and in July was a flying officer.

However, he was obviously an above average pilot, for he was retained as an instructor rather than being sent off to France, which was probably why he survived his baptism of fire in 1918. For his work as an instructor he was awarded the Air Force Cross.

Finally able to break free from training, he was posted to 85 Squadron, at this time commanded by Maj Edward Mannock DSO MC, and equipped with SE5A scouts. Mannock had earlier been with 74 Squadron, and interestingly, Longton shot down his first enemy aeroplane, a Fokker DVII, on the same date as Mannock scored his first with 85 Squadron – 7th July 1918 – and in the same fight at 2020 hours over Doulieu.

With 85 Squadron, Longton was credited with six aerial victories by 22nd August and received the DFC. He was then posted to 24 Squadron, another SE5A unit, as a flight commander. Between 8th and 30th October he accounted for a further five enemy machines shot down; all eleven of his victories were of the destroyed variety. For these actions he received two Bars to his DFC, the first Englishman so honoured.

Walter 'Scruffy' Longton (centre) with members of 85 Squadron in 1918.

In 1919 Walter married Lily Eleanor Miller, who had enrolled as an ambulance driver in the RFC in 1916. She was also to serve in the WAAFs in WW2. Walter Longton decided to remain in the RAF after the war, receiving a permanent commission, training for and taking part in the RAF Pageant at Hendon on 3rd July 1920. That same year he competed in the Aerial Derby but did not finish the race. Longton became a well-known figure at many flying events, obviously tolerated by his RAF masters, between 1920-1927. He was written up in *Flight* magazine on 29th June 1922 because of his 'crazy' flying in an Avro 504K at the RAF Pageant that year. In 1923 he won the Grosvenor Challenge Cup air race in a Sopwith Gnu and also flew the English Electric 'Wren' at Lympne in the light aircraft trials. Two aeroplanes were shown at Lympne in October, and he shared the first prize with the Air Navigation & Engineering Co. Ltd's 'Anec', when it covered the eighty-seven-and-a-half miles (140.8 km) on one imperial gallon (four-and-a-half litres) of petrol.

On 3rd July 1925 Longton flew a Martinsyde in the Fourth King's Cup, but was forced to retire. Nothing had hindered his RAF career and he was promoted to squadron leader on 1st January 1924. However, his luck ran out flying a Blackburn B1 'Bluebird' (G-EBKD) during an air race at Ensbury Park, Bournemouth on Monday 6th June 1927. On one early flight, a local farmer took a pot-shot at his aeroplane as it flew over his land, hitting a wing; a photograph of Walter and the damaged wing exists. Later, in the major air race, he and another competitor collided manoeuvring during a turn; both aircraft crashed killing the two men instantly. Longton was buried at Upavon Cemetery, Wiltshire. He was thirty-four years old.

His wife Lily spent most of her life as a ladies' companion and of course, had an interest in flying, and even accompanied the Irish aviatrix Mary Bailey (1890-1960) to a competition and altitude tests in the Netherlands in the 1920s. She remained very close to the Longton family and died in 1983. Bailey personally flew a Cirrus Moth from England to the tip of South Africa and back in early 1928 and was appointed Dame Commander of the Order of the British Empire (DBE). In WW2 Bailey served with the Women's Auxiliary Air Force.

Air Force Cross (*London Gazette* 2nd June 1918)
In recognition of distinguished service rendered during the war.

Distinguished Flying Cross (*London Gazette* 2nd November 1918)
On 22nd August this officer led his formation of six machines to attack an equal number of enemy scouts. All the latter were accounted for, four being crashed and the remaining two driven down out of control. A brilliant performance,

'Scruffy' Longton, after WW1, as a freelance racing pilot.

reflecting the greatest credit on this officer as leader, and all who took part in the engagement. During the last seven weeks, Lieutenant Longton has destroyed seven [sic] enemy aircraft.

Bar to Distinguished Flying Cross (*London Gazette* 8th February 1919)
Between 29th September and 9th October, this officer carried out twelve tactical reconnaissance missions, bringing back most valuable information; he also displayed great gallantry in attacking enemy troops on the ground. On 9th October, when on a low patrol, he observed a machine-gun nest which appeared to be the sole obstacle to our cavalry advance. Having informed the cavalry and field artillery of the situation, he co-operated with the former in their attack, and, after the enemy had been driven out, pursued them with machine-gun fire as they retreated.

Second Bar to DFC (*London Gazette* 3rd June 1919)
In recognition of general distinguished service during the war.

JAMES ARCHIBALD FINDLAY MACLACHLAN

Mac was born at Styal, Cheshire, on 1st April 1919, appropriately the first anniversary of the formation of the Royal Air Force. He was the second of six children (four boys and two girls) born to Hugh and Helen MacLachlan. Sadly, his father died in 1928 when Mac (he was also known as Jay in the family) was only nine, and his mother and her children moved to Southampton to be near her parents, where Mac went to Monkton Combe School, near Bath, and later King Edward Evangelist School in Southampton. At the age of seventeen, he joined the RAF in March 1937, determined to become a pilot. By this time he was living in East Grinstead, Surrey.

He started his training at No. 10 E&RFTS at Yatesbury, on Tiger Moths, then to Uxbridge, where he became a pilot officer on probation with a short-service commission for four years. On to No. 3 FTS at Grantham in Lincolnshire, flying Harts and Audax biplanes, and by November he passed out with an 'above average' assessment. There followed a posting to 88 Squadron, which was equipped with Fairey Battle bombers, at Boscombe Down.

The day before war began, his squadron was posted to France as part of the Advanced Air Striking Force, landing at Auberive on 2 September 1939, from where they began flying reconnaissance flights to the Franco-German border, before moving to an airfield near Reims on the 12th. Surviving a brutal winter, Mac's squadron was thrust into battle with the invasion of the west on 10th May 1940. During the next two weeks Mac had his share of dangerous bombing attacks, desperately trying to stem the tide of German armour and infantry as they pushed inexorably towards the French coast. The squadron also made night raids against railway traffic, but nothing was going to stop the enemy advance and all too soon it was a case of flying back to England, while further to the north the Dunkirk evacuation was taking place.

Back in the UK, 88 Squadron was sent to Northern Ireland, but the good news was that Mac had been awarded the DFC for his efforts in France. With the Battle of Britain about to begin volunteers from Bomber and Coastal Commands were asked for to join Fighter Command. A handful of 88's pilots did so, Mac being among those selected. His first squadron was 145, based at Drem in Scotland, which was on rest from the south of England. A further call for volunteers to move to fighter squadrons in the south came, and once more Mac did just that, finding himself with 73 Squadron at RAF Debden. He just managed to see some action as the Battle petered out but had his first combat on 7th October. He had no firm success, but did claim to knock some pieces off a couple of Me 109s, but then came another chance to volunteer, this time to go to the Middle East.

Within days Mac found himself aboard the carrier *Argus* headed for the island of Malta where he joined 261 Squadron with the rank of flight lieutenant.

On 16th November 1940, the twelve Hurricanes on the carrier were prepared to fly off the next morning, but the distance to Malta was too great and a number of Hurricanes ran out of fuel and were lost. Mac only just made Takali airfield with about four gallons of petrol left, and immediately went down with a high temperature, so was whisked off to hospital for a few days. Without seeing any action over Malta, he went back to Gibraltar but returned to the island on 5th January 1941, and to 261 Squadron.

On 9th January 1941 he shot down two Macchi 200 fighters of 6° Gruppo, and ten days later scored a brace of Ju 87s. Not content with this he also shot down a Cant Z506B, a Ju 88 and possibly a CR42 biplane fighter. One of the Italian Macchi pilots he shot down on the 9th was Capitano Luigi Armanino, who baled out and ended up in a Maltese hospital. A month later when Mac was wounded, he found himself in the next bed to the Italian!

Enemy aircraft also attacked the island at night and on the night of 8th/9th February, during two sorties, Mac shot down two Ju 88s, although the first of these was in fact a He 111. Mac received a Bar to his DFC for his actions. However, on the 16th, MacLachlan was himself shot down during a scrap with Me 109s. During the combat he failed to spot a 109 coming in from behind. Badly hit, he was seriously wounded in his left arm and forced to bale out. Luckily he landed on the island and not in the sea. He quickly ended up in hospital but within a day or so it became clear his forearm could not be saved and it was amputated. Mac had been shot down by the German ace Oberleutnant Joachim Müncheberg of JG6.

As soon as it was possible, Mac returned to the UK and attended the artificial limb unit at Roehampton. Effectively out of the war, Mac became determined not only to fly again but to get back into combat. This did not seem feasible but his desire to do so overcame all, and fitted with a suitable prosthetic which enabled him to engage the throttle controls with this false left arm, he was back flying before the end of the year.

For a pilot so badly injured he could have easily remained away from operational flying, but Mac MacLachlan ignored any advice to this effect and did his utmost to return to flying against Germany, which ultimately cost him his life. Before that event, however, he had proved himself and carved a niche within the annuls of the RAF.

'One-armed Mac', having proved his point, was given command of 1 Squadron that was engaged on night-intruder operations at this stage of the war, with Hurricane II fighters. This was following a brief attachment to 3 Squadron in October in order to gain some experience of night-intruder operations. Once OC of 1 Squadron, he began ranging over a darkened northern France, where pilots would try to engage German bombers returning from raids upon England, as they came into land at their home airfields, which would light up their runways. Mac was successful on a number of occasions, notably on 26th/27th April 1942, shooting down a Do 17 at Evreux and damaging another at St. Andre. On 3rd/4th May he shot down a Do 217 and a He 111 at Dinard airfield and on 3rd/4th June, bagged two Do 17s and damaged two others at St. Andre. He was also able to spot and attack several trains, claiming at least seven and on one occasion set fire to a barge on the River Seine.

In May he was awarded the DSO and in July received the Czech War Cross for his support of Czech pilots within his squadron. He was then rested, being posted to No. 59 OTU as an instructor. A posting to an air fighting development unit (AFDU) followed in 1943. News also came that his brother Gordon, himself a fighter pilot with 616 Squadron, had been killed in action over Brest during a Ramrod operation on 16th April 1943, shot down by Fw 190s of JG2.

'Mac' MacLachlan, CO of 1 Squadron, giving an 'Agincourt Salute' to the insignia he carried on his night-intruding Hurricane. Note Mac's prosthetic where his left arm should have been, which he used when controlling the aircraft's throttle.

MacLachlan was even more keen than ever to take the war to the enemy, and his flair for intruding gave him the idea of doing so in daylight, and his aircraft of choice was the new North American P-51 Mustang fighter which AFDU were testing. In company with Flt Lt Geoffrey Page DFC, who had been badly burnt in August 1940 but had also managed a return to operational flying, they planned a daylight intruder sortie for 29th June. They were highly successful and between them they accounted for six enemy aircraft south of Paris. Mac's share was two Hs 126 observation aircraft, a Ju 88, and another of this type shared with Page. Page claimed a further two observation machines.

On 18th July they attempted a second intruder sortie, covered this time by a flight of Hawker Typhoons, but as they reached the Dieppe area, Mac's Mustang began to leave a trail of smoke. He was forced to land at high speed in a small field, those above seeing his machine shedding pieces of metal before coming to a stop. There was no movement from the wreck. Mac had in fact been badly injured and was taken to a German field hospital, but died on the 31st. He was buried at Pont L'Éveque Communal Cemetery. He was twenty-four years old. A second Bar to his DFC had been announced the day before his last flight.

Distinguished Flying Cross (*London Gazette* 16th July 1940)

> **Recommendation:** 'During May 1940, this officer has taken part in five night and three day operational flights in Battle aircraft. In the face of strong opposition and under adverse conditions he has shown magnificent courage and devotion to duty. On every occasion he has carried out his attacks with skill and determination.'

Bar to DFC (*London Gazette* 11th February 1941)

During intensive operations one day in January 1941 this officer destroyed four and possibly five enemy aircraft. Ten days previously he destroyed two enemy aircraft, one of which he had pursued for many miles out to sea. Flt Lt MacLachlan has set a fine example of courage, initiative and leadership.

Distinguished Service Order (*London Gazette* 29th May 1942)

During the early part of the war, this officer served in the Middle East where he destroyed eight enemy aircraft. Following an injury, his left arm was amputated, but within a few weeks, he was flying again. Since his return to England, Sqn Ldr MacLachlan has trained intensively in night flying operations and has achieved much success. One night in April 1942, he shot down a Dornier 217 over northern France and damaged another near an enemy aerodrome. One night in May 1942, near Dinard, he destroyed a Dornier 217 and a few minutes later he shot down a Heinkel 111. The latter burst into flames on impact with the ground, causing a fire which could be observed from a distance of ten miles. Sqn Ldr MaLachlan has attacked goods trains and barges with damaging effect. He is a gallant and skilful pilot whose example is an inspiration to all pilots.

Second Bar to DFC (*London Gazette* 30th July 1943. Joint with Flt Lt A. G. Page DFC.)

Recently these officers in the course of an operation over enemy occupied territory, shot down six enemy aircraft, three of which were destroyed by Sqn Ldr MacLachlan and two by Flt Lt Page, while the other was destroyed jointly. The operation, which was planned by Sqn Ldr MacLachlan, was brilliantly executed and his successes were worthily earned.

The Czech Military Cross (Announced 30 July 1943)

I write this to inform you that our Ministry of National Defence has the intention of submitting to the president of the Czech Republic, the Czech Military Cross 1939 to be conferred upon Sqn Ldr J. A. F. MacLachlan.

HAROLD BROWNLOW MORGAN MARTIN

(617 Squadron)

The second of three children of Irish-born Joseph Harold Osborne Martin MD and Coline Elizabeth Martin (née Dixon) from New South Wales, Australia, Harold was born in Edgecliff, Australia, on 27th February 1918. He was educated at Randwick High School, Sydney Grammer School and Lyndfield College. Leaving Australia in 1937 he travelled to England, intent on studying medicine, and where he became something of a gentleman horse rider.

With the arrival of war, Harold joined the Cavalry Division of the Australian Army, but then volunteered to join the RAF on 28th August 1940, training at No. 2 EFTS and then 11 SFTS in February 1941. After operational training unit, his first operational unit was 455 Squadron in October 1941, which flew Handley Page Hampden bombers. With this squadron he completed thirteen operational sorties before being sent to 50 Squadron in April 1942. This unit flew the twin-engine Avro Manchester bombers, but later re-equipped with Avro Lancasters. Completing his first tour of operations in October, Martin received the DFC. He remained on the squadron as an instructor with its conversion flight. This led to a posting to the Rolls-Royce School of Instruction and then to No. 1654 Heavy Conversion Unit.

In late March 1943 he was posted to 617 Squadron at RAF Scampton, which had been formed especially under Wg Cdr Guy Gibson DSO DFC, to train and take part in attacking Germany's dams that fed water and power to the Ruhr factories. The crews of this new squadron were almost entirely made up of experienced pilots and aircrew, for the training would be specialised in low-level flying in order to release bouncing bombs against the dam walls.

The history and achievements of 617 Squadron are well known and documented in books and on film. Suffice it to say that Martin played his part in the raid, for which he received the DSO. The squadron continued flying specialised attacks on difficult targets and upon completing his second tour of operations, he received a Bar to his DFC. At one stage he was acting CO of 617.

Following a rest period, 'Mickey' Martin, as he was called, joined 515 Squadron that flew Mosquito night-fighters, part of 100 Group. This came at the same time as his award of a Bar to his DSO, and for his success in night-fighting, he received a Second Bar to his DFC in November 1944. He had destroyed two

AVM Harold 'Mickey' Martin (right) pictured with AVM Peter Fletcher at Abingdon in November 1967. (MoD)

enemy aircraft in the air, three and one damaged on the ground. Prior to this, in September, he was posted to the Middle East to attend the staff college at Haifa, Palestine, then returned to HQ 100 Group, where he saw out the war. He had flown eighty-three sorties in the war, forty-nine on bomber ops.

Immediately after the war he flew transport aircraft, flying Dakotas, Stirlings and Avro Yorks till 1947, and also the new transport Mosquito. That year saw him fly a Mosquito in a record-breaking flight to Cape Town in twenty-one hours and thirty-one minutes, being awarded the Britannia Trophy, and then an Air Force Cross. He also flew a Mosquito across the Atlantic, leading a flight of six de Havilland Vampires, in their first jet crossing of this ocean. There followed a number of important appointments: air attaché in Tel Aviv 1952-55, ADC to HM Queen Elizabeth II 1964, becoming air vice-marshal in 1966, AOC 38 Group Air Support Command, 1967-70, C-in-C RAF Germany and CO NATO 2nd TAF 1970-73. In 1974 he became air member for personnel till he retired from the service on 31st October 1974. He then worked for Hawker Siddeley as an advisor, until 1977.

He had been appointed CB in 1968 and knighted KCB in 1971 with the rank of air marshal. He had married Wendy Laurence Walker on 14th October 1944, a widowed civil servant, who was the daughter of the New Zealand artist Ida Rentoul Outhwaite. They had two daughters. Harold 'Mickey' Martin died on 3rd November 1988.

Leonard Cheshire VC DSO DFC said of him: "He was the ideal wartime pilot. He had superb temperament, was quite fearless and innovative in his thinking. He was meticulous in his flying discipline and never did make a mistake."

Distinguished Flying Cross (*London Gazette* 6th November 1942)

Recommendation: 'Fg Off Harold Brownlow Martin, an Australian, is the captain of an outstandingly successful and efficient crew who have consistently bombed their targets from a low altitude and brought back photographs of the target area. He is exceptionally courageous and determined and always bombs from a height at which he not only can identify his target, but also has a reasonable chance of hitting it. To complete his task successfully in spite of the strongest opposition is always his one thought and to do this he has often made long flights across enemy territory at night at very low altitudes in the region of 100 feet, having considered during his pre-flight planning that this was the course of action best calculated to achieve his mission.

'On the night of 12th/13th August, he and his crew took part in a very successful attack on Mainz, dropping their bombs from 5,500 feet and scoring direct hits upon the target. Again on the night of 15th/16th August they attacked Düsseldorf from 6,000 feet having spent nearly thirty minutes picking up the target, they were heavily engaged by the defences throughout, but pressed home the attack in a most determined and resolute manner. The aircraft was hit in many places when over the target area and one engine caught fire and had to be feathered.

'On the night of 17th/18th August they were detailed to attack Osnabrück and here, in spite of very poor visibility, they found and bombed their target from 6,500 feet and again brought back a photograph of the target. On the night of 24th/25th August 1942, they were detailed for a special mission which called for a very high standard of navigation, and crew co-operation. They were successful in their task and again brought back a photograph of the target. Fg Off Martin's valour and courage in the face of the enemy is of the highest order and I consider him to be well worthy of the award.'

Distinguished Service Order (*London Gazette* 25th May 1943)

On the night of 16th May 1943, a force of Lancaster bombers was detailed to attack the Möhne, Eder and Sorpe dams in Germany. The operation was one of great difficulty and hazard, demanding a high degree of skill and courage and close co-operation between the crews of the aircraft engaged. Nevertheless, a telling blow was struck by the successful breaching of the Möhne and Eder dams. This outstanding success reflects the greatest credit on the efforts of the following personnel who participated in various capacities as members of aircraft crew.

There followed a list of awards given to 617 Squadron aircrew.

Bar to DFC (*London Gazette* 12th November 1943)
In September 1943, Sqn Ldr Martin was detailed to participate in a low-level operation at night. Early in the engagement the leader of the formation was shot down, nevertheless, despite appalling weather, Sqn Ldr Martin, with grim determination persisted in his effort to locate the target. The search lasted for eighty-four minutes in the target area but Sqn Ldr Martin persisted until able to make an attack. An outstanding leader, this officer has always shown great courage and resolution.

Bar to DSO (*London Gazette* 31st March 1944)
Since being awarded a Bar to the Distinguished Flying Cross this officer has completed numerous sorties and has continued to set the highest example of courage and devotion to duty. He is a brilliant and fearless leader, whose iron determination in the face of the fiercest opposition has won great praise. One night in February 1944, Sqn Ldr Martin captained an aircraft detailed to attack a target in southern France. During the run up to the target his aircraft was repeatedly hit. One member of the crew was killed and another one was wounded. Sqn Ldr Martin pressed home his attack, and afterwards flew the damaged bomber to an airfield where he effected a masterly landing in difficult circumstances. He displayed great skill and resolution throughout, and great courage and devotion to duty.

Second Bar to DFC (*London Gazette* 14th November 1944)
As flight commander, the sterling and audacious operational work achieved by this officer, combined with his ardent fighting spirit, is worthy of the highest praise.

JAMES ATTERBY McCAIRNS

Jim McCairns was born at Niagara Falls, USA on 21st September 1919, son of Thomas and Kate E. McCairns. His parents were English, his father merely working in the United States, employed in the engineering business. The first time Jim came to England was in 1922, his family on a four-month visit. The family finally returned permanently to England in September 1930, living at No. 20 Chapelgate, Retford, where Jim attended the town's Edward VI Grammar School.

Deciding on an RAF career, Jim joined the RAFVR in March 1939. Once trained as a fighter pilot, he was posted to 611 Squadron at the end of 1940 with the rank of sergeant pilot. His squadron became part of the Biggin Hill Wing in 1941, and took its share in the offensive operations over France. However, on the afternoon of 6th July, flying on Circus No. 35, escorting six Short Stirling bombers attacking Lille, 611 flew as the cover wing and were engaged by Me 109s. The wing, in a running fight with fighters from JG26, claimed three 109s shot down but lost three of their own men, McCairns being one of them. Presumably hit by cannon fire from a 109, McCairns managed to crash land on the beach at Gravelines and was promptly taken into captivity. His canopy had jammed on landing, and German soldiers had to release him from the cockpit, so it was fortunate his aircraft did not catch fire.

After initial interrogation he was sent to Oflag IX-C prisoner-of-war camp at Spangenberg, but on 22nd January 1942 he effected an escape. He evaded the Germans and crossed into Belgium where he was picked up by the Resistance and handed over to an SOE agent, who first told him about the black-painted Westland Lysanders that were used to bring agents to and fro from England, and occasionally flew evaders back too. For McCairns, however, there was no quick trip back home, and he was taken across France by a Frenchman, Charlie Morelle. Morelle had been a cavalry lieutenant with the French army and taken prisoner in 1940. He escaped his captors and began work as a guide with the French Comet escape line. Morelle got McCairns across the Pyrenees and into Spain where he made his way to Gibraltar. Sadly Morelle was arrested in Brussels in May 1942 and died in Dachau concentration camp a few days after the war ended. McCairns was interviewed by a man from MI9, who passed on a message to England about some of the agents that had helped him thus far.

McCairns was eventually returned to England, arriving on 30th April, where he was awarded the Military Medal on 14th August 1942, having been commissioned on 1st May. He also received the French Croix de Guerre. His next appointment was on a lecture tour, talking of his experiences in escape and evasion to men who might easily find themselves in a similar position one day.

It was virtually impossible for a successful evader to resume operational flying over Europe, but remembering his conversation with Morelle about the black Lysanders, he applied to join one of the squadrons that did this clandestine work, was accepted and was finally posted to 161 Squadron which operated within the realms of SOE. So successful did he become that he was awarded both the DFC and Bar in 1943, followed by a second Bar in 1944. One operation was on the night of 16th/17th November 1943. He and Sqn Ldr Hugh Verity took two Lysanders into France, landing two SOE agents, and returned with six passengers.

Completing a long tour of duty with 161 Squadron, McCairns was rested but his desire to return to operations eventually led to flying Hawker Tempest fighters with 3 Squadron. He and Flt Lt H. K. Hughes probably destroyed a Me 109 on 28th February 1945. Moving to 56 Squadron, on the morning of 15th April 1945,

Jim McCairns sitting on the edge of his Lysander cockpit in which he flew clandestine missions into occupied France with the SOE.

GALLANTRY IN ACTION

flying in company with Flight Lieutenant N. D. Cox, McCairns spotted what he
thought was a German Me262 jet, but was actually an Arado 234. They attacked
and destroyed the jet near Kaltenkirchen airfield.

Jim McCairns survived what for him had been a successful flying war, encom-
passing a mass of variety, from Spitfire pilot, to prisoner of war, an escapee and
evader, flying clandestine operations over France, and finally as a Tempest pilot
with 2nd TAF.

Sadly his luck ran out in 1948. Flying Mosquito NF30s with 616 Squadron at
RAF Finningley, on 30th June, with a ground crewman, Aircraftman 2nd Class
Edward Shaw, aged nineteen, in the second seat, they did some low flying. Flying in NT423, the aircraft's port engine overheated and failed due to a glycol
coolant leak. McCairns allowed the speed to fall below critical level, stalled, and
flicked over and crashed inverted into the ground. Both men were killed instantly. McCairns had a wife, Moira.

Distinguished Flying Cross (*London Gazette* 16th April 1943)
This officer has completed many sorties, most of them of a hazardous nature.
He is a courageous and determined pilot, who has set an example worthy of the
highest praise.

Bar to DFC (*London Gazette* 13th August 1943)
This officer has completed numerous sorties, displaying a high degree of skill
and determination throughout.

Second Bar to DFC (*London Gazette* 14th January 1944)
Since being awarded a Bar to his Distinguished Flying Cross, Flt Lt McCairns
has participated in a large number of successful operational missions. He is a
model of efficiency and his example of determination and devotion to duty has
won great praise.

Other Honours
Military Medal (awarded 14th August 1942)
For escaping from Stalag IX-C and returning to England via Spain. He was shot
down in Spitfire P8500 on 6th July 1941.

French Croix de Guerre.

DESMOND ANNERSTY PETER McMULLEN

From Godstone, Surrey, where he was born on 6 December 1917, he attended Cheltenham College between 1928-1931. In 1937 he decided to join the RAF and was granted a short-service commission on 31st May of that year. Once fully trained he was posted to No. 1 Air Armament School at RAF Manby in July 1938, and then to 54 Squadron in September, just in time to become operational as the war started.

Usually known as 'Des' or 'Mac', he and his fellow pilots in 54 had become quite a team, and among them were pilots such as Colin Gray (q.v.), Al Deere, George Gribble, Wonky Way, Johnnie Allen and Prof Leathart; all would do well, especially in the early months of the war which began at the time of Dunkirk.

Officially the Dunkirk fight began on 26th May 1940, but 54 Squadron had already had contact with enemy aircraft a few days earlier. On 24th May McMullen claimed one Me 109, while sharing another with two other pilots, but neither were confirmed. Two more unconfirmed victories were claimed the next day, Me 110s, but finally on the 26th, Mac had a Me 110 confirmed as destroyed and two days later he shared a Do 17 bomber.

Des McMullen pictured with his wife and mother in the background. (Roddy McMullen via Battle of Britain London Monument)

With the evacuation over, everyone waited for the Battle over Britain to begin. Mac opened his account during the battle on 4th July with one enemy aircraft damaged, while on the 24th he had one Me 109 confirmed and a second unconfirmed. 54 Squadron's intelligence officer must have been really strict! The month of August saw McMullen add three more victories to his name, plus several more as probably destroyed or damaged. A couple more as September began but then he was posted to 222 Squadron. During this month he shot down three more with even more damaged, and in October three more, with two others shared plus the inevitable damaged opponents. On 1st October he was awarded the DFC. One more kill on 8th November, but then he was posted again, when he became an instructor with No. 55 Operational Training Unit and in December took a similar job with 57 OTU.

He then became a flight commander with 151 Squadron, so moving from Spitfires to Hurricanes. But then the squadron was equipped with Defiant two-seat night-fighters, which carried a gunner with four Browning machine guns in a turret behind the pilot's cockpit. In the early weeks of 1941, with Britain's night defences poor, Hurricane pilots were needed to try and engage hostile night raiders, and Mac shot down three enemy bombers at night, plus a probable, for which he received a Bar to his DFC. Two of his gunners were Flt Lt Stan Fairweather, and a WW1 veteran with the DFC and DCM, Sid Carlin, who had

Plt Off Des McMullen when with 54 Squadron at the time of the Battle of Dunkirk. Seated in front is Flt Lt J. A. 'Prof' Leathart DSO.

lost a leg in the army earlier in WW1. Regrettably, 'Timber Toes' Carlin was killed during an air raid on the aerodrome on 9th May 1941. He was fifty years old, and had also flown a few trips on Wellingtons with 311 Czech Squadron as a rear gunner.

Back on Spitfire in the summer of 1941, Mac became a flight commander with 266 Squadron, where he remained until November. His score mounted during operations over France in the summer of 1941 and following a rest (as a flying instructor!), in March 1942 he was attached to 602 Squadron, and then to 124 Squadron, on 16th May 1942, and finally to 64 Squadron, all posts being supernumerary. Following a rest, and the award of a second Bar to his DFC, in July 1942 he took command of 65 Squadron until September, seeing action over the Dieppe Raid on 19 August. Posted out to North Africa he became wing leader of 324 Wing but almost immediately was posted to a staff job, and did not see any further front-line action. In August 1943 he went to 53 Operational Training Unit and the following month was posted to HQ 93 Group for fighter-liaison duties.

He remained in the RAF post-war but broke a leg badly playing rugby for the RAF on 23rd June, which resulted in him having one leg two inches shorter than the other. Once recovered, he became a liaison officer between the RAF and USAAF, based on Malta. During this tour the Suez crisis occurred, and he had his work cut out because the Americans did not support the British and French.

McMullen retired on 16th December 1957 as an acting wing commander. By this time he had married Stella and they had a son Roderick. He and his family lived in the village of Kirdford, Sussex in the 1960s. He died on 1st July 1985.

Distinguished Flying Cross (*London Gazette* 1st October 1940)

Since the commencement of hostilities this officer has been continuously engaged on operational flights, including the Dunkirk operations, the protection of shipping and intensive air fighting over this country. He has destroyed seven enemy aircraft and shared in the destruction of others. He has displayed high qualities of leadership and determination.

Bar to DFC (*London Gazette* 7th March 1941)

Recommendation: 'Flt Lt McMullen now has thirteen confirmed victories to his credit in addition to ten probables and six damaged. This splendid record has been achieved by this officer's courage, keenness and great devotion to duty, coupled with exceptional skill.

'His fighting spirit and exceptional keenness have done much to help build up a spirit in his squadron which is second to none. I strongly recommend that this officer's services be rewarded by the award of a Bar to his DFC.'

This recommendation was put forward by Wg Cdr Basil Embry, Commanding RAF Wittering, countersigned by AVM R. E. Saul, AOC 12 Group, Fighter Command and finally by AM W. Sholto Douglas, at HQ, Fighter Command.

Second Bar to DFC (*London Gazette* 12th December 1941)

This officer has participated in operational sorties over occupied France and Holland and has always evinced the keenest desire to engage the enemy. Since being awarded a Bar to the Distinguished Flying Cross, Flt Lt McMullen has destroyed fifteen hostile aircraft bringing his total to at least eighteen, three of which were gained at night.

ROBERT WENDELL McNAIR

Always known as 'Buck', he was born in Spring-field, in Annapolis County, Nova Scotia, Canada, on 15th May 1919, to Kenneth Frank and Hilda May McNair. He had an older brother Franklyn (Frank) and a younger sibling, Ken. His father had been gassed in WW1, and post-war he had worked on the Canadian Pacific Railway. Buck's early schooling was in a one-room schoolhouse in Lake Pleasant but when he was nine, the family moved to North Battleford, Saskatchewan and a year later moved again to Alberta. After another move to Ed-monton, Buck went to the Kenora Public School. In his spare time he worked on a farm and later got a job with Canadian Airways.

With his interest in aviation, he managed to meet a pilot from WW1, who took him for his first flight. From then on he was hooked. When war came he tried to join the RCAF, and after some difficulty at being released from Canadian Airways, finally got the nod, and was soon starting his flight training in mid-June 1940. He started training at the No. 1 FTS in Toronto, and later in Windsor, Ontario, the home of No. 7 EFTS. Once fully trained he received his 'wings' and a commission, and boarding the SS *California*, set sail for England in March 1941.

Arriving in Grangemouth on 12th May, he moved to No. 58 Operational Training Unit where he got his hands on a Spitfire, and with this stage complete he was posted to 411 Squadron RCAF at RAF Digby. Two Canadian-manned squadrons, 411 and 412, needed to complete a 'working-up' period, so it was not until September that 411 moved down to West Malling, in 11 Group. However, things did not start too well, for on the 11th, he and another pilot flew off in a Magister. When the Maggie landed, Buck was not in it. The official story was the he had fallen out, but in reality he had wanted to see what it was like to bale out, which he did successfully.

Buck's first combat success came on 27th September on a sweep over France, attacking and damaging a Me 109F. His first confirmed kill came on 13th October, another 109 plus a damaged on another sweep. However, his own Spitfire was badly hit from another 109, but when he baled out, he was pretty low, his 'chute only opening seconds before he hit the sea. In doing so he hurt his back, something that would cause him some later concern.

Sweeps, patrols and Ramrods continued into the winter, but in February 1942, volunteers were requested to go out to the Middle East. A number of pilots were keen to go, including Buck, and his request was finally approved, and he was off to Gibraltar. Within a few weeks, Buck and others were flying off HMS *Eagle*, headed for the island of Malta. When he arrived he was assigned to 249 Squadron. The new pilots had flown in the first Spitfires to operate on Malta.

Before the month was out, Buck had begun scoring, and had been credited with a Me 109F and a Ju 88A4 destroyed and three other enemy aircraft damaged. In April he claimed two more victories plus six more probably destroyed or damaged. Malta was often referred to as 'a fighter pilot's paradise' and it was certainly very different from what any of them had experienced flying from southern England. Everything was in short supply, including good food, and the island and its airfield were under almost daily bomb attacks. Nevertheless, Buck McNair thrived on the action, and in May and June he added three more confirmed victories to his score, that now reached eight. He was lucky to survive a bomb hit on the hotel used as a mess, the Point de Vue, in Rabat, on 21st March, and his luck held.

At the end of his time on Malta, he was ordered back to England, where he found himself back with 411 Squadron on 1st July 1942, as a flight commander. It took a while for him to get into the swing of scoring again but over Dieppe he managed to knock pieces off a couple of German aircraft. In September he left the squadron on medical grounds. He had had a debilitating time on Malta and his back problems after his Channel bale out hadn't improved. He was found medically unfit for operational flying and packed off to Canada, where he was sent on a money-raising bond tour. He was then posted to 133 Squadron near Vancouver, which flew Hurricanes. He was continually agitating to get back to the war. He finally made it and in April 1943 he was back in England, sent to 403 Squadron and was soon flying on operations.

In May he was given command of 416 Squadron but the following month he was moved again, this time to command 421 Squadron, which he led until October. In June and July Buck was scoring victories again, adding two Me 109s and two Fw 190s to his tally. However, on 27th July Buck's engine stopped over the Channel and caught fire. With no way of reaching the English coast, he was forced to bale out, which he did, but his face suffered some superficial burns, which affected his eyes. Rescued by ASR Walrus, he was sent off to hospital, and while he was treated for his facial burns, kept quiet about his eyesight in case it grounded him.

Once passed fit again he was flying once more adding four more confirmed victories by early October, plus a couple more damaged. On 15th October he was given command of 126 Fighter Wing operating from Biggin Hill, which he led until 12th April 1944. He was taken off operational flying, which annoyed him as everyone knew that the invasion of France was imminent, but he threw himself into staff work, at first with No. 17 Wing HQ, as wing commander ops and on 1st January 1945 was sent off to the Staff College. Already decorated with three DFCs he was awarded the DSO in April 1944. His victory score stood at sixteen destroyed, three probables and fifteen damaged.

While with 126 Wing, Buck had met Barbara Still, who worked at the American embassy in London. They married on Easter Sunday, 2nd April 1944 and were to have two sons, Keith and Bruce.

After the war Buck decided to continue serving in the RCAF holding a number of important positions not only in Canada, but also Germany and Japan. His final posting was with the Canadian High Commission in London, between 1968 and January 1971, when he retired. In 1947 the French government bestowed upon him the Croix de Guerre and made him a recipient of the Légion d'Honneur. These were not his last awards for in December 1953, serving in Canada with No. 1 ADCC, he was a crew member in a four-engine Canadiar North Star aeroplane of 426 Squadron, flying from Vancouver to Montreal. The North Star was basically a DC4 but with Merlin engines, and thirty-five minutes into the flight, in bad weather, one engine began to overheat and the pilot decided to return to Vancouver.

Coming in to land, with the aircraft beginning to ice-up, the engine finally stopped, and in getting down the nose wheel buckled and one wing hit the ground. The aircraft ended up inverted with passengers hanging from their seats. Most of the passengers scrambled clear just as the aircraft caught fire, and Buck was instrumental in pulling several people clear, despite being soaked in petrol. All fifty-two passengers, including women and children, were safely evacuated. For his efforts he received the Queen's Commendation for Brave Conduct.

In the mid-1960s it was discovered that Buck was suffering from a blood disorder that was eventually diagnosed as leukaemia. He died on 3rd January 1971, in London, and was buried in Brookwood Cemetery with full military honours and as the mourners stood by the graveside a lone RAF aeroplane flew low over them, waggling its wings. I wrote a biography of Buck McNair (*Buck McNair, Canadian Spitfire Ace,* Grub Street, 2001). My last words of this book read: 'Robert "Buck" McNair had lost his last fight, but one which he had fought and lost with dignity and with the same bravery and fortitude he had shown in wartime. Valhalla is full of such men.' Buck was inducted into the Canadian Hall of Fame on 8th June 1990.

Distinguished Flying Cross (*London Gazette* 11th May 1942)
This officer is a skilled and courageous pilot. He invariably presses home his attacks with the greatest determination irrespective of the odds. He has destroyed

at least five and damaged seven enemy aircraft; four of these he damaged in one combat.

Bar to DFC (*London Gazette* 30th July 1943)
This officer is a skilful and determined fighter, whose record of achievement and personal example are worthy of high praise.. Sqn Ldr McNair has destroyed ten hostile aircraft (five of them whilst serving in the Middle East) and damaged a number of others.

Second Bar to DFC (*London Gazette* 26th October 1943)
Sqn Ldr McNair is a tenacious and confident fighter, whose outstanding ability has proved an inspiration to the squadron he commands. He has completed a large number of sorties and has destroyed fifteen and damaged many other enemy aircraft. His keenness has been outstanding.

Other Honours
Distinguished Service Order (*London Gazette* 14th April 1944)
Since being awarded a second Bar to his Distinguished Flying Cross, Wg Cdr McNair has completed many further operational sorties and destroyed another enemy aircraft, bringing his total victories to at least sixteen enemy aircraft destroyed and many others damaged. As his wing's officer commanding, he has been responsible for supervising intensive training in tactics. The results achieved have been most satisfactory. The wing under his leadership, destroyed at least thirteen enemy aircraft. Throughout, Wg Cdr McNair has set a magnificent example by his fine fighting spirit, courage and devotion to duty both in the air and on the ground. He has inspired his pilots with confidence and enthusiasm.

Croix de Guerre and Légion d'Honneur (*Canadian Gazette* 20th September 1947)

Queen's Commendation for Brave Conduct (*Canadian Gazette* 7th August 1954)
Wg Cdr McNair was flying as a crew member in one of the crew rest positions of North Star 17503 when it crashed at Vancouver, British Columbia, on 30th December 1953. The aircraft ended its crash landing run in an inverted position and as a result, all crew and passengers found themselves suspended in mid-air in an upside-down position. Self-preservation was uppermost in the minds of practically everyone because of the imminent danger of fire or explosion but Wg Cdr McNair, cognisant of the large number of passengers being carried and the state of turmoil that must be existing, threw caution to the winds, remained in the aircraft and fought his way through to the passenger compartments.

Here, he set to work, restored calm and through prodigious effort assisted all passengers in evacuating the aircraft as quickly as possible. Still not content, Wg Cdr McNair remained in the aircraft and personally searched through the debris on the off-chance that someone might have been overlooked. Only then did he abandon the aircraft.

It is to be remembered that this officer was soaked in gasoline at the time of this incident from an overturned Herman Nelson heater, a condition which would immediately bring to mind the fact that he had been badly burned by fire in his aircraft during the war and therefore should have been acutely aware of his precarious position under the present set of circumstances. The fact that the aircraft did not explode or did not take fire should not be allowed to detract in any way from the magnitude of Wg Cdr McNair's deeds, for it was only by an act of God that neither calamity occurred.

CHARLES MICHAEL MILLER

Miller was born at the Curragh, County Kildare in Ireland on 18th June 1919. His father was in the Indian army. He attended Cambridge University and was in the university air squadron from October 1937 to September 1939, when he was called for service. Sent to RAF Cranwell where he remained until April 1940, in June of that year he was posted to the Middle East where he joined 9 Squadron, flying Vickers Wellington bombers. With this squadron he won the DFC.

Later he was assigned to 148 Squadron, also equipped with Wellingtons, where his services brought him a Bar to his DFC. Squadron operations covered a wide variety of targets, not only along the North African coast, but also flying from Malta, it attacked enemy bases in both Sicily and Italy. On 20th December 1940, he and his crew attacked the airfield at Castel Benito. His air gunners strafed aircraft as they flew low over the base, and two Italian S-79 aircraft were seen to blow up and left on fire. At the end of his tour, Miller became the personal assistant to the air officer commanding in the Mediterranean.

In August 1941 he returned to England, where he flew with 24 Squadron of Air Transport Command until July 1942. His next move was in complete contrast to his earlier postings, for he went to No. 54 Operational Training Unit to learn all about night-fighting, and, promoted to squadron leader, he became a flight commander with 29 Squadron, operating night-fighter Beaufighter IFs in August.

His next move was to 530 Squadron with Havocs but he soon returned to 29 in January 1943. He scored two victories on the night of 26th/27th February, downing a pair of Do217 bombers. His radar operator on this night was Flt Lt J. Crowther. He was promoted to wing commander, taking command of No. 51 Operational Training Unit at Turnwood Farm, and received a second Bar to his DFC in July. In August he went to No. 63 OTU at RAF Honiley where he commanded until February 1944. He was then sent to command 85 (Night-Fighter) Squadron. With 85 he claimed two further night kills, a Ju 88 in April and a Me 110 in June, with radar operators Capt L Lovestad (Norwegian) and Fg Off R. O. Symon. He made his last operational flight on 27th September and in November received the DSO.

Miller had become ill, suffering with diabetes, which forced him to leave 85 Squadron in October and eventually he was invalided out of the service on 24th February 1945. After the war he joined the De La Rue Company, the printers of playing cards and later he became a sugar broker with Czarnikov Ltd, where he rose to deputy chairman. He died in April 1982 from cancer of the liver

Distinguished Flying Cross (*London Gazette* 17th January 1941)

Fg Off Miller has made twenty-six operational flights, on nineteen of which he has been captain of aircraft. He has invariably displayed the greatest determination and judgement in finding and attacking his target, frequently in very adverse weather conditions. On those occasions on which it has been impossible to find the primary target, he has shown marked persistence and discrimination in the selection of the last resort target. The work done by Fg Off Miller has been particularly valuable because on several occasions the bombing of the crew which he leads, started fires which were of the greatest assistance to other crews in locating the targets. His chief successes were at Hanau on 28th September, Bremen on 8th October, Berlin on 14th October and Hamburg on 21st October when lasting fires were started by his attacks. He is the squadron photographic officer and this has necessitated a second run over the targets, frequently in the face of strong enemy ground defences. He secured a valuable night photograph of shipping in Hamburg on 11th October and his keenness and perseverance in the art of night photography have done much to advance this science and so provide proof of the accuracy of the various bomber sorties.

Bar to DFC (*London Gazette* 11th February 1941)

This officer was pilot of an aircraft detailed to attack an enemy aerodrome. He carried out four accurate attacks despite intense opposition from light and heavy anti-aircraft guns. On returning to his base, Fg Off Miller offered to re-arm his aircraft and make another flight to the same target, although he knew that one aircraft had already been shot down by anti-aircraft guns. He again obtained good results, in spite of his seeing another aircraft shot down. He had continually shown keenness, determination and courage of the highest order.

Second Bar to the DFC (*London Gazette* 27th July 1943)

Since Wg Cdr Miller took over command of the squadron six enemy aircraft have been destroyed and two damaged. Wg Cdr Miller completed a large number of night operational patrols during this period, many of them in adverse weather, and personally destroyed two enemy aircraft. He received the DFC in January 1941, and was awarded a Bar in February 1941.

The recommendation for this second Bar reads:

'Wg Cdr C. M. Miller DFC and Bar, joined 9 Squadron and carried out his first bombing trip on 21st June 1940 by bombing Göttingen aerodrome. Altogether this officer carried out forty bombing trips in Wellingtons which included, Berlin, Hamm, Hamburg and Kiel and whilst a member of 148 Squadron in Malta bombed Tripoli and Palermo among other targets.

'On 1st September 1941, Wg Cdr Miller returned to this country and joined 24 Squadron. During his tour with this squadron this officer carried out 479 hours flying and carried important personages which included the Secretary of State for Air, Queen Wilhelmina of Holland, King Peter of Jugoslavia, Lord Louis Mountbatten, General Sikorski, General Paget, and Viscount and Lady Halifax. Some of this officer's trips included Iceland and Gibraltar.

'In September 1942, Wg Cdr Miller joined 29 Squadron in supernumerary capacity and assumed command of the squadron on 21st January 1943. Since that date this officer has carried out sixty night operation patrols, many of them in adverse weather conditions and has destroyed two Dornier 217s by carrying out a special technique on German mine-layers, which the squadron have now perfected and which has produced further results. Whilst this officer has been in command of 29 Squadron he has shown great dash and keenness and has been an inspiration to all who served under him. Many of his patrols have been carried out under extreme adverse weather conditions, very often against the advice of his flight commanders, but because of his keenness to engage the enemy nothing has deterred this officer from attempting to destroy the enemy wherever he may be.'

This recommendation was made by the station commander of RAF West Malling, Wg Cdr Peter Townsend DSO DFC, on 8th June 1943, and countersigned by Gp Captn D. G. Morris DFC, station commander of RAF North Weald on 13th June.

Distinguished Service Order (*London Gazette* 17th November 1944)
During a long and varied operational career, this officer has consistently displayed exceptional leadership and skill in both offensive and defensive operations. Recently, in offensive operations, the squadron has destroyed at least thirteen enemy aircraft and damaged others without loss to themselves. The successes achieved are mainly due to this officer's careful planning and personal example.

ARTHUR ALEXANDER O'LEARY

Born in Hastings, Sussex, on 4th January 1921, he received his education at St. Josephs, Eastbourne, and, upon moving to Mitcham, Surrey, the Central School in Carshalton, Surrey. In 1938 he enlisted in the Anti-Aircraft Seachlight Company, Territorial Army, at Hackbridge, South London. Mobilised in September 1938, he decided to join the RAF, applied on his eighteenth birthday and when war was declared he began training as an air gunner, with 217 Squadron, a general reconnaissance unit based at St. Eval, in Cornwall.

He was then sent to France to join the Advanced Air Striking Force as a ground-radio operator, and following the retreat from France, he volunteered for aircrew duties, completing a short airborne interception radar course at Yatesbury, before being sent to 604 Squadron in July 1940. Flying as a radar operator on night-fighter missions during the winter of 1940-41, on 20th December 1940, his Beaufighter was hit by return fire from a German bomber, which wounded O'Leary in the leg and forced him and his pilot to bale out.

He almost had to repeat this episode on the night of 1st May 1942. Sent up after enemy raiders, they closed in on one north of Swindon, but return fire slammed into their aircraft, again wounding O'Leary, in five places. However, his pilot, Pilot Officer I. K. S. Joll, with help from O'Leary, managed to get their aircraft safely back to base. With their radio and intercom out of action, the wounded O'Leary crawled forward and homed the Beaufighter back to Middle Wallop on the AI beacon, using the emergency intercom code on the aircraft's hooter. He was awarded the DFM.

After a period in hospital, O'Leary returned to operational flying and in October 1941 was posted to 89 Squadron, which was forming, where he teamed up with Plt Off N. E. Reeves. This squadron was headed for the Middle East, and on 1st December it left Portreath and headed for Egypt, via Gibraltar and Malta. However, on reaching Malta, six crews were retained to perform night-fighting duties. He and Nevil Reeves achieved several successes between July and early September, five Ju 88s and an Italian Cant Z1007. The last 88, on 6th September occurred during a daylight escort to Beaufort torpedo bombers engaged on a shipping strike. When they finally got to Egypt, both men were awarded the DFC, O'Leary having risen to the rank of warrant officer. They had also flown intruder missions over Sicily.

In December, they were sent as part of a forward detachment to Benina air-field, where they flew in the defence of Tripoli. Here they shot down three fur-ther enemy aircraft and damaged another to received Bars to their DFCs. During his activities, O'Leary had been involved in fourteen victories.

They returned to England in May 1943 and instructed at No. 62 Operation-al Training Unit before returning to operations with 239 Squadron, flying in support of Bomber Command over Germany, intercepting German night-fighter aircraft. Now flying Mosquito aircraft they managed to destroy a Do217 and four Me 110s. O'Leary had been commissioned in April 1944. Reeves received the DSO while O'Leary was given a second Bar to his DFC.

At the end of their tour, O'Leary was posted to ground control approach de-velopment unit on 29th November 1944 and left the RAF as a flying officer in 1946. He later emigrated to New Zealand, and worked as a housing officer at Massey University in Palmerston North. He died on 21st April 1987.

Distinguished Flying Medal (*London Gazette* 30th May 1941)
On the night of 1st May, 1941, Sgt O'Leary was the radio operator in a Beau-fighter which was being flown by Fg Off Joll. When closing in, the enemy aircraft fired a burst from its tower gun wounding Sgt O'Leary in five places. The pilot continued to attack and again opened fire, damaging the enemy air-craft. Fire from the enemy aircraft had put the R/T and intercommunication out of action. The pilot was uncertain of his position and needed homing aids to bring him back to base. Sgt O'Leary, though so badly wounded in one leg that on admission to hospital he was posted on the dangerously ill list, made his way forward and told the pilot that he would home the aircraft back to Middle Wal-lop on the AI beacon, using the emergency communication code on the aircraft hooter. This was successfully accomplished and Fg Off Joll landed his aircraft at Middle Wallop. Sgt O'Leary displayed great courage and fortitude and not only gave his pilot a successful interception but was directly instrumental in bringing the aircraft safely back to base. On a previous operational flight, Sgt O'Leary's pilot was wounded in the head and he himself wounded in the leg and on this occasion he had to abandon aircraft by parachute.

Distinguished Flying Cross (*London Gazette* 16th February 1943)
During night-flying operations this observer has taken part in the destruction of seven enemy aircraft. He has always set a splendid example of skill, courage and devotion to duty.

Bar to DFC (*London Gazette* 14th May 1943)

Warrant Officer O'Leary is an observer of exceptional merit. He has invariably displayed great courage and keenness and has taken part in the destruction of fourteen enemy aircraft at night.

Second Bar to DFC (*London Gazette* 14th November 1944)

This officer has completed many operational flights and has participated in the destruction of four enemy aircraft. His exceptional ability as a navigator, determination and cheerful confidence in times of stress set an excellent example to all.

The recommendation for this award by the AOC of No. 100 Group, was as follows:

> 'A gallant officer and a skilful and daring aircrew. As navigator/radio since the award of his last decoration, he has completed a further forty-three sorties, of which the last twenty-five were in his present squadron on Bomber Support night-fighter duties. During these latter sorties he enabled his pilot to destroy four enemy night-fighters. I recommend him for the award of a second Bar to his Distinguished Flying Cross.'

NEVIL EVERARD REEVES, O'Leary's pilot, came from Naunton, Upton-on-Severn, Worcestershire, born in 1920. After attending Hanley Castle Grammar School he enlisted into the RAFVR in early 1939 and commissioned in December 1941. He and O'Leary were sent out to Malta in June 1942 and by September had shot down six enemy aircraft. In December they were sent to Benina to defend Tripoli. On January 1943 the pair were back in England, Reeves serving as a flight commander with 239 Squadron, in 100 Group, the team accounting for a further four enemy night-fighters. In late 1944 Reeves joined BSDU and in 1945 commanded 169 Squadron. Sqn Ldr Reeves was killed in a flying accident, flying a Meteor F4 (VW782) at the Central Flying Establishment, on 27th January 1949. He had been awarded the DSO, DFC and Bar.

ROBERT WARDLAW OXSPRING

I first came into contact with Gp Capt Oxspring in 1967, when we corresponded about his father, Maj Robert Oxspring MC and Bar, a WW1 ace. However, I only met him once, and that was in the offices of William Kimber & Co in 1984, who were one of my publishers in those days. They had just released the group captain's own book about his life, *Spitfire Command*, and so it was a chance meeting, but we had a good old chat, and I got a signed copy of his book.

Bobby, as he was always known, was born in Sheffield on 22nd May 1919, living within the shadow of Sheffield Wednesday's football stadium. Having an early desire to become a pilot, his final education was received at the De La Salle College, fortunately with sufficient qualifications to apply. He was accepted for a short-service commission although he had to wait six months to be called. Once he began training, he soloed and then went to No. 4 E&RFTS, followed by a stint at No. 2 FTS, Brize Norton. Once fully qualified, Bobby was posted to 66 Squadron based at RAF Duxford, one of the first two squadrons to be equipped with Spitfires. He had his first flight in a Spitfire on 2nd February 1939. His father had been a flight commander with 66 in the Great War.

Like all RAF squadrons there followed a period of intense training, as the likelihood of war seemed inevitable. Once war did come, training intensified but then, in April 1940, with Gladiators and Hurricanes being sent to Norway, experienced pilots needed to be chosen from several RAF squadrons to reinforce them. Bobby was the one selected from 66 Squadron. However, he was one of four pilots left behind when the others went, and before they could get away too, the Norwegian campaign had come to a swift end. The Battle of France began on 10th May that eventually ended with the evacuation from Dunkirk only a couple of weeks later. Bobby rejoined 66 on 19th May, at Manston and celebrated his twenty-first birthday on the 22nd.

He got in a couple of patrols over the beaches but then it was all over and 66 returned to Duxford. The squadron then moved to Coltishall as the battle began further south, but Bobby had his first action on 29th July off Lowestoft. Leading Blue Section, control vectored them on to a He 111 flying north at 15,000 feet, just east of a convoy 66 Squadron were on their way to protect. He and his two wingmen attacked and the bomber finally crashed into the sea. No. 66 remained

out of the main battle area till they were needed to reinforce 11 Group, moving
down to Kenley. Over the next few weeks, Bobby was in almost daily action
against the hordes of enemy aircraft, but he was successful. By the middle of
October, he had destroyed eight German aircraft and damaged another four, and
was awarded the DFC. On 25th October, he was shot down by a Me 109, having
to take to his parachute, and suffering slight wounds.

Bobby featured in the wartime publication *Ten Fighter Boys* (1942) with one
chapter covering each of ten pilots who flew with 66 Squadron. His chapter is
under the title of 'Bob'.

He remained with the squadron until April 1941 at which time he was posted
to No. 59 Operational Training Unit as an instructor. In September he returned
to operations going briefly to 616 Squadron, then to 41 as a flight commander.
In January 1942 he received a posting to 91 Squadron as commanding officer,
but in July took command of 72 Squadron. He damaged a Fw 190 on 26th July
but then his squadron was ordered to the Middle East to take part in the Tunisian campaign. He remained as CO until April 1943, being heavily involved in
air combats over and around the area, engaging German and Italian aircraft. He
brought his score to fourteen, with a further thirteen damaged, receiving a Bar to
his DFC in September 1942. He was posted to HQ, 242 Group having ended his
tour and receiving a second Bar to his DFC in February 1943.

He returned to England late in 1943, going to HQ Fighter Command, working
in the Tactics and Training Branch until March 1944 when he commenced his
third tour of operations as leader of No. 24 Wing. On 1st January 1944 he was
given the Dutch Airman's Cross. His wing was involved in engaging V-1 rocket
bombs in June and July 1944, Bobby himself accounting for four of them flying
a Spitfire XIV. In September he led 141 Wing, then the Detling Wing, on long-
range escorts to RAF bombers heading into Germany. In May 1945 he was sent
to the Central Flying Establishment before attending the Command and General
Staff Course at Fort Leavenworth, Texas. When he returned to the UK he converted to jets and took command of 54 Squadron in May 1948, the squadron in
which his father had also served in WW1.

He led six of his squadron's Vampires as an aerobatic team across the Atlantic, the first jet crossing, and began a goodwill tour of Canada and the USA,
for which he received the Air Force Cross in the New Year Honours List of 1st
January 1949. By this time he had left 54 Squadron, commanded 73 Squadron
from January to November 1949, then served in the Middle East. He attended
the Flying College at RAF Manby in 1951. In 1953 he led a Meteor Wing in the
Queen's Coronation Review flypast. From 1955 to 1958 he was with the US
Air Defence Command before going to the Air Ministry until 1960, followed

by a post at the new Ministry of Defence between 1963-65 as a group captain. In 1965 he was given command of RAF Gatow, in Berlin, Germany, before retiring on 23rd February 1968.

He and his wife Joy (whom he married on 28th October 1942) retired to Lincolnshire, where he died on 8th August 1989. He was buried in Cranwell Parish Church Cemetery.

Distinguished Flying Cross (*London Gazette* 8th November 1940)

One day in September, 1940, Flight Lieutenant Oxspring was engaged on an offensive patrol with his squadron. Whilst acting as rear guard, he sighted and engaged several Messerschmitt 109s 3,000 feet above. After driving them off, he led his section in an attack against a large formation of enemy bombers and succeeded in destroying a Dornier 17 at short range and also damaging two Heinkel 111s. He has at all times led his section with skill and determination, and has destroyed six enemy aircraft.

Bar to DFC (*London Gazette* 18th September 1942)

This squadron commander has rendered much valuable service. His skill, whether in attacks on the enemy's ground targets and shipping or in air combat, has been of a high order. He has destroyed at least seven enemy aircraft.

Second Bar to DFC (*London Gazette* 16th February 1943)

During initial operations from forward airfields in North Africa, Sqn Ldr Oxspring led his formation on many sorties. He destroyed one enemy aircraft, bringing his total victories to eight. His outstanding devotion to duty and fine fighting qualities have been worthy of high praise.

Other Honours

Dutch Airman's Cross (Vliegerkruis) (*London Gazette* 10th January 1946)
Officially credited with 13.33 victories in the air and four V-1 missiles destroyed. Flew with 66, 616, 72, 222 and 41 Squadrons RAF.

Air Force Cross (*London Gazette* 1st January 1949)

HERBERT VICTOR PETERSON

From Calgary, Alberta, Canada, Peterson was born in 1920 and upon leaving school was employed as a clerk. He joined the RCAF in May 1940, attending No. 1 ITS from 22nd July to 14th September of that year. From this course he was placed fifth out of 193 students. Moving to 9 EFTS in October he soon soloed on a Finch II machine and was assessed as average, but had good reports from all his instructors. Over the winter of 1940-41 he attended No. 15 SFTS with Avro Anson aeroplanes, gained his 'wings' and was posted to the UK.

His first squadron was at RAF Leeming, No. 10, equipped with Armstrong Whitworth Whitley twin-engine bombers, arriving on 14th July 1941, as a warrant officer. He began his tour of bomber operations, and in December the squadron changed over to Handley Page Halifax four-engine night-bombers. However, on this new type he did not get off to a good start. On 14th December, having just three hours, five minutes on type, as he was preparing to take off in R9376 from the Skipton satellite, he applied full power to all four engines with brakes on, intending to build up a running start. The bomber had been delivered without ammunition and in consequence was slightly nose heavy. As he pushed the stick forward in order to bring up the tail, the Halifax went onto its nose, causing some damage. He was suspended from flying for two weeks.

Nevertheless he was not put off and in April 1942, during two attacks on the German naval base at Trondheim, Norway, where *Tirpitz* was based, his bomber was badly hit by flak on the second night, 27th, but Peterson got his aircraft back to England, and completed a successful emergency landing. He had bombed from 250-300 feet and some of the aircraft's damage included an eighteen-inch square hole in the tail, leads to petrol cock shot away and one engine knocked out. For this he received the DFC. Peterson went on to complete a tour of operations, including a very dicey trip to Essen on 5th/6th June 1942 – his twenty-sixth operation. His aircraft was under intense AA fire which knocked out one engine and a damaged windscreen caused injury to his left eye through a piece of Perspex. Continuing on he regained the English coast despite more heavy flak over the Dutch coast, and landed at an emergency airfield. For this he received a Bar to his DFC.

On nearing the end of his tour, Peterson and 10 Squadron were sent on detachment to the Middle East in July, based at Aqir, Palestine. It was listed as 10/227 Squadron that by September became 462 Squadron. From Aqir they

Members of 10 Squadron in May 1942. From left to right: Sgt C. J. Hayes, WO1 H. Peterson, Flt Sgt B. H. J. Davor (AG) and Flt Sgt J. G. Le Claire (AG).

flew raids on Tobruk in their Halifaxes. Tour expired he returned to England in November where he became an instructor at No. 1659 Conversion Unit at RAF Topcliffe. He remained here until he was repatriated to Canada in June 1944.

Following this rest period Peterson returned to England in September 1944, where he was posted to 429 (Bison) Squadron RCAF, flying Halifax IIIs from RAF Leeming, Yorkshire. By the end of the war he had flown a further twenty trips, between 21st November 1944 and 22nd April 1945. The following month he was recommended for a second Bar to his DFC. His CO, Wg Cdr E. H. Evans wrote of him on 14 May 1945: "Has completed a second tour as flight commander, ran a very efficient flight and when given responsibility does a very good job. His skill and ability in flying duties was held in high esteem by all squadron personnel." At the start of 1946, he was with 426 Squadron, a long-range troop transport unit.

Peterson remained in the RCAF after the war and by 1948 was with the Northwest Air Command HQ, at Edmonton, then went to the Staff College in Toronto, that September. In June 1949, posted to K Flight, at Trenton and in 1951, still at Trenton, he was OC Training Command Communication and Rescue Flight. February 1952 found him at No. 1 Air Navigation School, Summerside, and in 1953 he was on training duties as OC Air Training Wing at Canadian Joint Air Training Centre, Rivers. In 1955 he was at Chatham. Posted to 401 Squadron at Montreal in May 1959, and in 1960 he served at No. 4 Operational Training Unit, at Trenton, where he also attended the Otter Conversion Course, No. 102 K Flight in early 1961. The following year he was at Air Force HQ for attachment to the Congo with United Nations forces. Several times he was recommended for promotion to wing commander, but never attained this rank.

Posted to Air Defence Command at St. Hubert in December 1963 he remained here until he retired from the RCAF on 24th May 1967. Herbert Peterson died in Boucherville, Quebec, 9th August 1983.

Distinguished Flying Cross (*London Gazette* 29th May 1942)
WO Peterson has completed many operational sorties of which thirteen have been as captain of aircraft. One night in April 1942 he was detailed to attack the German naval base at Trondheim. On arrival over the target, in spite of the intense barrage of anti-aircraft fire which he encountered, he dived to very low altitude and pressed home his attack. On the following night he carried out another low-level attack on the same target. His aircraft sustained severe damage and one engine was put out of action. With great skill and judgement, Warrant Officer Peterson succeeded in flying his aircraft to an emergency landing ground where he made a safe landing.

Bar to DFC (*London Gazette* 30th June 1942)
One night in June 1942, WO Peterson was the captain of a Halifax aircraft detailed to attack Essen. Whilst over the target the aircraft was held by strong searchlight cones and subject to intense anti-aircraft fire. The port engine was hit and ceased to function, the windscreen was also damaged and a piece of Perspex entered WO Peterson's left eye. Nevertheless he continued to take evasive action and eventually set off on the return journey. Whilst over Holland, flying at 11,000 feet, he was attacked by an enemy fighter. His rear gunner delivered a short burst which caused the enemy aircraft to burst into flames and dive away out of control. When crossing the Dutch coast the aircraft was again subjected to anti-aircraft fire and the starboard engine was put out of action. Despite WO Paterson's injuries and the severe damage sustained by the aircraft he succeeded in flying back to this country and landing at an aerodrome with which he was unfamiliar. WO Peterson displayed fine courage and determination throughout.

Second Bar to DFC (*London Gazette* 26th October 1945)
This officer has served in both the African and European theatres of war. Since the award of the Distinguished Flying Cross he has attacked many of the most heavily defended targets in Germany. On several occasions his skill and fortitude were mainly responsible for the safe return of his aircraft and crew. Sqn Ldr Peterson is a flight commander of outstanding ability whose fine leadership and organization have been reflected in the high standard of operational efficiency maintained by his flight.

NOEL THOMAS QUINN

Painting by William Pidgeon, 1968
(RAAF)

The son of Matthew Joseph and Mary Frances (née Galvin) Quinn, of New South Wales, Australia, Noel was born in Cessnook, on 16th March 1916. Educated at De La Salle College, and at Hawkesbury Agricultural College, Richmond. In 1934, his goal was to go into farming, for which he achieved the diploma of agriculture. He began by managing his father's sheep farm near Muswellbrook, but with the coming of war, he enlisted as an RAAF cadet on 4th September 1939.

Once trained as a pilot the Japanese war had started and Quinn found himself posted to 2 Squadron, and was in action during the withdrawal from the Netherlands East Indies. In February 1942 he returned to Australia for test pilot duties. In July he was sent to Richmond, NSW. In August, flying a Hudson off Moruya, he helped save a trawler that had come under attack from a Japanese submarine. That same month he was posted to 14 Squadron in Western Australia. On 6th February 1943, he married Ann Violet Cameron Campbell, in Melbourne.

In April 1943 he was with 8 Squadron flying Bristol Beauforts, but also flew with 622 and 6 Squadrons before taking command of 8 Squadron on 4th December 1943. They were based on Goodenough Island, off the New Guinea coast in September and by November he had flown thirty-one operations and eight strikes. During several torpedo attacks he had damaged a Japanese cruiser on one occasion, for which he received the DFC.

His next command was as CO of 14 Squadron in November 1943. On 4th December during an attack on the Japanese base at Rabaul, Quinn led six Beauforts. Whilst attacking a ship in the harbour his aircraft either hit a mast or a cable and crashed into the sea. He and one of his crew, Plt Off R. B. O'Loghlen, survived and were picked up by the Japanese. Flt Sgts I. L. Mainland and D. McDonald were lost. While a prisoner, Quinn was often flogged by his captors but he survived, but O'Loghlen was later drowned when a ship that was taking him to a prisoner-of-war camp was sunk. Later he was flown to Japan for further questioning. One of his pilots later wrote of this raid:

'I was flying on the port side of Sqn Ldr Quinn. We searched the Duke of York Island area and then came down the coast from Tawui Point to Praed Point. We then turned into Blanche Bay (Rabaul Harbour) on a course of 270°. At 1938 hours I sighted a ship of 6,000 to 7,000 tons and I turned to starboard and attacked. I dropped [the torpedo] at approximately 1,000 yards, dead abeam and turned away to port. My gunner reported an explosion approximately thirty seconds later. I looked and saw a large fire burning on the ship – smoke and flames being very clearly seen. From that point I had to concentrate on flying my aircraft and did not see the ship again.'

Surviving his captivity he remained in the RAAF and held various posts. During 1950-52 he attended the RAF Flying College at RAF Manby in the UK, having been promoted to wing commander in March 1950. In 1952-53 he served during the crisis in Malaya, taking command of 1 Squadron RAAF, which were equipped with Avro Lincolns. For his command and part in operations against the communist insurgents, he received a second Bar to his DFC.

He returned to Australia in August 1953 and became CO of the School of Land/Air Warfare, at Williamtown, NSW, and in 1948 was promoted to group captain. He then became an honorary ADC to the governor general until 1961, followed by the appointment as air attaché between 1963 and 1965 at the Australian embassy in Jakarta. Once more he returned to his native Australia,

Noel Quinn (fourth from left in the front row) pictured with members of 8 GR course at Laverton, August 1940. (RAAF via Andrew Thomas)

serving in air and defence posts until his retirement on 16th February 1967, with the honorary rank of air commodore.

He settled in Brisbane with his wife and family, of which there was one son and one daughter. Noel Quinn died of cancer on St. Lucia on 13th October 1985.

Distinguished Flying Cross (*London Gazette* 14th December 1943)
In recognition of gallantry displayed in flying operations against the enemy in the South-West Pacific.

Bar to DFC (*London Gazette* 25th June 1946)

> **Recommendation:** 'On 4th December, 1943, Sqn Ldr Quinn, commanding officer of 8 Squadron, was detailed to lead a flight of six Beaufort aircraft in a torpedo attack against a Japanese convoy expected to arrive in the vicinity of the Duke of York Islands at last light. Information had also been received that a 12,000-ton merchant vessel carrying bombs and ammunition would arrive at Rabaul approximately one hour ahead of the convoy.
>
> 'On arrival at the target area where visibility was very poor, the convoy could not be located, and he directed the flight to break formation and act independently.
>
> 'Sqn Ldr Quinn proceeded into the inner harbour flying very low and, on sighting the stern of a large merchant vessel, he made a slight climbing turn and released the torpedo. At the same time, his aircraft met some obstruction, later discovered to be a cable, and crashed into the water. The vessel exploded and sank almost immediately, and Sqn Ldr Quinn, with one member of his crew who had been thrown clear of the wreckage, was picked up and taken prisoner by the crew of a Japanese launch which was collecting survivors.
>
> 'Sqn Ldr Quinn displayed exceptional skill and courage in making this dangerous and daring attack which succeeded in sinking the primary target.'

This recommendation is dated 12th October 1945, once Noel Quinn had returned safely from captivity and the story could be told.

Second Bar to DFC (*London Gazette* 22nd June 1954)
In recognition of gallant and distinguished service in Malaya.

MACK DONALD SEALE

Seale was born on 11th December 1920, in Murwillumbah, New South Wales, Australia. After leaving school he worked for the Bank of New South Wales in their Gundagai branch. He was keen to join the RAAF but his bank manager thought he should remain with the bank. However, in 1942, when a recruiting train came through Gundagai, he went aboard and enlisted during his lunch hour. Although he dreamed of being a pilot, he was re-mustered as a trainee navigator, and completed his training in Winnipeg, Canada. Shipped to the UK aboard the *Queen Elizabeth*, he finished his work on Wellingtons and finally converted to Lancasters. With Bomber Command in England, his first squadron was No. 460, RAAF, flying Avro Lancasters, operating from RAF Binbrook, Lincolnshire. He completed a tour of thirty operations and was awarded the DFC.

His pilot on this tour was Plt Off Henry T. Scott and raiding Hagen on 1st October 1943, Scott was temporarily blinded by flak over the target. A shell had burst right in front of the bomber, the windscreen being shattered by fragments of shrapnel. Perspex splinters showered into the cockpit and one piece lodged into Scott's eye. Nevertheless he completed the bomb run and Scott, regaining his sight, got them home. Scott received the DFC for this effort.

Following a rest and instructional period he returned to 460 and completed another tour, being only required to fly twenty operations. For this tour his pilot was Flt Lt John H. C. Clark DFC. Seale was awarded a Bar to his DFC, before being sent to No. 357 (Special Duties) Squadron, north of Kolkata, India. Here he flew Consolidated Liberator VIs in Burma, where the task was to drop supplies to British and Gurkha troops behind the Japanese lines. Completing a further twenty operational sorties he was awarded a second Bar to his DFC just after the war.

He left the RAAF in April 1946 and returned to Australia. Married to Lee, they had a daughter. One of Seale's hobbies was photography. In 2015 he was interviewed for an article in the Sunshine Coast's *Profile* magazine for Remembrance Day. As he recorded: 'One tour of operations was thirty trips and that was the first tour. If you were silly enough to do [volunteer] a second tour that was twenty, if you got through fifty you could uncross your fingers.'

Distinguished Flying Cross (*London Gazette* 10th December 1943)

Bar to DFC (*London Gazette* 8th December 1944)
Now on his second tour of operations, Fg Off Seale has flown on many more operational sorties since the award of the DFC. He has attacked some of the enemy's most heavily defended targets in Germany In the face of intense enemy opposition, this officer has accomplished his tasks with determination, skill and courage. The excellent results obtained are a testimony to his outstanding ability.

Second Bar to DFC (*London Gazette* 5th March 1946)
This officer has completed a large number of operational flying hours and has participated in three tours of operational duty. As squadron navigation officer he has worked with great efficiency and enthusiasm. Flt Lt Seale has always reached his target, even in the most adverse weather. He completed three long-range sorties to Malaya, dropping stores and personnel by parachute, in the Singapore area. Throughout, Flt Lt Searle has set a magnificent example of determination and devotion to duty.

His address was given as 39 Norfolk Street, Killara, NSW, at the time the governor of New South Wales, Lieutenant-General Sir John Northcott, presented him with his second Bar at Government House, Sydney, on 26th February 1947.

JOHN BEAN SHEPHERD

From Edinburgh, the son of William and Rosetta Shepherd, Northfield Farm Road, he was born on 20th July 1919. In November 1937 he joined the Royal Auxiliary Air Force, serving with 603 Squadron until 1939, as an aircraft hand. When the RAux-AF introduced a scheme to train its own NCOs as aircrew, he re-mustered as an airman under training pilot with the rank of LAC, and posted to No. 11 E&RFTS, Perth. Called up on 24th August 1939, on the eve of war, he completed his training and emerged as a sergeant pilot. He was posted to 234 Squadron at RAF Middle Wallop on 13th September 1940.

He was commissioned on 21st August 1941 and during that year managed to shoot down a couple of enemy 109 fighters and damage another plus two Ju 88s. In early 1942 he was posted to 118 Squadron, and saw action over the Dieppe show in August, shared a Do217 bomber, and received the DFC the following month.

He was promoted to flight commander in March 1943, added two more 109s to his tally and at the end of his fighter tour received a Bar to his DFC in August and was sent on rest. In June 1944 Shepherd went to 610 Squadron, flying Spitfire XIVs and saw action against the V1 flying bomb menace, shooting down seven of these buzzbombs, between 20th June and 4th August. Following the squadron's visit to an armament practice camp at Warmwell in February 1945 he was given temporary command of the squadron, but 610 was soon to be disbanded. He therefore was sent to 41 Squadron at Eindhoven in Holland and in the fighting as the war progressed to the end he added further victories to his score, all fighters including three long-nose Fw 190Ds, and received a second Bar to his DFC shortly after the peace was finally won. He had been a flight commander with 41, and been made CO on 31st March 1945.

His final score was eight destroyed, five shared destroyed, two probables and three damaged, plus those seven rocket bombs. On 14th April 1945 he had shot down a Me 110 that was towing a Me163 rocket fighter near Norenholz airfield. First he shot down the 110 and then, having been released, the Komet (163).

At the start of 1946, the squadron having changed over to Hawker Tempest Vs, he took his squadron to Germany as part of the occupation forces. On 22 January, flying Tempest NV640 from RAF Wünsdorf, his engine cut on take-off for a few seconds, then failed completely. Shepherd retracted the undercarriage and made a perfect belly landing on the airfield, but the Tempest slid on to some frozen earthworks and his safety harness snapped. Shepherd was thrown forward into the windscreen and tragically suffered fatal injuries. The fault to his aircraft was the failure of six sparking plugs in an engine that had yet to be modified to overcome a problem that had been known with the plugs.

Distinguished Flying Cross (*London Gazette* 22nd September 1942)

This officer has taken part in many sorties over enemy-occupied territory and in several reconnaissance missions and attacks on shipping. He has destroyed at least two enemy aircraft. In the combined operations at Dieppe, Flt Lt Shepherd assisted in the destruction of a Dornier 217. He has at all times displayed great skill and determination.

Bar to DFC (*London Gazette* 27th August 1943)

Since being awarded the Distinguished Flying Cross, this officer has undertaken a large number of sorties and has displayed inspiring leadership and great keenness throughout. He has participated in several successful attacks on enemy shipping and, in addition, has destroyed two enemy aircraft bringing his victories to four. He has set a worthy example.

Second Bar to DFC (*London Gazette* 14th September 1945)

Sqn Ldr Shepherd is now on his third tour of operational duty. Since the award of a Bar to the Distinguished Flying Cross he has destroyed seven enemy aircraft and seven flying bombs. He has also destroyed 160 enemy transport vehicles. Intense anti-aircraft opposition has never in any way deterred him from completing his missions. As a squadron commander, Sqn Ldr Shepherd has set a fine example to all under his command.

EDWARD BARNES SISMORE

Known universally as either Ted or 'Daisy', Sismore was born in Kettering, Northamptonshire, on 23rd June 1921 and educated at Kettering County School. At the age of eighteen he joined the RAFVR and trained to be an NCO observer.

His first posting was to 110 Squadron and he became engaged in low-level anti-shipping sorties and attacking ports along the coast of France and the Low Countries. After thirty such operations he was awarded the DFC, and following a rest joined 105 Squadron commanded by Wg Cdr Hughie Edwards VC. In December 1942 he teamed up with pilot Sqn Ldr Reggie Reynolds with whom he flew numerous long-range, dangerous missions, including the RAF's first daylight raid on Berlin, a round-trip of 1,100 miles. The bombers were briefed to bomb at exactly 1100 hours, the time Hermann Göring was due to address a rally commemorating the tenth anniversary of Hitler's regime.

March 1943 saw Sismore became a Gee-H instructor at Swanton Morley, but he returned to operations later. During 1943 Reynolds and Sismore led many daylight attacks in their Mosquito aircraft and when Reynolds was given command of 139 Squadron, Sismore continued as his navigator. Another long-distance raid of note was to Leipzig on 27th May 1943. Facing heavy AA fire their aircraft was hit and Reynolds wounded, but they carried out their task and returned home. Reynolds received a Bar to his DSO and Sismore the DSO.

Transferred to 21 Squadron as navigation leader in early 1944, Sismore planned the attack on Amiens prison in order to release French Resistance prisoners. On the raid he flew as navigator to AVM Basil Embry, OC 2 Group. On 31st October, flying with Reynolds once more, they led a force of twenty-four Mosquitos to attack the Gestapo HQ in Denmark, which was a complete success. Both men received Bars to their DFCs. On 20th March 1945 Sismore led a low-level raid on another Gestapo HQ, in Copenhagen. For these last raids, Sismore received his second Bar to his DFC. Sismore was appointed Knight of the Danish Order of Danneborg (1949) and also given the Air Efficiency Award.

Post-war, Sismore continued his association with the Mosquito and was selected to be navigator for an attempt at the speed record flying from London to Cape Town, with pilot Sqn Ldr Micky Martin DSO DFC (q.v.). Taking off on 30th April 1947, he completed the 6,011-mile journey, with stops at Libya and Kenya to refuel, in twenty-one hours and thirty-one minutes, thirty seconds. Both men were awarded the Royal Aero Club's Britannia trophy.

In 1951 Sismore trained as a night-fighter pilot and two years later took command of 29 Squadron, the RAF's first jet night-fighter unit, flying Meteor NF11s. For his work in developing night-fighter tactics with jets, he received the AFC. This was followed by commanding an advanced flying school and in 1959 went to HQ, British Forces in the Middle East. While so employed he was heavily involved in the RAF's counter-insurgency operations against dissident sheikhdoms. Promoted to group captain in 1962 he commanded RAF Brüggen, Germany, and two years later he converted onto the Victor bomber prior to being appointed as senior air staff officer (SASO) at the Central Reconnaissance Establishment.

An air commodore by 1971 he commanded the Royal Observer Corps and later became director of the UK's Air Defence Team. He retired on 23rd June 1976 and joined Marconi as a service advisor and during the Falklands conflict he quickly mobilised air defence radar over the islands. He had married Rita in 1946 and they had one son and one daughter. Rita passed away in 2006. In retirement, Sismore spent much of his time supporting RAF charities and playing golf.

Following a stroke, Ted Sismore died in Chelmsford, Essex, on 22nd March 2012, at the age of ninety. He was recognised as the finest wartime low-level

Ted Sismore and Reginald Reynolds.

navigator, taking part in many daring raids, including those mentioned, and especially the raid on Berlin in daylight, the Amiens attack, and the two Gestapo HQ missions.

REGINALD WILFRED REYNOLDS was born in Cheltenham, on 6th January 1919 and educated at Clifton College. When he was eight years old the sight of a Gypsy Moth landing in a nearby field in Winchcombe, stimulated his passion to become a pilot. After a year working for the Gloster Aircraft Company he joined the RAF on a short-service commission in August 1937.

In August 1938, now a pilot, he joined 144 Squadron, flying Hampden bombers and during the Phoney War, flew on operations on shipping sweeps and once France had fallen, dropped mines in Baltic waters, and bombed the invasion barges in French ports. After thirty missions he received the DFC and spent six months as an instructor. Back on ops in April 1941, as a flight commander, he formed the nucleus of the first RAAF bomber squadron, No. 455, to be formed in the UK, and flew a further twelve missions.

Completing another stint as an instructor, where he even added another trip on 31st July 1942 in a Whitley to bomb Düsseldorf, when a maximum effort was called for. Later in the year he converted to Mosquito aircraft, joined 105 Squadron, and teamed up with Ed Sismore. Over the following nine months the pair flew many daylight raids against targets in France, the Low Countries and Germany, often at low altitudes. On 27th May 1943, Reynolds led fourteen aircraft in an attack on the Schott Glass Works and Zeiss Optical Instrument Works at Jena, the longest low-level daylight raid flown thus far. As the bombs were released, their aircraft was hit, damaging one engine and wounding Reynolds in the hand and leg, while another piece of shrapnel ripped the collar of his jacket. By this time Reynolds had received the DSO and DFC, and after this raid, he was awarded a Bar to his DSO, while Sismore was awarded the DSO.

In January 1944, Reynolds became wing commander flying in No. 140 Wing of the 2nd TAF, again with Sismore. Both men helped plan the raid on the Amiens prison. On 31st October he led twenty-four Mosquitos to bomb the Gestapo HQ situated in the Aarhus University in Denmark.

After attending the RAF Staff College he went to Canada in September 1945, based at Dorval, near Montreal, working with No. 45 Group, responsible for ferrying aircraft across the Atlantic. He left the RAF in January 1946, and a year later joined the Dutch airline, KLM, flying Constellations on the north Atlantic route. He returned to Canada in 1951 and had several flying jobs including flying executives for the Comstock Corporation, and later flying Piper Twin Cherokee aircraft for a radio and news company.

He married Mary in Montreal, and they had two daughters, and lived in Ontario. Retiring in 1983, he had amassed some 22,000 flying hours, in sixty different aircraft types. Reggie Reynolds died on 25th November 2017, his wife having died in 2010.

Distinguished Flying Cross (*London Gazette* 16th February 1943). Group citation for one DSO, six DFCs and three DFMs
On 30th January 1943, two forces of bombers were detailed to attack Berlin, one during the morning and the other during the afternoon. To reach the German capital necessitated a flight of more than 500 miles, mostly over heavily defended territory. Close co-operation and precise timing were essential but, such was the skill exhibited, that the target was reached and the attacks delivered within seconds of the specified time. That complete success was achieved, despite opposition from the ground defences, is a high tribute to the calm courage, resolution and endurance displayed.

Distinguished Service Order (*London Gazette* 18th June 1943)

>**Recommendation:** 'On 27th May, 1943, this officer was navigator of the leading aircraft of a formation of fourteen detailed to attack targets at Jena, Germany, in daylight.
>
>'The total distance was 1,100 miles, over 500 of which were to be covered at very low level in daylight, through strong defences, both from the ground and the air, in occupied and enemy territory.
>
>'Weather conditions were met as expected, being very clear over the first part of the route, but deteriorating badly towards the target. Visibility was reduced to less than a mile for the last 300 and was not more than half a mile for the last forty. In spite of these difficulties, Fg Off Sismore navigated with extreme accuracy, and finally brought the formation over the target along the pre-arranged run. The attack was made at low level in the face of heavy anti-aircraft defences and balloons.
>
>'Over the target itself, a light anti-aircraft shell burst in the aircraft, wounding the pilot. Fg Off Sismore coolly rendered first aid, and

helped the pilot to maintain control of the aircraft. He then continued his accurate navigation, and the aircraft returned safely to base.

'This officer was navigator of the leading aircraft of a formation which attacked Berlin in daylight, arriving precisely at the scheduled time. Since then he has completed eleven successful sorties.'

Bar to DFC (*London Gazette* 15th December 1944). Joint citation with acting Wg Cdr R. W. Reynolds DSO* DFC, awarded First Bar to the DFC.

As pilot (Reynolds) and navigator (Sismore) respectively these officers have taken part in numerous sorties against a wide variety of targets. In October 1944, they took part in a most successful attack on a vital German target. In this well executed operation, these officers displayed skill and resolution of the highest standard.

Second Bar to DFC (*London Gazette* 22nd June 1945)

In March, 1945, Sqn Ldr Sismore was the navigator in the leading aircraft of a large formation detailed to attack the Gestapo headquarters at Copenhagen. The operation, necessitating a flight of more than 1,000 miles, demanded the highest standard of navigational ability. In this direction, Sqn Ldr Sismore's work was outstanding and contributed materially to the success obtained. Again, in April 1945, this officer flew with great distinction in an attack against a similar target at Odense. This officer, who has completed much operational flying, has rendered very valuable service.

Other Honours
Danish Order of Danneborg, Degree of Knight, by Frederick IX, King of Denmark, 18th March 1949.

Air Force Cross (*London Gazette* 31st May 1956)
When commanding 29 Squadron.

STANISLAW SKALSKI

Born in the village of Kodyn, north of Odessa, Russia, on 27th October 1915, his father sent him and his mother to Zbaraz, near Lvov, in Poland, following the Russian Revolution. He went to school in Dubno, and in his teens (1934) he learnt to fly gliders and powered aircraft the following year. Deciding on a military career, Skalski became a cadet at Deblin in 1936, being commissioned two years later.

Served with the 4th Air Regiment at Torun, then 142 Eskadra, flying PZL P-11c fighters. Following the German attack on Poland on 1st September 1939, Skalski was in immediate combat, shooting down an Hs 126 observation aircraft that first day, and by the 4th he had shot down a total of six German aircraft. With the Polish collapse, his unit moved to Romania, from where he escaped to Marseilles, France, via Beirut. From France he was sent to England in January 1940 and began training in RAF customs, language and tactics, initially going to No. 1 School of Army Co-operation at Old Sarum, and then to No. 6 OTU, until he was posted to 501 Squadron, then to 302 Polish Squadron on 3rd August.

His squadron was not operational, so he requested a transfer to one that was, and in consequence, found himself sent back to 501 Squadron RAF on the 27th, flying Hurricanes. He flew with 501 for just over a week during the Battle of Britain, adding seven more victories to his total, plus a couple of damaged, but in gaining his last three on 5th September, he was himself shot down, by a Me 109, and suffered burns. Six weeks later he insisted on leaving hospital, returning to his squadron in October.

In March 1941 he was posted to 306 (Torun) Squadron, flying Spitfires, and promoted to flight commander in June. During the summer of 1941 he was constantly in action in Fighter Command's battles over northern France flying sweeps and circus operations, adding the destruction of five Me 109s between July and mid-September. Following a rest he began a second tour in March 1942 with 316 Squadron, where he shot down a Fw 190 and damaged two more enemy fighters before being sent to command 317 Squadron. His tour of duty ended in November, and he was sent to No. 58 Operational Training Unit as chief flying instructor.

Eager to get back to the action, he formed the Polish Fighting Team in early 1943, moving to North Africa, equipped with Spitfire IXs. Once in North Africa the team, made up of volunteers, were attached to 145 Squadron, RAF, and during the spring, Skalski added three more victories to his tally, plus another damaged. With the defeat of Axis forces in Tunisia, and having taken command of 601 Squadron in July, he was based on Malta. In this post he became the first Polish airman to command an RAF squadron.

By this time he had been awarded, in December 1940, the Polish Virtuti Militari, the Cross of Valour with three Bars by September 1941, and the British DFC in September 1941, with a Bar in November 1942. For his work in North Africa, he received a second Bar. In October 1943, returning to England he took command of No. 131 Polish Fighter Wing, and in April 1944 took over 133 Wing, equipped with Mustang IIIs. On 24th June he caused two Me 109Gs to collide and crash without him having fired a shot. With these victories he became the highest-scoring Polish fighter ace.

Awarded a further VM, 4th Class (Golden Cross) in 1944, he was taken off operations and left for the USA to attend a course at the Command and General Staff School. Returning to the UK in February 1945 he became wing commander operations with 11 Group HQ. He had been awarded the DSO in August 1944, and in 1947 returned to Poland. He was initially appointed inspector of flying techniques at Polish air force HQ, but then, like many other Polish veterans who had fought with the British, was arrested by the Communists and imprisoned. He remained in prison from June 1948 to April 1956, spending a year under threat of execution for espionage.

Finally released he rejoined the PAF, flying MiG fighters, eventually rising to the rank of general. In 1968 he took charge of the aeroclub of Poland for the next four years. He retired from the PAF with the rank of general in 1972, and lived in Warsaw. He did not marry, and died in that city aged eighty-nine, on 12th November 2004.

Distinguished Flying Cross (Approved 11th December 1941)
This officer has taken part in twenty-five offensive sweeps. He has been credited with ten enemy aircraft destroyed, three enemy aircraft probably destroyed, and one enemy aircraft damaged. On 17th September 1941, while returning from a sweep, he saw four Me 109s diving to attack another Polish squadron flying at a lower height. He attacked the e/a immediately, and destroyed two of them, but he himself was, in turn, attacked by other e/a which arrived on the scene, and only escaped by skilful evasive action.

Bar to DFC (Approved 10th September 1942)
This officer has been engaged on operational flying since 1940 and has participated in seventy-nine sorties over enemy territory. Sqn Ldr Skalski led his squadron in the combined operations at Dieppe, on 19th August, 1942, when the squadron destroyed at least seven enemy aircraft without loss to themselves. This achievement

reflects the greatest credit on this officer's excellent leadership and the confidence he has inspired in those under his command. He has personally destroyed eleven enemy aircraft, probably destroyed four and damaged two others.

Second Bar to DFC (Approved 1st July 1943)
Sqn Ldr Skalski has continued to display inspiring leadership, courage and devotion to duty which have contributed largely to the success achieved by his squadron. Whilst serving with his present squadron, Sqn Ldr Skalski has destroyed three enemy aircraft and damaged others.

Distinguished Service Order (Permission to accept this award granted by the Polish president on 26th May 1945.)

Recommendation for excellent leadership of a Fighter Wing (133) in eighty-seven operational flights in May, June and July 1944. Since the day of his last award this officer carried out eighty-seven operational flights bringing down two enemy aircraft and giving proof of great gallantry, keenness and self control. This wing under his leadership shot down on operations over Germany and Normandy forty-one enemy aircraft, two probables and eleven damaged, and carried out a series of successful bombing operations assisting considerably the landing operations on the beach head.

The recommendation also noted Skalski as having flown a total of 324 sorties, covering 416 hours and thirty minutes.

Polish Decorations
Virtuti Militari, Golden Cross 4th Class, 25th September 1944[1]

Virtuti Militari, Silver Cross 5th Class, 23rd December 1940

Krzyż Walecznyth, Cross of Valour, four times. Cross of Valour & Bar, awarded on 23rd September 1941. Second and third Bars awarded on 23rd December 1940.

Order of Polonia Restituta, Knight's Cross

Order of the Cross of Grunwald, 3rd Class

---

[1] Only about a dozen members of the Polish air force were awarded the 4th Class of the VM during WW2. Classes 1-3 were only awarded to high ranking commanders for winning important battles or campaigns.

ROSS MACPHERSON SMITH

One of three brothers born to Andrew and Jessie (née Macpherson) Smith, Ross was born on 4th December 1892, at Semaphore, South Australia. Both parents were from Scottish stock, Andrew coming from Moffat, Dumfries, and Jessie's family hailed from Kengussie, Inverness, although she was born in New Norcia, Western Australia. Andrew Smith was the station manager of the Mutooroo Pastoral Company, a property of some 3,000 square miles (7,700 km). Ross was the middle son, Keith being the eldest, while Colin was the youngest.

Both the eldest boys went to Queen's School in Adelaide, but early in the 1900s both lads attended the Warriston School, Moffat, Scotland, their father's birthplace. They were accompanied by their mother, who lived locally for the two years they were there. On return to Australia, Ross joined the Australian mounted cadets and in 1910 was selected to tour Britain, and the USA, as a South Australia representative. Following this very educational experience, Ross became a warehouseman for Messrs Harris, Scarfe and Co, in Adelaide.

With the coming of war, Ross enlisted as a private in the 3rd Australian Light Horse, becoming a sergeant on 1st October 1914. In May 1915 he landed with his regiment on Gallipoli, but like so many other young men, decided that war flying was a far better option, so managed a transfer to the Australian Flying Corps. Brother Keith also became a pilot, but Colin joined the 10th Battalion, Australian Infantry. He was killed in action in October 1917 in France, aged twenty-two.

Once trained as an observer, Ross Smith was posted to 67 (Australian) Squadron, serving in both Egypt and Palestine, quickly making his mark. He and his pilot were awarded MCs for rescuing a downed brother pilot, and then Ross trained to be a pilot in July 1917. Back with 67 Squadron, flying Bristol F2b fighters, he took part in all manner of operations, including air fighting, although for his first victory, on 1st September, he was flying a BE2e observation aircraft. A Bar to his MC was gazetted in March 1918.

With the formation of the RAF in April 1918, his squadron became 1 Squadron, Australian Flying Corps, flying bombing, photographic and offensive patrols, and on the latter, he achieved a further ten victories flying the Bristol Fighter. The last of these victories came on 19th October 1918, he and his observer,

Ross Smith pictured seated in BF2b No. B1146 in 1918 while with 1 Squadron AFC in Palestine. He was known as 'Hadji'.

Lt A. V. McCann, forced down a German two-seater. Smith landed nearby and covered by McCann and his machine guns, sauntered over to the German machine, ordered the crew to stand clear, set the DFW on fire, then returned to his machine and took off for base. For his actions during 1918, he received the DFC and two Bars. (Amazingly all gazetted on the same date, 8th February 1919.)

Known as 'Hadji', Ross was wounded twice during his time with 1 AFC, once, in September 1917, an enemy bullet puncturing both cheeks and knocking out teeth, but he survived. He also flew on occasions with Lawrence of Arabia, not in BF2bs but in a large Handley Page bomber. Smith also flew bomb raids in the HP. However, he did once fly Lawrence in a BF, on 16th May 1918, to an Arab HQ in readiness for an expedition to Azrak. Another feat was to make the first flight from Cairo to Calcutta in 1918, for which he received the Air Force Cross in the 1919 Birthday Honours.

The war over, Ross and brother Keith got together in response to an announcement by the Australian prime minister, Billy Hughes, that an air race with a £10,000 prize would be given to the first aeroplane to fly from London to Australia in thirty days or less. The boys asked the Vickers Aeroplane Company to supply them with a Vickers Vimy, and enlisting the help of two RAF sergeant mechanics, W. H. Shiers and J. M. Bennett, took off from Hounslow Heath on 12th November 1919, reaching Darwin on 10th December – twenty-seven days and twenty hours, with actual flying time being 135 hours. The four men shared the prize money and both brothers were knighted KBE. Both Bennett and Shiers also received decorations, Bars to their AFMs.

Sadly Ross Smith did not live long enough to fully enjoy his celebrity status for on 14th April 1922, he was killed in a flying accident, along with Sgt Bennett, preparing for an attempt at a round-the-world flight, in a Vickers Viking. Sir Keith Smith continued to be associated with aviation, working in Sydney as an agent for Vickers, and also became vice president of British Commonwealth Pacific Airlines (taken over by Quantas in 1954). Then becoming a director of Quantas and Tasman Empire Airways, Ltd. He died of cancer in December 1955, aged sixty-four.

Military Cross (*London Gazette* 11th May, 1917)
For conspicuous gallantry and devotion to duty when his pilot (R. F. Ballieu) descended to the rescue of an officer who had been forced to land. On landing he held the enemy at bay with his revolver, thus enabling his pilot to rescue the officer and safely fly away his machine.

Bar to MC (*London Gazette* 26th March 1918)
For conspicuous gallantry and devotion to duty. He was one of two pilots who carried out a remarkable series of photographs in one flight, completely covering an important area of 45 square miles. On a later occasion he successfully bombed an important bridgehead from low altitude, and his work throughout, as well as his photography, has been invaluable by the most consistent gallantry.

Distinguished Flying Cross (*London Gazette* 8th February 1919). Joint citation with Lt W. A. Kirk, awarded DFC.
During the months of June and July these officers accounted for two enemy machines, and they have been conspicuous for gallantry and initiative in attacking ground targets, frequently at very low altitudes. The keenness and fine example set by these officers cannot be over-estimated.

Bar to DFC (*London Gazette* 8th February 1919)
During the operations prior to October 1918, he took part in numerous engagements involving flights of 150 to 200 miles, and succeeded in doing extensive damage to the enemy's hangars, railways, etc. Capt Smith displayed most consistent gallantry with marked ability in all his work, whether bombing by night or day or in personal encounters in the air. Whilst operating with the Sharifian forces he destroyed on enemy machine and brought down two others out of control in the desert.

Second Bar to DFC (*London Gazette* 8th February 1919)
On 19th October this officer, with Lt A. V. McCann as observer, engaged and drove down an enemy two-seater. As it appeared to land intact he descended to a low altitude and, with machine-gun fire, forced the occupants to abandon the machine; he then landed alongside it, and while his observer covered the enemy officers, he set light to their machine and completely destroyed it. To have effected a landing in an unknown country, many miles in rear of the enemy's advanced troops, demanded courage and skill to a very high order.

Other Honours
Air Force Cross (*London Gazette* 3rd June 1919)

Most Honourable Order of the British Empire – Knight Commander (KBE) (*London Gazette* 26th December 1919). Ross and Keith Smith.
In recognition of the valuable services rendered to aviation by their successful flight in the Vickers-Vimy-Rolls from England to Australia.

MAURICE MICHAEL STEPHENS

The son of an army officer, Mike Stephens was born in Ranchi, India, on 20th October 1919. He was however educated in England, being sent to Xaverian College, Clapham, south London, and later attending Xaverian College at Mayfield, Sussex.

In 1936 he joined the Port of London Authority, and while so employed represented it at rugby, swimming and rowing. However, his thoughts turned to aviation and in 1938 he was accepted to RAF Cranwell, where his sporting interests helped with not only rowing, but boxing too. Between times he learnt to fly and in 1940 received a commission and posting to 3 Squadron, that was about to go to France as the Germans had begun their blitzkrieg in the west on 10th May.

Two days later, Stephens downed three enemy aircraft, two Ju 87s and a Do 17 while on the 14th, he added a further three; a Ju 87, one Me 109 and a Hs 126. He had also been made a flight commander. Such was the confused state during the battle of France that 3 Squadron's record keeping became a nightmare, and while Stephens continued to attack enemy aircraft, the details were somewhat obscured. A Dornier on the 18th with another on the 20th, but on this date he also damaged another Hs 126 and probably got another three victories, either Dorniers or Messerschmitts. Confirmations may have been missed, but he achieved some ten kills before the squadron was forced to return to England. For his actions he received the DFC and Bar.

In July 1940 his flight became the nucleus for 232 Squadron, and he was chosen as its commanding officer. This was formed in the north, and over Scapa Flow on the morning of 23th August, he and another pilot attacked a He 111 on a reconnaissance mission and shot it down near the Orkneys. However, his Hurricane, P3104, was damaged by return fire but he managed to get home. It was the squadron's first victory.

In December, the Battle of Britain over, Stephens answered the call for volunteers to go to Greece which was being hard pressed by the Italians. Sailing on the carrier HMS *Furious*, it was diverted to North Africa where he joined 274 Squadron in February 1941. He was then sent to Turkey with orders to get Turkish fighter pilots onto a war footing, remaining there for eight months, four of which were with a Hurricane unit in western Turkey, the other four with another unit near Izmir. He twice reported shooting down two Italian S-84 recce aircraft over the Bulgarian border, but they were never included in his overall score of victories, even though he inspected the wreckage of both aeroplanes and even sent samples of ammunition back to England in the diplomatic bag. He had, after all, been in civilian clothes, and was flying unofficially.

In November 1941 he returned to the desert war going to 80 Squadron as CO. On 9th December his Hurricane was set ablaze and Stephens was wounded in both feet. As he was about to bale out, the attacking enemy fighter overshot him, so he dropped back into his seat and shot it down. Baling out, he was picked up by Polish soldiers who confirmed seeing his victim go down. He had thought it had been a Me 109 but as none were lost this day, it was probably an Italian MC202. The Poles took him into Tobruk and to hospital, where he remained until January 1942. However, he was awarded the DSO.

Posted to RAF HQ in Nairobi, Kenya, he did not return to Egypt until the autumn, being attached to the newly arrived American 57th Fighter Group that flew P-40 Warhawks. Stephens then volunteered to go to Malta, arriving in early October 1942, being attached to 249 Squadron, flying Spitfires. In the first two weeks of October he shot down three enemy aircraft, shared two more and damaged two others. During one of these actions, on the 12th, he was shot down and baled out into the sea. He was rescued by ASR launch. The following day he was given command of 229 Squadron, celebrating by downing an Italian fighter and damaging two Ju 88s. This was followed by two more kills on the 15th. He did not get off scot-free on the date, for his Spitfire was damaged in combat and he had to fly through an AA barrage over Grand Harbour in order to crash land at Takali airfield. This all resulted in his second Bar to his DFC.

In November he took command of the Hal Far Wing before returning to England in January 1943. He attended the Central Flying School at Hullavington, took an instructor's course and became CFI at No. 3 Operational Training Unit in early 1944. In April 1945 he went to the USA on liaison duties and that September attended the RAF Staff College. He then returned to Turkey to become an instructor at Ankara in 1948. Back in England once more he lectured on air force law at RAF Cranwell and as a wing commander he was posted to EMMO in London, and in 1951 was posted to Supreme Headquarters Allied Powers, Europe, in Paris and became the first RAF officer to join the newly founded NATO. This was followed by tours at Cranwell and Gütersloh, Germany, then Air Ministry before returning to SHAPE in 1960.

He joined the aero engines division of Rolls-Royce in Paris before becoming a consultant with Pilkingtons and Lucas, finally retiring to the south of France in 1980. He returned to England in 1992. Mike's two brothers both served with Bomber Command during the war, and he married Violet May Paterson in 1942, who died in 2002. They had a son and a daughter. Mike Stephens died on 23rd September 2004, aged eighty-four.

Distinguished Flying Cross (*London Gazette* 31st May 1940)

This officer has destroyed four enemy aircraft in May, 1940, and led his flight with courage and skill.

Bar to DFC (*London Gazette* 31st May 1940)

This officer has continued to lead his flight against formations of enemy aircraft of much superior numbers with such good leadership that he rarely lost any members of his formation. In addition, Plt Off Stephens brought down four more enemy aircraft recently, bringing his total to eight.

Distinguished Service Order (*London Gazette* 30th October 1942)

In December 1941, this officer led a bombing and machine-gun attack on enemy mechanical transport in the Acroma area. Following the attack, Sqn Ldr Stephens observed the fighter escort in combat with a force of enemy fighters, but, whilst attempting to participate in the engagement, his aircraft was severely damaged by an enemy fighter pilot whose cannon fire exploded the starboard petrol tank which, with the oil tank, burst into flames. The same burst of fire wounded Squadron Leader Stephens in both feet and blew out the starboard side of the aircraft's cockpit. Squadron Leader Stephens then prepared to abandon the aircraft but, when halfway out of the cockpit, he observed the enemy aircraft fly past him. He immediately regained his seat and shot down the enemy aircraft. Sqn Ldr Stephens finally left his crippled aircraft by parachute and landed safely on the ground where he beat out the flames from his burning clothing. Although he had landed within 300 yards of the enemy's lines, he succeeded in regaining our own territory within three-quarters of an hour. Throughout, this officer displayed great courage and devotion to duty. Previously, Sqn Ldr Stephens led his squadron on operations which were of the greatest value during the battle for Tobruk. His leadership and example proved an inspiration.

Second Bar to DFC (*London Gazette* 3rd November 1942)

From the 8th to 15th October 1942, this officer has destroyed five enemy aircraft in air combats over Malta. On one occasion he followed an enemy bomber down to sea level and, after pursuing it out to sea for some twenty miles, shot it down into the water. He was afterwards attacked by six enemy fighters but he destroyed one of them and fought the others off. Although his aircraft was badly damaged he flew it to base and made a crash landing. This officer has greatly enhanced the gallant reputation he so worthily holds.

ALISTAIR LENNOX TAYLOR

Taylor, who was the first RAF airman to be awarded three DFCs during WW2, was born in Worcester, on 12th March 1916, and educated initially at the Worcester Cathedral Choir School then at the town's King's School in January 1931. His parents were Alfred Herbert and Marie Isobel Taylor of 'Belmont', Merriman's Hill, Worcester and later Barnes Hall, while later still, of Alderton, Gloucestershire. On leaving school in 1933 he began work as an electrical engineer, for J. G. Smithson & Co. Ltd., a company making electric controllers.

His school magazine mentions him on several occasions, especially in 1932 when he joined the school Cricket 2nd XI, and described him as a 'sound and steady batsman, but a poor judge of a run. Slow in the field, thereby losing runs which he found it difficult to make up for'. He also sang in the school choir, and in 1933 joined the 1st XI at cricket where he received his colours, and won the general knowledge prize.

Deciding upon a flying career, he joined the RAF on 16th November 1936, and was commissioned. With his first squadron, No. 266, he was selected in April 1938, along with two other pilots, to give a demonstration flight of close-formation flying before the OC, No. 1 Bomber Group. With the RAF he also played Rugger for No. 6 FTS and captained one of the RAF's seven-a-side teams, which won the annual competition, beating the headquarters team in the final.

When the war began, he was a trained bomber pilot, flying Fairey Battles with 226 Squadron. Sent to France, he operated during the Phoney War and following the German blitzkrieg in May, after the loss of France, Taylor was sent to 212 Squadron. No. 212 used a variety of aircraft for reconnaissance work including Blenheims and Spitfires. In June it was absorbed into the photographic reconnaissance unit. By this time Taylor had been awarded the DFC.

On 21 May 1940, Taylor married Margaret Reid, eldest daughter of Mr and Mrs E. B. Morgan of 40 Redlands Road, Reading, Berkshire, setting up home in that town.

Taylor was employed on numerous reconnaissance missions over the next year, flying PRU Spitfires and later de Havilland Mosquitos. By the autumn of 1940 he had been awarded a Bar to his DFC, for operations often at low level across western Germany, the Low Countries and Norway. Once he began operating with the Mosquito he needed a navigator, and this was Sgt Sidney Edward Horsfall.

In early 1941 Taylor became the first airman in WW2 to be awarded a second Bar to his DFC. Taylor was also the first PR pilot to complete 100 operational sorties, sixteen of which this team successfully completed over Norway during October 1941. On 4th December 1941, Taylor and Horsfall took off from Wick in Mosquito W4055 at 1015 hours to fly a PR mission to Trondheim, Norway. They encountered heavy AA fire and may have been damaged, but they were then intercepted by Unteroffizier Rudolf Fenton of the 1/JG77 and shot down into the sea at 1520 hours, near Stavanger. They did not survive and they do not have known graves. Taylor, who had the nickname of 'Ice', was twenty-five years of age.

His old school magazine noted: 'We also learned with deep regret that Sqn Ldr A. L. Taylor DFC and two Bars, who has been missing since January, must now be presumed to have been killed. Shortly before he was reported missing he had been mentioned in despatches for his signal services in aerial photography.'

Distinguished Flying Cross (*London Gazette* 30th July 1940)
The recommendation for this award dated 30 June 1940, reads:

> 'During the last three months this officer has carried out daylight re-connaissances over enemy territory in an unarmed aircraft. Many of these flights have penetrated as much as 300 miles behind the enemy front line and on some occasions even more, resulting in supplying information of the greatest value of the enemy's concentrations, sup-plies, fortifications and movements.'

Bar to DFC (*London Gazette* 8th October 1940)
In September, 1940, this officer carried out a successful photographic recon-naissance of the Dortmund-Ems aqueduct. Flying Officer Taylor took off from his base in dense fog but, flying through this, he reached his objective and se-cured valuable photographs from a height of 6,000 feet. He has, during the last two months, carried out a number of exceptionally successful reconnaissances, including one over Kiel which was considered the most valuable reconnais-sance completed for the navy during the war. Other work by this pilot includes photographs of Cap Gris Nez and Flushing taken from a height of 400 feet. He has completed sixty photographic missions and in this class of operations he is outstanding.

Second Bar to DFC (*London Gazette* 7th March 1941)
Mentioned in Despatches (*London Gazette* 1st June 1941)

KEITH FREDERICK THIELE

'Jimmy' Thiele was born in Christchurch, New Zealand, on 25th February 1921, attending Waltham Primary School and the Christchurch Boys' High School. His first job was as a junior reporter for the *Star-Sun* newspaper but with the coming of war, he joined the RNZAF in December 1940, when he was nineteen.

Once trained as a pilot, and now in England, he was posted to 405 (Vancouver) Squadron, RCAF, flying Wellington bombers. He flew twenty-one operations over Germany before his squadron re-equipped with Handley Page Halifax bombers, and completed his tour with eleven raids with these aeroplanes, making a total of thirty-two in all, for which he received the DFC. After a rest he moved to 467 Squadron RAAF to begin another tour. He had a number of adventures during his tours, including a mission to bomb the three German battleships during their dash up the Channel on 12th February 1942. Trying to locate them in thick cloud late in the day, when they were spotted it was too late to bomb and despite several attempts to relocate them, they had to reluctantly turn for home. Only his rear gunner had managed to get off a burst as they crossed over one of the ships. Then there was the night his rear gunner became unconscious through lack of oxygen, but he continued to the target, while two of his crew got the gunner from his turret, bringing him to the front of the bomber. Thiele dived to a low level while crewmen tried to revive him, but the man did not recover. Soon after take-off on a trip to Nuremberg, one engine developed a glycol leak which then turned into a fire. Closing down the engine, he jettisoned most of his incendiaries and carried on with his 4,000-lb 'cookie' and just a few incendiaries, and bombed his target. On another raid, with 467, to Duisburg (12th/13th May), his aircraft was damaged by an anti-aircraft shell that exploded beneath the fuselage; then they were caught and coned by searchlights. Escaping from these, Thiele reached the target but they were hit again, knocking out the starboard outer engine. This was followed by another hit, this time knocking out the starboard inner engine and ripping open the side of the Halifax alongside the pilot and bomb-aimer's positions. Thiele was also struck in the head by a shell fragment. However, he got himself and his crew back to England but had to crash land soon after crossing the coast. It was his fifty-sixth and final operation. He received a Bar to his DFC and the DSO. During his tours, he had attempted to attack German ships which tried to slip along the Channel on

12th February 1942 as already explained, and had flown on all three of the 1,000 bomber raids to Cologne, Essen and Hamburg.

Once back on flying he began operating with Ferry Command in Canada until late in the war, at which stage he managed to get himself onto fighters in 1944, posted to 41 Squadron flying Spitfire XIIs. During the V1 crisis that summer he shot down one. Converting to Hawker Tempests he joined 486 Squadron in Holland but in December moved to 3 Squadron claiming two victories before the year was out. In the new year he took over command of the squadron, claiming ground victories in January. However, on 10th February his Tempest (NV644) was hit by ground fire and he was forced to bale out suffering burns to face and wrists. He was taken into captivity but in March, with the war nearing its end, he and another prisoner managed to walk out of their camp and finding a couple of bicycles, were soon peddling their way west.

Thiele later managed to get hold of a motorbike and continued to head towards Allied lines, finally reaching American troops at Remagen. Back with his squadron he was deemed unfit for operational flying, but in May he received a second Bar to his DFC.

After returning to New Zealand, he left the service in December 1946, and went back to being a journalist. Later he moved to Australia and became an airline pilot with Quantas, while also enjoying sailing. In fact when he was eighty, he sailed across the Tasman Sea in order to see New Zealand's first America's Cup defence. He had retired to Bundaberg, Queensland and died in Sydney on 5th January 2016 aged ninety-four, survived by his daughter.

Distinguished Flying Cross (*London Gazette* 11th August 1942)

> **Recommendation:** 'Sqn Ldr Thiele has been attached to this squadron for eight months during which time he has completed twenty-five successful sorties. On every occasion he has shown great skill and has pressed home his attacks regardless of opposition. His keenness and efficiency have been an inspiration to other member of the squadron. He has always been a leader and has just proved a thoroughly courageous and skilled flight commander. In view of this officer's excellent record and number of operational trips, it is strongly recommended that he be awarded the DFC.'

Distinguished Service Order (*London Gazette* 14th May 1943)

> **Recommendation:** 'This officer has, at all times, displayed outstanding keenness and determination during operations. The majority of his sorties

have been attacks on well-defended and distant targets which have all been highly successful. On one occasion, during an attack on Berlin, his rear-gunner lost consciousness from lack of oxygen, but Sqn Ldr Thiele proceeded with the mission although two of the crew were fully occupied with the unconscious man. Later he returned to this country at a very low altitude, in an attempt to succour the gunner.

'While on a flight in March 1943, his port engine caught fire early on the outward journey. The flames were extinguished however, and the whole flight was accomplished with success. His outstanding courage and devotion to duty and confidence have earned the admiration of all.'

Bar to DFC (*London Gazette* 28th May 1943)

One night in May, 1943, this officer captained an aircraft detailed to attack Duisburg. When nearing the target area, the aircraft was subjected to anti-aircraft fire and severely damaged when a shell burst underneath the fuselage. Despite this, Sqn Ldr Thiele flew on to the target. Whilst making his bombing run the aircraft was illuminated by searchlights, but this captain maintained a straight course in order to ensure accurate bombing. Just as the bomb-aimer had completed his work, the aircraft was repeatedly hit by fragments from bursting shells. One burst destroyed one of the engines, whilst shortly afterwards a second engine was disabled. The windscreens on the starboard side of the pilot's and bomb-aimer's cabins were shattered. Although he was dazed by a blow from a shell splinter, which struck him on the side of the head, Sqn Ldr Thiele skilfully extricated the damaged bomber from a perilous situation and endeavoured to fly it to base. Shortly after crossing the English coast he was unable to maintain height but, displaying superb airmanship he struggled on and succeeded in effecting a crash landing at an airfield. In most hazardous circumstances, Sqn Ldr Thiele displayed courage, skill and determination of a high order.

Second Bar to DFC (*London Gazette* 8th May 1945)

This officer's operational record is outstanding. As pilot of a bomber he completed two tours of duty during which he took part in very many attacks on enemy targets. Since joining his present squadron, Sqn Ldr Thiele has taken part in a large number of sorties, involving attacks on a wide range of enemy targets. He has personally been responsible for the destruction of numerous locomotives, barges and mechanical vehicles. In air fighting he has shot down two enemy aircraft. This officer has displayed the highest qualities of skill, together with great bravery and iron determination. His example has inspired all.

KENNETH ROBERT TRIGGS

Born in Lewisham, south-east London on 6th November, 1919, son of Robert A. and Kate F. (née Eve) Triggs, living at 3 Liskeard Gardens, Greenwich, London. Robert Triggs worked for his uncle Horace, who owned a jewellers shop, as an assistant, a business that had begun in 1860. Upon leaving school, Kenneth became an engineer working in the air conditioning sector. When war came he joined the RAFVR (020704) and became a sergeant, trained as a navigator in South Africa, and received a commission on 25th May 1941.

His first squadron was No. 40, flying bomber operations with Vickers Wellingtons, mainly in the Middle East, for which he received the DFC in late 1942. He was part of Warrant Officer William Craig Brodie's crew. Brodie, who came from Glasgow, had won the DFM with 38 Squadron at Shallufa, where 40 Squadron was reformed and several aircrew from 38 were posted across.

After a rest he was posted to 692 Squadron in 1944, flying Mosquito B.IV bombers for which he was mentioned in despatches in January 1944. Triggs teamed up with his old pilot from 40 Squadron, now Sqn Ldr W. C. Craig DFM. Flying with this unit he received a Bar to his DFC in late 1944 and a second Bar as the war ended. He had been promoted to flying officer on 24th May 1942 and then flight lieutenant on 24th May 1943. Meantime, Brodie had received the DFC and then the DSO.

One memorable mission they flew was on the night of 14th/15th January 1945. A total of eighty-three Mossies headed for Berlin this night, fourteen

692 Squadron photographed in 1944. Kenneth Triggs is ninth from the left in the middle row. Ninth from the left in the front row (in front of Triggs) is Sqn Ldr W. C. Brodie DFC, DFM, Triggs' pilot (Aircrew Remembered)

Mosquito B.XVI bombers of 692 Squadron taking off from RAF Graveley at 2109 hours each carrying a 4,000-lb 'cookie', led by Sqn Ldr William C. Brodie DSO DFM, with Kenneth Triggs as his navigator, in MM182. One aircraft aborted, suffering a burst tyre on take-off, and one Mosquito was lost. Another ran short of fuel upon returning, and although the crew baled out, both were killed. Returning crews found bad weather over their home bases, and in all five Mosquitos from the Berlin operation crashed in England.

Nine of 692's aircraft dropped their loads on Berlin, while three others bombed secondary targets (Bonn and Cologne). Over Berlin the sky was clear and good results achieved both on marking the target for Main Force bombers and bombing, despite light AA fire and the presence of night-fighters. Brodie added the DFC to his list of awards.

Kenneth Triggs survived the war and died in 1972.

Distinguished Flying Cross (*London Gazette* 6th October 1942)

This officer is a navigator of outstanding merit. His work has contributed materially to the great success of many of the operations in which he has taken part, some of which have been of a daring character. He has always set a high example to his fellow navigators.

Mentioned in Despatches, 14th January 1942

Bar to DFC (*London Gazette* 17th November 1944)
Group citation of three awards of the DSO, one Bar to DFC and four awards of the DFC

One night in October 1944, a force of bombers was detailed for an important low-level mining operation requiring considerable skill and accuracy in flying. The target was strongly defended by heavy and light anti-aircraft guns, searchlights and balloons. Undeterred by these hazards and the most adverse weather, the operation was completed successfully. The success achieved reflects the greatest credit on the following personnel.

Distinguished service order
Wg Cdr R. J. Gosnell DFC, 571 Squadron
Acting Sqn Ldr W. C. Brodie DFM, 692 Squadron
Acting Sqn Ldr E. J. Greenleaf, 571 Squadron

Bar to DFC
Acting Flt Lt K. R. Triggs DFC, 692 Squadron

DFC

Flt Lt W. I. Drinkall, 692 Squadron
Acting Flt Lt A. W. Lockhart RCAF, 692 Squadron
Fg Off R. W. McLernon, 571 Squadron
Fg Off J. R. Wood RCAF, 692 Squadron

Second Bar to DFC (*London Gazette* 17th June 1945)

Since the award of a Bar to the Distinguished Flying Cross, this officer has completed his second tour of operations, including a number of attacks against well
defended targets in Germany. By his outstanding ability, courage and devotion
to duty, Flt Lt Triggs has contributed materially to the success of those missions.
His skill, courage and initiative have been worthy of the highest praise.

ROBERT ROLAND STANFORD TUCK

I met Bob Tuck in 1979. I was writing a book on Sailor Malan and requested an interview in order to get his recollections on this famous South African fighter pilot. He was more than accommodating, even happy to collect me from his local railway station and drive me to his house, right on the beach at Sandwich in Kent. The first thing I noticed was that his house was not locked, and secondly that several people were walking along the beach just a few yards away. It was only when Tuck had to refer to his old flying logbooks, that I saw they were placed on a nearby sideboard, which amazed me. That such treasures just sat in plain view, in an unlocked house, with people walking by, remains in my mind till this day.

Bob Tuck was born in Catford, south-east London, on 1st July 1916 – the first day of the bloody Battle of the Somme. He was the second son of Captain Stanley Lewis Tuck, the head of an export business and Ethel Constance (née Baker) his wife. Jack was the eldest boy and a sister Peggy was the eldest sibling. Stanley Tuck had served in the Queen's Royal West Surrey Regiment in WW1 and had taught his son to shoot at the age of twelve, to become quite an expert in rabbit and pheasant shooting. Bob was educated at St. Dunstan's College, Reading, although he seems to have concentrated on sport and shooting rather than academic excellence.

At the age of sixteen he joined the Merchant Navy as a cadet with Lamport and Holt, sailing mostly on the South American meat runs. His skill at shooting sharks with a Lee Enfield .303 rifle impressed his skipper. However, in 1935 he answered a newspaper advert asking for young men to join the RAF, applied, and was accepted that September. He went through the usual training, flying Avros, Tutors, Harts and Audax aircraft at No 3 FTS, where often his proficiency as a pilot was 'above the average'. However, he suffered a mid-air collision on 17th January 1938 and had to take to his parachute, landing safely, although his right cheek had been slashed through by a flying wire, leaving him with a scar. The other pilot was killed.

In September 1938 he was posted to 65 Squadron at RAF Hornchurch, where he flew Gauntlet fighters. By August 1938, he was being assessed as 'exceptional'. He had another collision on 4 November but only slightly damaged his machine. In early 1939 his squadron were scheduled to receive Spitfires, so he was attached to 19 Squadron to convert onto them. However, it was not until

Bob Tuck in front of his Spitfire in May 1940.

March that the new aircraft began to arrive and from then on, with war looming, training continued apace. On 1st May 1940, Tuck was posted to 92 Squadron, as a flight commander.

His first combat action came on 23rd May, with the Dunkirk operation about to begin in earnest. During a morning patrol over Dunkirk, Calais and Boulogne he shot down a Me 109 and in the afternoon shot down two Me 110s. Over the next few days he added to his score and was awarded the DFC. He remained with 92 Squadron during the Battle of Britain, and after a combat with a Ju 88 on 15th August, his aircraft caught fire and once more he had to take to his parachute. On 11th September he was given command of 257 Squadron, on Hurricanes. He and his pilots gained some fame by routing a raid by Italian aircraft on 11th November. By the end of the year he had some twenty victories and had received a Bar to his DFC. This was followed by the DSO in January 1941. He was also signing himself as R. R. Stanford Tuck.

In early 1941, still with 257, his squadron were often intercepting enemy bombers off the Norfolk coast, and he was also involved in some night sorties. As spring gave way to early summer, his squadron became involved in the early sweeps and circus operations over France, and then he was given command of the Duxford Fighter Wing, followed by command of the West Malling Wing. He used his parachute again on 21st June but not over France. Flying a convoy patrol he wrote in his logbook: 'Got browned off, went out to sea and when about 100 miles off Southend got attacked by three Me 109s. Shot down two and damaged the third, own machine damaged, had to bale out when nearing the coast on the way back.' On 7th August 1941 he claimed his last combat victory, a 109F, bringing his score to twenty-nine, including shares.

Towards the end of the year he was sent to the USA, test flying aircraft from companies such as Bell, Curtiss, Republic and Lockheed – P-39s, P-40s, P-47s, and P-38s. Returning to England he took command of the Biggin Hill Wing. On 28th January 1942 he flew on a ground-strafing mission over France, but his Spitfire was hit by ground fire, forcing him to crash land and be captured. He ended up in Stalag Luft III. He managed to escape on 1st February 1945, reached the Russian lines and remained with a Russian infantry unit for two weeks. He finally left and went through Poland to the British embassy in Moscow. Put aboard a ship at Odessa, he reached Naples on 3rd April. From here he was flown back to the UK in a Warwick, landing at RAF Lynham. He was back in the air on 15th May – in a Harvard. On 23th May he was still assessed as 'exceptional' by the CO of RAF Coleby Grange.

Posted to the Central Fighter Establishment at Tangmere, for duties with the Tactics Branch, Tuck was given the position of wing commander air combat.

Back on Spitfires and Tempests, he also got his hands on a Meteor jet, and later even Mosquitos. The Americans awarded him their DFC in June 1946. He continued to serve over the next few years in various capacities. He finally left the RAF in May 1949 and became a test pilot, including work on the English Electric Canberra jet-bomber. He also became a mushroom farmer with a friend, for the next twenty years. He had met his future wife, Joyce Baker-Harber (née Carter) in 1941, she being an ambulance driver. Once he had got back to England in 1945, they married by special licence within a week. They had two sons, Michael and Simon and moved to Eastry, in Kent. Retiring finally to Sandwich Bay in 1970, Joyce died in November 1985; Bob Tuck died on 5th May 1987, aged seventy.

Distinguished Flying Cross (*London Gazette* 11th June 1940)
During May, 1940, this officer led his flight in company with his squadron on two offensive patrols over northern France. As a result of one of these patrols in which the squadron engaged a formation of some sixty enemy aircraft, the squadron commander was later reported missing, and the flight commander wounded and in hospital. Flt Lt Tuck assumed command, and on the following day led the squadron, consisting of only eight aircraft, on a further patrol engaging an enemy formation of fifty aircraft. During these engagements the squadron has shot down ten enemy aircraft and possibly another twenty-four. Throughout the combats this officer has displayed great dash and gallantry.

Bar to DFC (*London Gazette* 25th October 1940)
Since 11th June, 1940, this officer has destroyed six enemy aircraft, and probably destroyed or damaged at least six more. One day in August, 1940, he attacked three Junkers 88s, destroyed two and damaged the third. Later in the month he intercepted two Junkers 88s at 15,000 feet, and in a head-on attack destroyed one. In a similar attack on the second, a cannon shell blew away his oil and glycol tank and a piece of his propeller, but he reached the coast and landed by parachute. In September 1940, he shot down one Messerschmitt 109 over the sea. Flt Lt Tuck has displayed gallant and determined leadership.

Distinguished Service Order (*London Gazette* 7th January 1941)
This officer has commanded his squadron with great success, and his outstanding leadership, courage and skill have been reflected in its high morale and efficiency. Since 4th October, 1940, he has destroyed four hostile aircraft, bringing his total victories to at least eighteen.

Second Bar to DFC (*London Gazette* 11th April 1941)

This officer has displayed conspicuous gallantry and initiative in searching for and attacking enemy raiders, often in adverse weather conditions. Since December 1940, he has destroyed three enemy bombers and one fighter, bringing his total victories to twenty-two.

American Distinguished Flying Cross, awarded 14 June 1946.

Tuck was also mentioned in despatches three times.

RALPH VAN DEN BOK

Born in London on 2nd September 1907, to a Dutch father and Australian mother, he attended Dulwich College, and pre-war worked in the London Stock Exchange. He joined the RAFVR in 1940 and after training, became a wireless operator/air gunner, and posted to 408 Squadron RCAF, equipped with Hampden bombers.

Ralph Van Den Bok. (214Squadron.org.uk)

He completed thirty bombing operations and was awarded the DFC. One mission was during the Channel Dash on 12th February 1942, the day German capitol ships made a dash along the English Channel to Norway from Brest. Ralph's pilot on this occasion was Sqn Ldr D. S. N. Constance RNZAF. The aircraft was badly damaged by AA fire and the radio was knocked out, but Van den Bok repaired it and got them home. However, on 28th October 1942, flying with the CO, Wg Cdr J. D. Twigg RCAF, on a raid to Saarbrücken they were on their way home when they were attacked by a German Ju 88 night-fighter, flown by Hauptmann Wilhelm Herget, of 9./NJG4, north-west of Philippeville, Belgium, at 2322 hours, his second victory of the night and his seventh overall. Herget would survive the war with seventy-one victories, fifty-seven during night actions. He received the Knight's Cross with Oak Leaves.

Twigg and their air gunner, Flt Lt I. Maitland DFC, were both killed, but Van den Bok and the navigator Flt Lt G. C. Fisher RCAF baled out as the aircraft crashed at Boussu-lez-Walcourt, 24 km SSW of Charleroi. Both men managed to evade capture and picked up by the French Resistance, were passed along by the Comet Line 55, to Paris, by Andre de Jongh and Jeanine De Greef.

They were spirited through France, into Spain and finally Gibraltar, from where Ralph was flown back to England on 2nd October. Fisher was evacuated by submarine on 21st September, arriving at Greenock on 5th October. Both men were decorated, Ralph with a Bar to his DFC, Gordon Fisher the DFC.

Van den Bok made the following report to MI9 on 4th October:

> 'I took off at 2000 hours on 28th August 1942 from Balderton, Notts, in a Hampden aircraft to bomb Saarbrücken. We were shot down by

a Ju 88 at about 2230 hours. I baled out and landed by parachute in a field at Cerfontaine, Belgium, unhurt all but for scratches on the leg. The aircraft crashed about five miles away. The rest of the crew were: Wg Cdr J. D. Twigg (killed), Flt Lt G. C. Fisher (navigator) (now on convoy from Gibraltar), Flt Lt I. Maitland DFC (rear gunner) (killed in aircraft before the crash).'

The report continued:

'I had lost my boots, and, after hiding my parachute, walked for ten minutes until I came to a hamlet called Les Violettes. I met some Belgian peasants who told me there were no Germans nearer than three kilometres. These people did not appear very helpful, but I later discovered that their attitude was due to caution, since one of them was the wife of a helper. I, therefore, slept in the woods near Ballonet. [This name stands for Bois d'Allonet.]

'I saw a farmer come out with an Alsatian dog. I whistled to the dog, which came and made friends with me. I then declared my identity to the farmer, and received help and shelter for three days. My host had a friend, who put me in contact with an organisation by means of which I was brought back to the UK.'

Once back in England, Van den Bok decided to become a pilot and being accepted, was sent to Canada to train, despite his age of thirty-seven. Back in the UK with his 'wings' up, he went to 12 Operational Training Unit then to 1657 Conversion Unit, and finally to 214 Squadron, flying American B17s on radio counter measures duty – jamming of German radio and radar. An acting squadron leader by January 1945, he completed seventeen sorties before the war ended, and received a second Bar to his DFC.

He remained in the RAF after the war but transferred to the Reserve on 29th May 1951 and finally relinquished his commission on 2nd May 1955. He joined the Standard Oil Company (Esso), employed to fly a Percival Proctor aircraft. In December 1957 he was involved in the Lewisham railway crash; a badly smashed leg turned gangrenous and had to be amputated.

By this time he had married, and had two sons, Paul and Adrian. Ralph died in Salisbury, Wiltshire, in 1976.

Distinguished Flying Cross (*London Gazette* 4th August 1942)

This officer has participated in numerous sorties against heavily defended targets, including Mannheim, Duisburg, Hüls, Bremen, Kiel and Hamburg. He was the wireless operator/air-gunner of a Hampden aircraft which participated in a low-level attack on the *Scharnhorst* during the battleship's escape from Brest. The aircraft was extensively damaged, including the wireless equipment, by the battleship's defences. Skilfully effecting repairs, Fg Off Van den Bok re-established communication with his base, thus rendering valuable assistance in the safe return of the aircraft.

Bar to DFC (*London Gazette* 24th November 1942)

In August 1942, Flt Lt Van den Bok and Flt Lt Fisher were wireless operator/air gunner and navigator respectively of an aircraft detailed to attack Saarbrücken. On the return flight the bomber was attacked by enemy aircraft, sustaining much damage. Flt Lt Van den Bok, who was wounded in the leg by a piece of shrapnel, and Flt Lt Fisher displayed outstanding courage, determination and fortitude. Both have completed many sorties and have invariably displayed similar qualities.

Second Bar to DFC (*London Gazette* 26th October 1945)

This officer has a distinguished record of operational flying. His enthusiasm for operational flying was not diminished by his experiences in evading capture after being shot down by anti-aircraft fire [sic] whilst over occupied Belgium during his first tour of duty. Since the award of a Bar to the DFC, Sqn Ldr Van den Bok has flown many sorties against strongly defended targets in Germany, including Berlin. He is an excellent captain of aircraft and flight commander, who has at all times set an inspiring example by his enthusiasm, courage, and devotion to duty.

REMY VAN LIERDE

Known as 'Mony' he came from Overboelaere, Belgium, born 15th August 1915. Joined the Aviation Militaire Belgium 16th September 1935 and trained as an observer, but then began training to be a pilot on 1st May 1937, qualifying in April 1938. With the rank of sergeant, he was posted to the 3rd Squadron, 1st Aviation Regiment at Goetsenhoven.

With the coming of war, Van Lierde flew a number of reconnaissance missions during the German invasion in May, in a Fairey Fox III biplane. However, on the 16th he was shot down by ground fire, wounded and taken into captivity in the hospital at Malines. Recovering from his wounds, he managed to escape. On 30th May 1940, he crossed into France and entered Spain, where he was arrested and put into prison. He escaped once again on 28th September, evaded recapture and eventually made his way to England, arriving on 20th July 1941.

He joined the RAFVR on 5th September, and trained at No. 57 Operational Training Unit before being sent to 609 Squadron on 6th January 1942. No. 609 was a squadron which had several Belgian pilots among its pilots. He had his first taste of action on 2nd June, intercepting and damaging a Dornier 217 over Skegness, flying a Spitfire Vb. The squadron then changed its equipment to the new Hawker Typhoon fighter.

Van Lierde's first confirmed victory was over a Me 109 on 20th January 1943, the RAF mounting standing patrols to combat German hit-and-run fighter-bombers, dropping bombs indiscriminately along the south coast of England. A married man, Van Lierde shot down a Ju 52 transport aircraft on 26th March, while en route to attack the German air base at Chièvres. The action was witnessed by a number of local inhabitants, including Van Lierde's wife, who surprised her husband after the war by showing him pieces of the downed Junkers at the end of their garden. On 14th May he was the first pilot to drop bombs from a Typhoon, and forced a He 111 to crash on its way home from a night mission. At the end of July he claimed another 109 and on 5th October added a Ju 88, and destroyed another of these on the ground.

His last victory was a Me 110, on 30th November, bringing his score to six plus one ground victory. Promoted to flight lieutenant in September, he left 609 on 22nd December with a posting to the Central Gunnery School at RAF Sutton Bridge, but returned to 609 on 7th February 1944 at Manston as master gunnery leader.

In April he was posted to 3 Squadron, flying Tempest V fighters, operating against the V1 menace. In all he destroyed forty-four of these 'doodlebugs' and shared in another nine, making him the second highest V1 killer. On 4th July he shot down four of these flying bombs, and the next day, during two sorties, shot down five. His V1 victories were scored between 16th June and 16th August, thirty-five destroyed with nine more shared. Having been awarded the DFC in June 1943, he received a Bar in July 1944.

Once the V1 period came to an end, Van Lierde took command of 164 Squadron on 20th August, taking it to France, and leading it till January 1945 against ground targets. From May he served in No. 84 Group Support Unit as Belgian liaison officer at 2nd TAF HQ. In July he received a second Bar to his DFC. That August he was given command of 350 Squadron, flying Spitfires, a unit that later was transferred to the Belgian air force. Commissioned into the Belgian air force in June 1946, he took command of the 1st Fighter Wing at Beauvechain, and from October 1947 to November 1950 he was head of the office of group operations, while also studying at the RAF College in 1948. He was appointed detachment commander at Chièvres, followed by commander of the 7th Fighter Wing on 1st December 1950. Three years later he was appointed to the operations group of chiefs of Staff, and in September 1953 became an aide to King Leopold III.

Now with the rank of lieutenant-colonel he was made deputy chief of Staff to the minister of defence in 1954. In November 1958, along with Capt Yves Bodart, he travelled to England, to test fly the Hawker Hunter at Dunsfold, becoming one of the first Belgian pilots to break the sound barrier. A full colonel in 1959 he commanded Kamina air base in the Belgian Congo, a post he held to June 1960. Returning to Belgium he became chief of operations of the chiefs of Staff while also commanding the 7th Fighter Wing. He retired in 1968 and died in Lessines, on 8th June 1990.

Distinguished Flying Cross (Approved 1st June 1943)
Has participated in many operational missions during which he has inflicted considerable damage to the enemy. In addition to destroying three enemy aircraft he has damaged seven locomotives and five enemy ships.

Bar to DFC (Approved 20th July 1944)
Since being awarded the DFC, this officer has destroyed a further four enemy aircraft and at least nine pilotless aircraft [V1s], and inflicted much other severe damage to the enemy. He has at all times displayed outstanding ability and has now participated in 250 sorties.

Second Bar to DFC (Approved 24th July 1945)

During July 1944, whilst with 3 Squadron, Sqn Ldr Van Lierde destroyed twenty-eight flying bombs. Since August, 1944, he has led his squadron in eighty-five sorties against enemy transport, armour, strong-points, troops and communications. His daring, vigour and skill in pressing home his attacks, often in the face of heavy anti-aircraft fire, have been an inspiration to his fellow pilots. During the period covered by his leadership the squadron has, inter alia, given close support to our advancing army in its most vital operations and it is largely due to Sqn Ldr Van Lierde's leadership and organising ability that the Sqn has been so successful in these operations.

Number of sorties flown thus far by Van Lierde was 420, covering 473 operational hours.

LANCE CLEO WADE

Born on 18th November 1916, in Broaddus, San Augustine County, Texas, Lance Wade was the son of Bill and Susan Wade. His older brother Oran, and others in the family, usually referred to him as 'LC'. In 1922 the family moved to Reklaw, Texas, where Lance attended the local school while helping with the family farm. At the age of seventeen he decided to become a pilot and began training at Tuscon, Arizona, with an aeroplane purchased with some friends. In 1934, aged nineteen, he joined the Civilian Conservation Corps (CCC) in Arizona, a public work relief programme for unemployed, unmarried men aged between the ages of eighteen to twenty-five, founded by Franklin D. Roosevelt during the US Depression era. Meantime he completed some fifty-four flying hours at the Spartan Air Base at Tulsa, used by the RAF as a refresher school.

With the coming of war in Europe, Wade tried to join the USAAF as a cadet but failed due to poor education standards, so he joined the RAF in Canada in December 1940, came to England and completed his flight training at No. 52 Operational Training Unit. Posted out to Egypt, he was sent to 33 Squadron with Hurricanes and downed his first two enemy aircraft, both Italian CR42 biplane fighters on 18th November. All his initial victories were Italian aircraft, his first German claim being over a Me 109 which he damaged on 21st December. By this date he had achieved four victories plus shares in two others. In attacks on airfields he had destroyed or damaged six more. One event on 5th December was when he was hit by ground fire during a ground-strafing attack, forcing him to crash land. A brother pilot landed in order to pick him up but this machine was damaged so both men had to walk back many miles before being picked up by friendly forces. In action over the Western Desert in 1942 his main opponents continued to be Italian machines and by the end of that year his score had risen to a dozen with more damaged.

Ending his tour, he was sent back to America to help evaluate US fighters and while attached to an RAF delegation in Washington, was introduced to President Franklin D. Roosevelt at the White House. After much feting in several US towns and his own hometown he returned to action in January 1943, posted as flight commander to 145 Squadron, flying Spitfire Vs. His next promotion was to commanding officer of the squadron and by the end of April 1943 his score had risen to more than twenty.

Now flying Spitfire IXs, 145 Squadron was involved in the invasion of Sicily and then came fighting on the Italian mainland. Over the latter Wade shot down two Fw 190s on 2nd October, and damaged three Fw 190s on the 3rd, although it seems II/SG4 lost a pilot in this action. Wade was promoted to wing commander and joined the staff of the Desert Air Force, but on 12th January 1944 he was killed in a crash flying an Auster III (MT415) at Foggia, Italy.

Initially buried in Mirandola, eighteen miles NE of Modena, his body was later taken back to America and buried in the McKnight Cemetery in Reklaw, Texas. Aged twenty-seven he had been nicknamed by the media as the 'Wildcat from Texas' and was the highest-scoring American pilot to serve only with the RAF. He had received the DFC and two Bars, and it had just been announced that he was to receive the DSO.

Distinguished Flying Cross (*London Gazette* 7th April 1942)
This officer has carried out fifty-four operations against the enemy, and has taken an active part in the squadron's very successful operations against enemy

transport columns and aerodromes. One day in November 1941, he took off with five other pilots to defend a forward airfield which was being attacked by twelve Junkers 88s, and destroyed one of them. On the same afternoon he led a section of two aircraft detailed to intercept a Savoia 79 escorted by six fighters. Plt Off Wade shared in the destruction of the enemy bomber after driving off the fighters. On another occasion, during an attack on Agedabia airfield in the face of intense opposition, this officer damaged three Caproni 42s on the ground and destroyed a Savoia 79, thus bringing his total to four enemy aircraft destroyed. Plt Off Wade was subsequently shot down himself, but rejoined the squadron after walking for twenty-five miles. He has displayed outstanding courage, and has done much to maintain the excellent morale of the squadron.

Bar to DFC (*London Gazette* 13th October 1942)
Since being awarded the Distinguished Flying Cross this officer has destroyed seven enemy aircraft thus bringing his total victories to fifteen. In September, 1942, during a reconnaissance patrol his aircraft was attacked by some eight Italian fighters. Flt Lt Wade, however, fought them off. By his skill and determination he contributed materially to the success of the reconnaissance and much valuable information was obtained. Flt Lt Wade's courage and devotion to duty has been an inspiration to all.

Second Bar to DFC (*London Gazette* 27th April 1943)
This officer is the leader of a squadron which has achieved much success in recent operations. During March, 1943, the squadron destroyed twenty-one enemy aircraft, four of which were shot down by Sqn Ldr Wade. By his great skill and daring, this officer has contributed materially to the high standard of operational efficiency of the squadron he commands. Sqn Ldr Wade has destroyed nineteen enemy aircraft.

Distinguished Service Order (*London Gazette* 25th January 1944)
Since being awarded a second bar to his DFC, this officer has continued to lead his squadron in operations against the enemy in the North African campaign and during the invasion of Sicily and the campaign in Italy. He has destroyed a further five enemy aircraft, bringing his total victories to at least twenty-five enemy aircraft destroyed and others damaged. An outstanding leader and fighter pilot, Wg Cdr Wade's great skill, courage and devotion to duty have largely contributed to the high efficiency attained by his squadron.

JAMES ELMSLIE WALKER

'Jimmy' Walker was a Canadian, born on 4th April 1919 at Claresholm, Alberta, the son of James and Helen Augusta Walker. After completing his education he became a bank teller in Edmonton, with the Canadian Bank of Commerce in 1936. With the coming of war, he wanted to join up in order to fly. Helped by the legendary WW1 fighter ace, Wilfrid 'Wop' May DFC, he enlisted in May 1940, started training at No. 2 SFTS, and was commissioned on 1st December that year then travelled to England on 14th December.

Once his training had been completed he was posted to 81 Squadron in August 1941 and was with this unit until 13th February 1943, including the time it fought in Russia, and in North Africa. No. 81 went to Russia aboard the carrier HMS *Argus*, flying off to become part of 151 Fighter Wing at Murmansk. On 12th September 1941 he downed a Me 109 and on 6th October claimed a Ju 88 probably destroyed.

Returning from Russia in November the squadron remained in England for a while, Walker shooting down a Fw 190 off Le Touquet on 2nd June, by which time he had become a flight commander. He saw action over Dieppe in August 1942 and was awarded the DFC. In November he moved to North Africa with 81 Squadron where he had considerable success in air combat against German and Italian aircraft. In just under a month, from 9th November to 6th December he claimed two destroyed, one shared, and several damaged. In January he bagged two more enemy aircraft before being posted to command 243 Squadron, part of 242 Group, adding a Bar to his DFC in March and a second Bar in July. In the final weeks of his tour he was engaged in actions over Tunisia. At the end of his tour his total victories came to at least nine and one shared, plus four probables and 12 and three shared damaged. All his latter victories were either Me 109s or Ju 87 Stuka dive-bombers. On 11th April his Spitfire was hit and set ablaze by return fire from a Stuka and he was forced to bale out at 6,000 feet, landed without injury and walked home. He had earlier experienced another downing, for on 26th February, his Spitfire was hit by anti-aircraft fire, damaging one wing and the oil cooling system, but he managed to glide down and belly-land just inside Allied lines.

Walker left 243 Squadron on 1st June 1943 and was given home leave to Canada in September. While there he married Barbara Joan Whitley on 16th

October. However, he was posted back to England on 29th November, starting a brief stay at RCAF Overseas HQ in London. Following this he was sent to the RAF Staff College on 6th December. On 3rd March he became wing leader of No. 144 Wing, as wing commander flying.

On 25th April 1944, flying an Auster (NK116) he flew an unauthorised low-flying trip to Tangmere with Sgt R. F. Teale RAF. Banking round some trees, the port wing struck the top branches of two trees and crashed. Teale was killed and Walker died later in hospital, and is buried in Brookwood Military Cemetery. He had just passed his twenty-fifth birthday.

Distinguished Flying Cross (*London Gazette* 11th September 1942)
This officer is a determined and skilful pilot. He has at all times shown a keen desire to engage the enemy. While serving in Russia, Flt Lt Walker destroyed one hostile aircraft. Since March 1942, he has led his flight continuously in all its operations.

Bar to DFC (*London Gazette* 19th March 1943)
In operations in North Africa, Sqn Ldr Walker has destroyed four enemy aircraft. By his great skill, leadership and untiring efforts, this officer has won high praise.

Second Bar to DFC (*London Gazette* 9th July 1943)
Sqn Ldr Walker assumed command of his squadron at a difficult period and, by his fine leadership and excellent example, was responsible for bringing it to its present day high standard of efficiency. He has been largely instrumental for the many successes achieved by the squadron and has himself destroyed at least four enemy aircraft and damaged others.

ADRIAN WARBURTON

'Warby' as he became known, was born in Mid-dlesborough, on 10 March 1918, the son of Commander Geoffrey Warburton DSO RN, and his wife Murial. He had a sister, Alison, five years older than him. His father was a submarine captain, and in fact, Adrian was christened aboard his father's submarine, while serving in Malta. Considering Adrian's future, it was a special place to be received into the church.

Both children received their education in Bournemouth, England, Adrian going to Sangeen School till about fourteen, later the Warburtons lived in Park Avenue, Enfield, Middlesex. Meantime, Adrian was sent to St. Edward's boarding school in Oxford. In 1937, he enlisted in the Territorials as a private into the Royal Tank Corps (22nd London Armoured Car Coy), but a year later changed his mind and joined the RAF and received a short-service commission. His initial pilot training was at No. 10 E&R FTS at Prestwick leaving in January 1939 to go to No. 8 FTS at Hullavington.

He was then posted to the Torpedo Training Unit at Gosport, so it seemed likely he would become a torpedo pilot with Coastal Command. This became reality in October 1939 with his posting to 22 Squadron at Thorney Island, equipped with the antiquated Vickers Vildebeest biplane. Fortunately the squadron was soon to convert to the Bristol Beaufort twin-engine torpedo aeroplane. That October he met a barmaid in a local hostelry, Eileen 'Betty' Mitchell and they were married in Westminster on 28th October. However, it did not last long and they more or less lived apart.

Adrian Warburton was often unconventional, and did not get on with his CO, so when Adrian completed a general reconnaissance course at Squires Gate, near Blackpool, No. 2 School of General Reconnaissance, the CO, having to choose three crews to convert to the Glenn Martin 167F Maryland in order to form 431 Flight, selected Adrian. As soon as the conversions took place, three Marylands were sent off to Malta.

On his first dozen sorties, Warby flew half of them as navigator, often to Fg Off James Foxton. Their area of duty was in and around the Italian harbour at Taranto or along the Greek coast, looking for enemy shipping. On 12th October, in the pilot's seat of AR707, they were attacked by an Italian fighter, but they successfully evaded its fire. Warby had several encounters with hostile aircraft.

On 30th October he was observing around Brindisi and Taranto despite heavy AA fire when they ran into an Italian seaplane, which his gunners shot down. On 2nd November, on another recce mission, they were attacked by three CR42 biplane fighters, his rear gunner setting one of them smoking. A few days later they engaged a Macchi 202 fighter and this too limped away from his gunners' fire.

Then came the plan to attack the Italian navy in Taranto harbour on 11th November. On the 10th Warburton and crew flew to the harbour in bad weather and at very low level, which surprised the defences, and the crew were able to fly around the harbour plotting the positions of all the ships there – five battleships, fourteen cruisers and twenty-seven destroyers. The following day Fleet Air Arm Swordfish made torpedo attacks based on the information provided and put half the Italian navy out of action for the loss of two Swordfish.

On 10th January 1941, 421 Flight became 69 Squadron. He often flew with two NCOs, Sgts P. D. J. 'Paddy' Moren and Frank Bastard, both of whom received the DFM. To list all of Warby's achievements would somewhat overload this section of the book, but he was never afraid of a fight, and on 15th December 1940, even went down and strafed a surfaced U-boat he spotted off Syracuse. No. 69 Squadron also changed its Marylands for Baltimores and when Warby got his hands on a Spitfire in 1942, he found it not only a delight but fitted with cameras, he could improve on photographic technique.

In 1943 he left 69 and took command of 683 Squadron, formed from B Flight of 69, fully equipped with Spitfires. Photographing from a much higher altitude, the targets remained the same – Taranto, Palermo, Messina and Naples, but with the planned invasion of Sicily, it was back to low-level sorties. All too soon, as far as he was concerned, it was time for a rest. But rather than take one, he began to co-operate with USAAF units, especially when they let him fly one of their P38 PR Lightnings. On one occasion, soon after take-off he had engine trouble and had to crash land but got clear of the burning P38, got back to the airfield and was soon away in another P38. After flying several missions with the Americans, he was given command of a PR Wing at La Marsa but a motoring accident in Tunis ended this promotion and he was sent back to England.

Upon recovery he again visited his American friends and on 12th April 1944, managed to convince someone that he fly a P38 trip across Germany and having taken pictures of a target, pay a visit to friends on Sardinia. Taking off from Mount Farm, adjacent to RAF Benson, Oxfordshire, in a P38F5B (No. 42-67325), he was accompanied by another P38. Their task was to photograph Regensburg and Schweinfurt, Warby taking the latter, then rather than return, they would fly on to Sardinia and return to England over France the next day.

The two P38s headed south, and north of Munich they separated to each go to their respective targets. They were to meet up over Munich but Warby never showed. His companion called several times, but the radio remained silent, so he headed for Sardinia. Warburton was listed as missing.

For years it was all a mystery until a Mr Frank Dorber became obsessed with finding the answer. In due course he discovered that only two PR P38s had been lost this day, and eventually narrowed the search down to a place called Egling in southern Germany, finding records of a German AA battery having shot down an Allied aircraft on 12th April. In August 2002 an excavation of the site revealed remains of both a P38 and its pilot. These remains were buried in the Bavarian village of Gmund on 14th May 2003. On 12th April the following year, sixty years after his death, Warby had a small stone memorial placed near to the airfield he took off from in 1944, together with an RAF Honour Guard and members of the Royal British Legion and local branches of the RAFA. His widow, Betty, aged ninety-two, was also in attendance, although she had married twice since their failed marriage at the beginning of the war. Warby, of course, had a romantic association with a dancer and cabaret entertainer on Malta, who had originally come from Cheshire. Warby, the unorthodox 'King of the Mediterranean', was a month short of his twenty-sixth birthday.

Distinguished Flying Cross (*London Gazette* 11th February 1941)
This officer has carried out numerous long-distance reconnaissance flights and has taken part in night air combats. In October 1940, he destroyed an aircraft and again, in December, he shot down an enemy bomber in flames. Fg Off Warburton has at all times displayed a fine sense of devotion to duty.

Bar to DFC (*London Gazette* 9th September 1941)
This officer is a most determined and skilful pilot and has carried out 125 operational missions. Fg Off Warburton has never failed to complete the missions he has undertaken, and in the actions fought, he has destroyed at least three hostile aircraft in combat and another three on the ground.

Distinguished Service Order (*London Gazette* 29th March 1942)
This officer has carried out many missions each of which has demanded the highest degree of courage and skill. On one occasion whilst carrying out a reconnaissance of Taranto, Flt Lt Warburton made two attempts to penetrate the harbour, although as there was much low cloud this entailed flying at a height of fifty feet over an enemy battleship. In spite of the failure of his port engine and repeated attacks from enemy aircraft he completed his mission and made a safe

return. On another occasion he obtained photographs of Tripoli in spite of ene-my fighter patrols over the harbour. In March 1942, Flt Lt Warburton carried out a reconnaissance of Palermo and obtained photographs revealing the damage caused by our attacks. This officer has never failed to obtain photographs from a very low altitude, regardless of enemy opposition. His work has been most val-uable, regardless of enemy opposition. He has displayed great skill and tenacity.

Second Bar to DFC (*London Gazette* 3rd November 1942)

Since August 1942, this officer has completed numerous operational photo-graphic sorties, many of them at low altitudes and often in the face of opposition from enemy fighters. His work has been of the utmost value. In October, 1942, his gallantry was well illustrated when he directed an enemy destroyer to a din-ghy in which were the crew of one of our aircraft, which had been shot down. Although he was fired upon by the destroyer and engaged by Italian aircraft, he remained over the area until he observed the drifting crew were picked up by the destroyer.

Bar to DSO (Recommendation which led to the award in the *London Gazette* 6th August 1943)

'Wg Cdr Warburton has commanded 683 Photographic Reconnais-sance Squadron since its formation on 8th February, 1943 and prior to the formation of this squadron he commanded 69 Squadron. This officer has flown a total of 375 operational sorties involving 1,300 hours flying. From Malta he has completed 360 sorties with a total of 1,240 hours. During his tour of duty in Malta, he has covered all the Italian and Sicilian targets continuously, invariably obtaining 100% cover with his photography.

'In recent months, since he has commanded 683 Squadron, he has continued to operate on all the routine sorties required from a pilot of the squadron, selecting for himself the sorties which have been con-sidered of a more dangerous nature. On a recent operation, one cam-era became unserviceable. In order to ensure that full photographic cover would be obtained, he covered every target, including Taranto, three times being continuously chased by Me 109s.

'On 15th November, 1942, Wg Cdr Warburton was despatched on a photographic reconnaissance of Bizerta. He was attacked by Me 109s and with his aircraft damaged he force-landed at Bône. From there he went to Gibraltar, returning to Malta a few days later in a fighter aircraft. He encountered two Ju 88s on his return journey which he engaged, destroying one and damaging the other.

'On 5th December, this officer carried out a photographic reconnaissance of Naples. In spite of intense flak and enemy fighter opposition he covered the whole of the target area at 4,000 feet.

'On 18th May, he took low-level obliques of the whole of the Pantelleria coastline from a height of 200 feet. He was fired on continuously by the AA coastal batteries but succeeded in obtaining results which proved extremely valuable in the eventual invasion of the island.

'Wg Cdr Warburton has destroyed a total of nine enemy aircraft while flying armed reconnaissance aircraft and three on the ground.

'The importance of the results obtained by this officer in spite of intense enemy opposition and in all weathers cannot be too highly estimated. The success of operations carried out from this Island, the safe arrival and departures of convoys are largely dependent on the accuracy of photographic reconnaissance.

'Wg Cdr Warburton is to a great extent responsible for this successful reconnaissance. His personal enthusiasm for operations, his courage and devotion to duty have set the highest example to all with whom he was associated.'

American Distinguished Flying Cross (*London Gazette* 18th January 1944)
While on a mission to obtain urgently needed photographs of the coastline of Pantelleria on 3rd June, he distinguished himself through his resolute courage and calm efficiency under fire. Flying over the island at 200 feet, within easy range of every type of anti-aircraft battery and drawing fire of even the large coastal guns, Warburton photographed virtually the entire shoreline, gaining information of inestimable value to the Allied Forces which later invaded the island.

HAROLD ALFRED WHISTLER

The son of clergyman Alfred J. and Mary Maud Whistler, he was born on 30th December 1896 in Theddlethorpe, Lincolnshire. He was the fourth child, following one brother and two sisters. He completed his education at Oundle School before going to the Royal Military College at Sandhurst, Berkshire.

The family was living at the Rectory in Little Carlton, Lincolnshire, when Harold joined the Dorset Regiment, commissioned on 19th July 1916, but then transferred to the Royal Flying Corps. Once trained as a pilot (29th September 1916) he was posted to 3 Squadron, flying observation flights over the Western Front. On 17th December, flying a Morane LA (A270) along with Lt A. G. S. Ross as his Australian observer, they were attacked by a German aircraft and forced to crash land. He was forced down again, and wounded in action on 29th January 1917. In a Morane P (A239), with observer Corporal E. J. Hare they were flying a photographic sortie when they were shot up and forced to land. Whistler's observer was also injured in the landing.

Recovering from his wounds, 'Willy' Whistler, eventually ended up as a Sopwith Camel pilot, and went as a flight commander to the newly formed 80 Squadron, on 27th August 1917. The squadron moved to France in January 1918 and undertook much ground-attack, bombing and strafing sorties, particularly in co-operating with the Tank Corps as an anti-tank gun suppression unit. Not surprisingly the squadron, being exposed to plenty of ground fire, suffered heavy casualties. In aerial combat, Whistler became a veritable tiger in the air, and by far the most successful and outstanding fighter pilot on the squadron. By the war's end he had achieved twenty-three victories, of which thirteen were classed at destroyed, nine out of control, plus a balloon. These achievements brought him the DFC and Bar, and the DSO. In one action on 1st June with some Pfalz DIII scouts, the plywood behind his seat was set on fire by a tracer bullet but he put out the flames and landed safely.

After the war he decided to remain in the RAF, was given a permanent commission and one of his first posts was as an instructor at the RAF College, Cranwell. Whistler saw service in Iraq in 1927 to 1928, flying operations against the Nadj Bedouin tribesmen, flying DH9As out of Hinaidi with 55 Squadron, which he commanded. For his actions he received a second Bar to his DFC.

He subsequently instructed at the Central Flying School between 1930 and 1932, rising to the rank of wing commander in July 1934 and group captain in 1938. By 1940 he had become chief of Staff of RAF India as an acting air commodore. He was also a married man with a family.

With the beginning of WW2 he was recalled to England in 1940 to take up further positions of importance, with the promise of being promoted to air commodore. He took off from India as a passenger aboard an Imperial Airways HP42 (named 'Hannibal'), but it disappeared without trace over the Gulf of Oman on 1st March 1940, with eight people on board. He was forty-three years old.

Distinguished Flying Cross (*London Gazette* 2nd July and 3rd August 1918)
A very courageous and enterprising patrol leader, who has rendered valuable services. He has done exceptionally good work in attacking ground targets, which he engages at very low altitudes. During the past month his patrol attacked eight enemy scouts who were flying above him. He attacked a triplane and brought it down to crash, and whilst thus himself engaged another of his pilots destroyed a second enemy machine. The remainder of the enemy formation was driven off.

Distinguished Service Order (*London Gazette* 2nd November 1918)
During recent operations this officer has rendered exceptionally brilliant service in attacking enemy aircraft and troops on the ground. On 9th August he dropped four bombs on a hostile battery, engaged and threw into confusion a body of troops, and drove down a hostile balloon, returning to his aerodrome after a patrol of one and a half hours duration with a most valuable report. He has in all destroyed ten aircraft and driven down five others out of control.

Bar to DFC (*London Gazette* 8th February 1919)
This officer has twenty-two enemy machines and one balloon to his credit. He distinguished himself greatly on 29th September, when he destroyed two machines in one combat, and on 15th September, when, following two balloons [down] to within twenty feet of the ground, he destroyed one and caused the observer of the second to jump out and crash. He has, in addition, done arduous and valuable service in bombing enemy objectives and obtaining information. Capt Whistler is a gallant officer of fine judgement and power of leadership.

Second Bar to DFC (*London Gazette* 15th March 1929)
In recognition of gallant and distinguished service rendered in connection with the operations against the Akhwan in the Southern Desert, 'Iraq', during the period November 1927 to May 1928.

HAROLD EDWARD WHITE

By coincidence the first triple DFC winner recorded in this book is Mike Allen, and here, the last, is his pilot, Harry White. Born on 23rd May, 1923, and educated at Bearwood, Woking, White enlisted into the RAFVR in 1940, although it is thought he lied about his age, and trained as a pilot. He went to No. 54 Operational Training Unit as a sergeant in July 1941. Commissioned on 26th March 1942, he was first sent to 534 Squadron, where he met up with Mike Allen, remaining together as a night-fighting team for the rest of the war.

No. 534 was a Turbinlite unit with Havoc Is, the idea being for the Havoc crew to locate night raiders on its radar, and call in Hurricane fighters to shoot down the enemy aircraft that was now caught in the massive searchlight fitted to the Havoc. There were few successes by these Turbinlite units. However, White and Allen were then posted to 141 Squadron, which would become a bomber-support unit, flying into Germany to help pick off German night-fighters as they homed in on RAF Lancasters, Halifaxes and Stirlings. The apparatus that the radar operator (Allen) used could detect enemy aircraft and guide the pilot into an attacking position. The operation went by the name of 'Serrate'.

Flying Beaufighter VIFs, their first success came on the night of 3rd/4th July 1943, damaging a Me 110 over Aachen. On 15th/16th July, they got a 110 destroyed south-east of Reims, flown by the German ace Major Herbert Rauh of II.NJG 4. Rauh was a Knight's Cross winner with thirty-one kills. As the summer progressed they added another 110 as damaged to their score, then two Ju 88s in August and September. Two other German aces were shot down by White and Allen in August, Maj Wilhelm Dormann of III.NJG 1, who baled out, and Ltn Gerhard Dittmann of 12/NJG 1. Both White and Allen received the DFC.

In 1944 the squadron re-equipped with Mosquito IIs and north of Berlin on the night of 27th/28th January, the team shot down a Me 109 'Wild Boar' fighter.

On 15th/16th February they claimed a He 177 destroyed near Berlin and in March they scored a double on the night of 18th/19th, both Ju 88s. They damaged another 88 before the month was out and in April shot down a Do217. In May they shot down another Ju 88 and a Me 109 and two more Ju 88s towards the end of July. This brought their total victories to twelve and three damaged. It was not all plain sailing, and White and Allen had several narrow escapes such as on the night of 17th August 1943 helping to protect the bomb raid on Peenemünde.

Members of 141 Squadron at the end of WW2. **From left to right (standing):** Flt Lt Henry 'Jacko' Jacobs DFC★; (fifth from left) Flt Lt 'Sticks' Gregory DSO, DFC; (seventh from left) Wg Cdr Bob Braham DSO★★, DFC★★, AFC, CD; (tenth from left) Harry White; (eleventh from left) Mike Allen. **Front row (from left to right):** Wg Cdr H. C. Kelsey DSO DFC★ and Sqn Ldr C. V. Winn DSO, DFC.

Near Hamburg they were attacked by a night-fighter that they then engaged and claimed as damaged, although post-war they discovered they had actually shot it down. Near Aachen on another occasion, White had got so close to his target – a 109 – that when it exploded his night vision was lost and for some minutes he was more or less blinded. One evening in January 1945, now flying Mosquito XXXs, soon after taking off on what was their ninety-first sortie, an engine failed and White was forced to crash land in a field, where it exploded in flames. Fortunately, a farmer and two of his labourers where nearby and managed to extricate both men from the burning wreckage. All three men received BEMs. Both White and Allen worked with bomber support development unit and both received Bars to the DFCs.

With the war at an end, White elected to remain in the RAF and qualified as an instructor, became a chief flying instructor. He was awarded the AFC in 1952 and the Queen's Commendation for Valuable Service in the Air in the New Year Honours List in 1954. He became commander of the flying wing at RAF Leeming in 1955. The following year he took command of 46 Squadron that was introducing the Gloster Javelin all-weather fighter into service. Between 1959 and 1967, he held various staff appointments in both the UK and the Far East. On his return he commanded RAF Buchan, near Peterhead, Aberdeenshire, which was a radar station/control and reporting centre, responsible for co-ordinating all aspects of air defence as part of the UK's air surveillance and control system (ASACS).

White spent two years on the planning staff of RAF Germany, and then made director of quartering, completing his service in charge of administration for the RAF in Germany. He retired as an air commodore on 29th November 1977, and appointed CBE on 1st January 1978.

Once retired, he became chief executive of Swale District Council in Kent, having been selected from more than eighty applicants. It was a post he held until 1988. He died on 25th March 1990, survived by his wife and two sons.

Distinguished Flying Cross (*London Gazette* 24th September 1943)
This officer has completed numerous sorties over enemy territory and has displayed great skill and determination throughout. In July 1943, he shot down a Messerschmitt 110, while during another sortie in August, 1943, he engaged three hostile aircraft in separate combats. In the latter engagement his opponent's aircraft was seen to spiral towards the ground in flames and explode on impact.

Bar to DFC (*London Gazette* 14th April 1944. (Joint citation with Fg Off M. S. Allen DFC. Awarded First Bar to the DFC.)
As observer (Allen) and pilot (White) respectively these officers have completed many sorties since being awarded the Distinguished Flying Cross. They have set a fine example of keenness and devotion to duty and have now destroyed at least five enemy aircraft at night. Their achievements have been worthy of much praise.

Second Bar to DFC (*London Gazette* 13th October 1944)
Since the award of the first Bar to the Distinguished Flying Cross, this officer has destroyed three enemy aircraft and damaged one while flying as a night-fighter pilot. His skill and daring in this capacity have been outstanding. On one sortie, while patrolling near Aachen, he destroyed a Messerschmitt 109 that exploded so near and with such brilliance that he was blinded for some moments. He has completed a large number of operational missions.

Other Honours
Air Force Cross (*London Gazette* 1st January 1952)

Queen's Commendation for Valuable Service in the Air (*London Gazette* 1st January 1978)

AIR COMMODORE PHILIP JEREMY ROBINSON OBE, DFC AND TWO BARS, MA

Born on 16th February 1973 and educated in Yorkshire, he was commissioned into the RAF as a pilot in 1992. He flew Chinooks in Germany with 18 Squadron, in the late 1990s and then with 7 Squadron at RAF Odiham from 1997.

He saw active service in Bosnia, Albania, Northern Ireland, Kosovo, Sierra Leone, Afghanistan, Iraq and Lebanon. As a flight lieutenant he received the DFC in 2001 for operations in Afghanistan, a Bar in 2003 for operations in Iraq and a second Bar in 2007 for further operations in Afghanistan.

He became station commander at RAF Odiham and the UK Chinook Force commander, 2015-17 and in 2017-18 attended the Royal College of Defence Studies. He was also made an Officer of the Order of the British Empire (OBE) in 2013.

Promoted to air commodore in October 2018 he is currently the assistant chief of Staff Operations at the Permanent Joint Headquarters in Northwood.

INDEX OF PERSONALITIES